2008 Supplement

to

FEDERAL CRIMINAL LAW AND ITS ENFORCEMENT

Fourth Edition

By

Norman Abrams

Professor of Law Emeritus
Acting Chancellor Emeritus
University of California, Los Angeles

Sara Sun Beale

Charles L.B. Lowndes Professor of Law
Duke University School of Law

AMERICAN CASEBOOK SERIES®

THOMSON

WEST

Mat #40702955

© West, a Thomson business, 2004, 2005
© 2008 Thomson/West
        610 Opperman Drive
        St. Paul, MN 55123
        1–800–313–9378
Printed in the United States of America

ISBN: 978–0–314–19002–4

 *TEXT IS PRINTED ON 10% POST CONSUMER RECYCLED PAPER*

ACKNOWLEDGEMENT

The authors wish to express their appreciation to those individuals who helped us with the preparation of this Supplement. Norman Abrams would like to thank Sergei Moudriak, UCLA '08 and Brian Tanada UCLA '10 for their very able research. Sara Beale would like to thank Michael Devlin, Duke '10 and Meghan Ferguson, Duke '10 for their very thorough research assistance. Professors Abrams and Beale would both like to thank Tal Grietzer for his outstanding assistance on the preparation of the manuscript.

N.A.
S.S.B.

July 2008

TABLE OF CONTENTS

CHAPTER 2

FEDERAL, STATE AND LOCAL CRIMINAL ENFORCEMENT RESOURCES

Page 12. Add and substitute as indicated below.

Elevation of the anti-terrorism mission in the Department of Justice has resulted in one major change in the Department's organization chart. The organization chart that appears on the next page is to be substituted for the chart that appears on p. 12 of the main volume. It shows the National Security Division in lieu of the Office of Intelligence Policy and Review which has been absorbed into the NSD. This chart is followed by another organization chart that presents the internal organization of the National Security Division. The reorganization is designed to consolidate the Department's national security efforts within one unit. The elevation of the anti-terrorism mission is described more fully in chapter 4.

U.S. DEPARTMENT OF JUSTICE

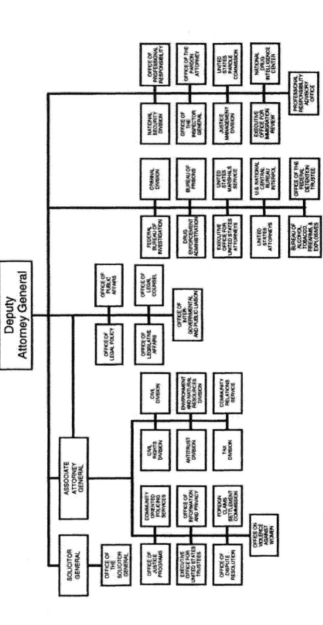

Attorney General

Deputy Attorney General

ASSOCIATE ATTORNEY GENERAL

SOLICITOR GENERAL

OFFICE OF THE SOLICITOR GENERAL

OFFICE OF PUBLIC AFFAIRS

OFFICE OF LEGAL POLICY

OFFICE OF LEGAL COUNSEL

OFFICE OF LEGISLATIVE AFFAIRS

OFFICE OF INTER-GOVERNMENTAL AND PUBLIC LIAISON

CIVIL DIVISION

CIVIL RIGHTS DIVISION

ENVIRONMENT AND NATURAL RESOURCES DIVISION

ANTITRUST DIVISION

COMMUNITY RELATIONS SERVICE

TAX DIVISION

COMMUNITY ORIENTED POLICING SERVICES

OFFICE OF JUSTICE PROGRAMS

OFFICE OF INFORMATION AND PRIVACY

EXECUTIVE OFFICE FOR UNITED STATES TRUSTEES

FOREIGN CLAIMS SETTLEMENT COMMISSION

OFFICE OF DISPUTE RESOLUTION

OFFICE ON VIOLENCE AGAINST WOMEN

NATIONAL SECURITY DIVISION

OFFICE OF THE INSPECTOR GENERAL

CRIMINAL DIVISION

FEDERAL BUREAU OF INVESTIGATION

BUREAU OF PRISONS

DRUG ENFORCEMENT ADMINISTRATION

UNITED STATES MARSHALS SERVICE

EXECUTIVE OFFICE FOR UNITED STATES ATTORNEYS

U.S. NATIONAL CENTRAL BUREAU INTERPOL

UNITED STATES ATTORNEYS

OFFICE OF THE FEDERAL DETENTION TRUSTEE

BUREAU OF ALCOHOL, TOBACCO, FIREARMS & EXPLOSIVES

OFFICE OF PROFESSIONAL RESPONSIBILITY

OFFICE OF THE PARDON ATTORNEY

UNITED STATES PAROLE COMMISSION

NATIONAL DRUG INTELLIGENCE CENTER

JUSTICE MANAGEMENT DIVISION

EXECUTIVE OFFICE FOR IMMIGRATION REVIEW

PROFESSIONAL RESPONSIBILITY ADVISORY OFFICE

NATIONAL SECURITY DIVISION

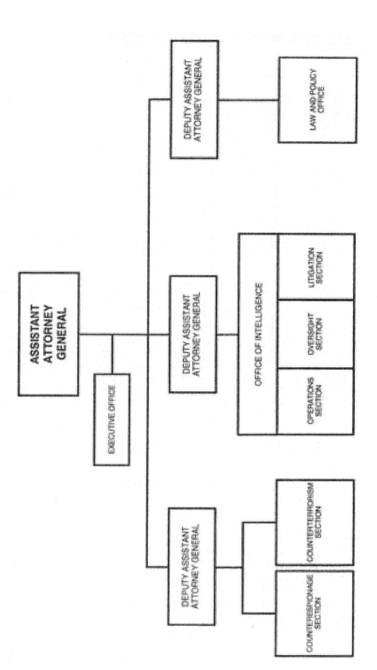

CHAPTER 3

SCOPE OF THE FEDERAL CRIMINAL LAWS

Page 41. Add to note 1b. (which begins on p. 38).

The Supreme Court in Gonzales v. Raich remanded the case to the Ninth Circuit to consider the plaintiff's remaining arguments in favor of a preliminary injunction. The court of appeals summarized its conclusions on remand as follows:

> We conclude that Raich has not demonstrated a likelihood of success on the merits of her action for injunctive relief. First, we hold that Raich's common law necessity defense is not foreclosed by *Oakland Cannabis* or the Controlled Substances Act, but that the necessity defense does not provide a proper basis for injunctive relief. Second, although changes in state law reveal a clear trend towards the protection of medical marijuana use, we hold that the asserted right has not yet gained the traction on a national scale to be deemed fundamental. Third, we hold that the Controlled Substances Act, a valid exercise of Congress's commerce power, does not violate the Tenth Amendment. Finally, we decline to reach Raich's argument that the Controlled Substances Act, by its terms, does not prohibit her possession and use of marijuana because this argument was not raised below. Raich v. Gonzales, 500 F.3d 850 (9th Cir. 2006).

See also Gonzales v. Oregon, 546 U.S. 243 (2006).

Page 55. In connection with note 2a.

See United States v. Logan, 419 F.3d 172 (2d Cir. 2005) where the court sustained the application of the federal arson statute to a rented fraternity house (fraternity members burned it down after being evicted by the landlord who had then rented it to a rival fraternity), rejecting the defendant's argument that the particular activity must substantially affect commerce. The court relied on Russell v. United States, 471 U.S. 858 (1985), a rental property case that had been cited approvingly by the Supreme Court in Jones.

Compare with the application of the "in commerce" formula statute, interpreted in United States v. Robertson, the following case:

UNITED STATES V. BALLINGER
395 F. 3d 1218 (11t[h] Cir. 2005)(en banc)

Before EDMONDSON, Chief Judge, and TJOFLAT, ANDERSON, BIRCH, DUBINA, BLACK, CARNES, BARKETT, HULL, MARCUS, WILSON, PRYOR and HILL, Circuit Judges.

Marcus, Circuit Judge

...

Ballinger was convicted under Title 18 U.S.C. § 247, which provides in relevant part:

> (a) Whoever, in any of the circumstances referred to in subsection (b) of this section-
>
> > (1) intentionally defaces, damages, or destroys any religious real property, because of the religious character of that property, or attempts to do so; or
> >
> > (2) intentionally obstructs, by force or threat of force, any person in the enjoyment of that person's free exercise of religious beliefs, or attempts to do so;
>
> shall be punished as provided in subsection (d).
>
> (b) The circumstances referred to in subsection (a) are that the offense is in or affects interstate or foreign commerce.

We understand Ballinger as having made three separate, though overlapping arguments for overturning his convictions under § 247. First, Ballinger says that § 247 is facially unconstitutional-that is, under no circumstances does Congress have the commerce power to proscribe the intentional destruction of religious property in or affecting commerce. Second, Ballinger claims that § 247 is unconstitutional as applied to his conduct-that is, even if Congress has the power to reach some offenses, it is not empowered to reach conduct like Ballinger's. Finally, the argument that Ballinger has cast as an as-applied challenge to the constitutionality of § 247 seems really to raise a question of statutory construction-namely, whether, by its specific terms, § 247 covers Ballinger's conduct. The substance of the argument is that "there was insufficient evidence to show that the offenses in this case were 'in or affecting commerce.'... The first two questions are easily resolved, ... the third is more involved.

...

The central question this appeal raises is whether § 247 is properly interpreted as prohibiting the use of the channels and instrumentalities of commerce to commit church arson, or whether the statute merely proscribes arsons in which the burning of the church itself occurs in commerce or affects commerce. Ballinger takes the position that arson is a purely intrastate activity that can rarely, if ever, be "in commerce." In this view, the crime of arson occurs only at the precise "point when the arsonist starts the fire," this point, therefore, is the only one relevant to determining whether the offense is "in commerce." "[T]ravel prior to the offense is not relevant," Ballinger maintains, because it is not part of the offense. Accordingly, he reads § 247's provision that "the offense is in or affects" commerce as requiring that the defendant commit the ultimate *actus reus* of igniting the church "in commerce." Ballinger is less than clear about what, precisely, he believes must transpire "in commerce" to satisfy the statute; what is clearly insufficient, though, in his view, is "[t]raveling [in interstate commerce] or using facilities or instrumentalities [of interstate commerce] before or after committing the offense." In other words, Ballinger envisions the statute as proscribing only those offenses in which the precise meeting of flame and church occurs in commerce-not those in which the offender relies on the channels and instrumentalities to carry out the offense. We disagree with this unusually limited reading of § 247.

...

The words "affecting commerce," as the Supreme Court has repeatedly explained, are "words of art that ordinarily signal the broadest permissible exercise of Congress' Commerce Clause power." ...

The words "in commerce," in sharp contrast, have a much narrower meaning. The Court has not defined the exact parameters of the term, which may vary by context, *see Am. Building Maintenance*, 422 U.S. at 277, 95 S.Ct. 2150 ("The phrase 'in commerce' does not, of course, necessarily have a uniform meaning whenever used by Congress."); it has, however, stressed repeatedly that "in commerce" is a phrase that expresses Congress' intent to invoke less than the full reach of its commerce power....

...

Thus, a statute employing the language "in commerce," the Court has said, covers "only persons or activities within the flow of interstate commerce." *Allied-Bruce,* 513 U.S. at 273, 115 S.Ct. 834 (quoting *Am. Building Maintenance,* 422 U.S. at 276, 95 S.Ct. 2150 (quoting *Gulf Oil,* 419 U.S. at 195, 95 S.Ct. 392)); ...

For more than 175 years of Commerce Clause precedent, this much has been clear: "Within the flow of commerce" denotes movement or people or things across interstate borders. *See, e.g., Gibbons v. Ogden,* 22 U.S. (9 Wheat.) 1, 189-90, 6 L.Ed. 23 (1824) ... Accordingly, the jurisdictional language "in commerce" invokes Congress' authority to regulate only the channels within which people and goods move through the flow of commerce, as well as the instrumentalities used to facilitate that movement-that is, the *Lopez* 1 and *Lopez* 2 powers. A statute that uses only the "in commerce" language stops well short of invoking Congress' *Lopez* 3 power to regulate activities outside the channels and instrumentalities of commerce that nonetheless substantially "affect" commerce.

In fact, the Supreme Court has rejected the suggestion that "in commerce" and "affecting commerce" may be conflated or read interchangeably....

...

The Supreme Court similarly declined to conflate the phrase "used in" with "affect" in *Jones v. United States,* a case interpreting the federal arson statute, § 844(i). In *Jones,* the Court assigned great significance to the particular commerce-modifying language selected by Congress, observing that "Congress did not define the crime described in § 844(i) as the explosion of a building whose damage or destruction might *affect* interstate commerce," but rather "require[d] that the damaged or destroyed property must itself have been *used in* commerce or in an activity affecting commerce." *Jones,* 529 U.S. at 854, 120 S.Ct. 1904.The Court refused to read § 844(i) so that "the statute's limiting language, 'used in' any commerce-affecting activity, would have no office," noting that "[j]udges should hesitate ... to treat statutory terms in any setting [as surplusage], and resistance should be heightened when the words describe an element of a criminal offense.").

Even if we had any doubt whether Congress was using "in commerce" and "affects commerce" as terms of art in this case, looking to the pre-1996 version of § 247 would erase all uncertainty on this score. Prior to its amendment in 1996, § 247 specifically prohibited the destruction of religious property when, in committing the offense, the defendant traveled in interstate commerce. The pre-1996 statute provided in pertinent part:

(a) Whoever in any of the circumstances referred to in subsection (b) of this section-

> (1) intentionally defaces, damages, or destroys any religious real property, because of the religious character of that property, or attempts to do so; or

> ....

shall be punished as provided in subsection (c) of this section.

(b) The circumstances referred to in subsection (a) are that-

> (1) in committing the offense, the defendant travels in interstate or foreign commerce, or uses a facility or instrumentality of interstate or foreign commerce in interstate or foreign commerce; and

> (2) in the case of an offense under subsection (a)(1), the loss resulting from the defacement, damage, or destruction is more than $10,000.

Pub.L. No. 100-346, § 1, 102 Stat. 644 (1988).

In amending the statute eight years later, Congress simply substituted in the jurisdictional language "that the offense is in or affects interstate or foreign commerce" for the original jurisdictional language that "in committing the offense, the defendant travels in interstate or foreign commerce, or uses a facility or instrumentality of interstate or foreign commerce in interstate or foreign commerce." All that Congress did was (1) employ the shorthand "in commerce" rather than describing the substantive requirement of use of the channels or instrumentalities of commerce; and (2) expand the jurisdictional hook to cover offenses that "affect" commerce, thereby invoking for the first time all of its commerce power.

...

Indeed, Ballinger's interpretation of § 247 would read the "in commerce" language out of the statute altogether. The Appellant's circumscribed construction of § 247 as applying only when the ultimate destruction of the church itself happens in commerce (or affects commerce) effectively excises the "in commerce" basis for jurisdiction from the statute. In fact, the Appellant argued explicitly to the *en banc* Court that "§ 247 applies only to cases having a substantial effect on interstate commerce, and does not apply to situations where the offense was committed or facilitated through the instrumentalities of interstate commerce, or through interstate travel." Although the Appellant offered at oral argument several strained examples of offenses he believed would be "in commerce," his argument in his brief that § 247 applies "only to cases having a substantial effect on interstate commerce" suggests that even he believes his interpretation of "in commerce" to be virtually impossible to satisfy.

The Appellant's remarkably constricted reading of the "in commerce" language effectively strips those words of any force at all. It is difficult to imagine a case that more classically depicts arson occurring in commerce than Ballinger's. If § 247's prohibition on destroying religious property in commerce does not reach Ballinger's four-state church-arson spree, there is implausibly little, if any, conduct it actually proscribes. To dream up an offense in which the final act of destruction actually occurs "in commerce" is difficult, if not impossible. Even if the perpetrator were to ignite a fire in Florida, for example, just over the Georgia state line, and wait for it to burn its way across the border to a nearby Georgia church, the offense, as the Appellant sees it, would still not be in commerce because the act of destruction, though set into motion in Florida, actually occurs in Georgia.

...

Moreover, Congress specifically intended the amended § 247 to reach offenses like Ballinger's. The House and Senate reports both state that "[u]nder this new formulation of the interstate commerce requirement, the Committee intends that where in committing, planning, or preparing to commit the offense, the defendant either travels in interstate or foreign commerce, or uses the mail or any facility of interstate or foreign commerce, the statute will be satisfied." H.R.Rep. No. 104-621, at 7 (1996), *reprinted in* 1996 U.S.C.C.A.N. at 1088; 142 Cong. Rec. at S7909 (joint statement of Sens. Faircloth and Kennedy and Reps. Hyde and Conyers).

Congress could not have made clearer its intention to exercise its full commerce power: the House Report specifically stated that § 247's "in or affects interstate or foreign commerce" language "grants Federal jurisdiction ... as to *any conduct which falls within the interstate commerce clause of the Constitution.*" H.R.Rep. No. 104-621, at 7, *reprinted in* 1996 U.S.C.C.A.N. at 1088 (emphasis added). The Senate Report reiterated that "it is the intent of the Congress to exercise the fullest reach of the Federal commerce power." 142 Cong. Rec. at S7909 (joint statement of Sens. Faircloth and Kennedy and Reps. Hyde and Conyers). Plainly, the statute is designed to cover all proscribed conduct that Congress may constitutionally reach. This is nothing more than the simple principle that the greater includes the lesser. Applying this general rule to the statute at hand leads inescapably to the conclusion that Ballinger has improperly read the statute as excluding his conduct: Congress invoked its full commerce power with the "in or affects commerce" language; Congress has the power, under the Commerce Clause, to reach conduct like Ballinger's; therefore, the statute covers Ballinger's offenses.

…

TJOFLAT, Circuit Judge, dissenting, in which BIRCH and HILL, Circuit Judges, join:

…

When Congress seeks to rely on interstate travel as a basis for exercising its authority under the Commerce Clause, it knows how to do so. As the panel majority noted, "[t]here are numerous federal statutes which do, explicitly, forbid movement in interstate commerce in order to commit a traditional common-law crime." *United States v. Ballinger,* 312 F.3d 1264, 1273 n. 8 (11th Cir.2002) (collecting statutes). And more important for present purposes, prior to its amendment in 1996, § 247 itself reached cases in which, "in committing the offense, the defendant travels in interstate or foreign commerce, or uses a facility or instrumentality of interstate or foreign commerce in interstate or foreign commerce." In 1996, this provision was deleted and replaced with the current § 247(b), which extends only to cases in which "the offense is in or affects interstate or foreign commerce."

The court, however, now reads the old interstate travel provision back into the statute, as if the 1996 amendment had never occurred, despite the fact that it is unable to cite a single case that holds that an offense is "in commerce" simply because the offender crossed state lines at some point prior to its commission. In reaching this conclusion, the court makes much of the narrowness of the contrary interpretation urged by the appellant and relies on the principle that, whenever possible, a statute should be read in a way that gives effect to all of its words. Indeed, the court faults the appellant for failing to identify satisfactorily those offenses other than his own that might be considered "in commerce." I am uncertain what, if any, church arson might be "in commerce." It is, however, clear to me that a church arson is not "in commerce" simply because the arsonist came from another state at some point prior to the offense. The rule that statutes should be read so as not to render words insignificant is a general principle of statutory interpretation, not an inflexible rule. Therefore, we need not do violence to the statutory language simply to satisfy ourselves that we have given all the words of § 247 a function. The court says that "Congress does not write statutes for the words-it writes them for the meaning." The court, in turn, has applied § 247's (perceived) meaning rather than its words.

...

My confusion as to the holding of this case can be summarized in a few short questions that the court seems to leave unanswered: First, under the court's interpretation of § 247, is it necessary to prove that the defendant traveled in interstate commerce with the intent to commit church arson? I think the court would answer, "no." If that is the case, then how close in time must the border crossing and the arson be for § 247 to apply? (And, as a matter of statutory interpretation, how are we to decide where to draw the line?) If, however, the court would answer my first question in the affirmative, what basis is there for concluding that Ballinger crossed state lines with the intent to commit church arson? Because all of these points remain unclear, the court's opinion remains unsatisfactory even if I assume that it reaches the correct result. Once these ambiguities are cleared away, we are again left with purely intrastate offenses and a federal prosecution of them that hangs solely on the offender's earlier crossing from one state into another. As such, the court's discussion of Ballinger's highway travels, gasoline purchases, and hotel stays, and its citations to cases sustaining convictions where the federal crime was the interstate travel itself, are simply irrelevant and serve only to obscure the real issue and to create an illusion of a connection to interstate commerce that simply does not exist in fact.

Because § 247 cannot properly be interpreted to reach Ballinger's conduct, and because it would be unconstitutional even if it could, I respectfully dissent.

BIRCH Circuit Judge, dissenting, in which HILL, Circuit Judge, joins:

As to the majority opinion, I respectfully dissent. I fully concur in Judge Hill's and Judge Tjoflat's dissents and add my following thoughts as well.

At its core, this case devolves into a simple, yet nuanced, question: does the Commerce Clause grant the United States Congress the power to proscribe the common law crime of arson by attaching the jurisdictional qualifier "in or affects interstate commerce" to the anti-church-burning statute, 18 U.S.C. § 247? As Judge Hill's thorough and well-reasoned dissent points out, the majority's noble effort to uphold the constitutionality of § 247 through statutory construction fails to consider what the statute actually penalizes, namely, a local common law crime against property. While I fully concur with his opinion and analysis, Judge Hill's arguments can be magnified even further when viewed through the lens of federalism, a concept which retains vitality and importance in our modern constitutional scheme, *see United States v. Lopez,* 514 U.S. 549, 575, 115 S.Ct. 1624, 1637, 131 L.Ed.2d 626 (1995). Recognizing that § 247 regulates by federal statute an area of criminal law traditionally reserved to the States, I write separately to emphasize that the principles of federalism implicated in this case should have led the majority to find that 18 U.S.C. § 247 represents an incursion into State police powers not sanctioned by the United States Constitution.

...

Page 64. At top of the page, add to note 3 (which begins on p. 57).

g. Just as Lopez had done, Gonzales v. Raich triggered an outpouring of law review commentary. The following is a small selection: Glenn H. Reynolds & Brannon P. Denning, *What Hath* Raich *Wrought? Five Takes,* 9 LEWIS & CLARK L. REV. 915 (2005); Douglas W. Kmiec, Gonzales v. Raich: Wickard v. Filburn *Displaced,* 2005 CATO SUP. CT. REV. 71 (2005); Jonathon H. Adler, *Is* Morrison *Dead? Assessing a Supreme Drug (Law) Overdose,* 9 LEWIS & CLARK L. REV. 751 (2005); Robert J. Pushaw, Jr., *The Medical Marijuana Case: A Commerce Clause Counter-Revolution?* 9 LEWIS & CLARK L. REV. 879 (2005); Randy E. Barnett, *Federalism After* Gonzales v. Raich: *Limiting* Raich. 9 LEWIS & CLARK L. REV. 743 (2005); Ernest A. Young, *Just Blowing Smoke? Politics, Doctrine, and the Federalist Revival after* Gonzales v. Raich, 2005 SUP. CT. REV. 1 (2005); Ilya Somin, Gonzales v. Raich: *Federalism as a Casualty of the War on Drugs,* 15 CORNELL J.L. & PUB. POL'Y 507 (2006).

h. Following the decision in Gonzales v. Raich, some lower federal courts relied on Raich (and the doctrine of Wickard v. Filburn) in sustaining federal criminal legislation in the child pornography arena. These cases involved jurisdictional language that was keyed to whether the offending image was produced with materials previously "mailed, shipped, or transported in ...commerce by any means, including by computer." See, e.g., 18 U.S.C. § 2251(a) and

§ 2252A(a)(5)(B). While some case law supported the conclusion that compliance with this type of jurisdictional commerce link alone was sufficient to sustain prosecutions under such statutes, see United States v. Mugan, 441 F.3d 622 (8th Cir. 2006) and eighth circuit cases cited therein, cases in other circuits applied the Raich decision in sustaining the application of the statute to intrastate production of pornographic images. See, e.g., United States v. Smith, 459 F.3d 1276 (11th Cir. 2006). Indeed, in Smith, the court of appeals originally overturned his conviction on the ground that the statutes in question [the two statutes cited supra] were unconstitutional exercises of commerce power authority as applied to his conduct. The government sought review in the Supreme Court and the high court remanded the case to the eleventh circuit "for further consideration in light of Gonzales v. Raich...," leaving an implication that the statutory jurisdictional provision by itself, in this context, was not a sufficient basis on which to ground commerce power jurisdiction.

To be compared with the foregoing decisions, see the material in the notes in this Supplement to p. 108 of the main volume (below) where the jurisdictional provisions in question required the transmission of the offending images themselves in commerce, and where the lower courts do not appear to have engaged in a Raich-based analysis.

i. The recent district court opinion in United States v. Waybright, —F.Supp.2d— 2380946 (D. Mont. 2008) presents a Lopez-Morrison-Raich issue in connection with the federal law requiring registration of sex offenders. Excerpts from the court's opinion follow:

Waybright was charged in a two-count indictment with failing to register as a sex offender, in violation of 18 U.S.C. § 2250(a). ...The indictment alleges Waybright, a person required to register under SORNA by reason of his West Virginia conviction for sexual abuse in the second degree, traveled in interstate commerce to Montana, and knowingly failed to register as a sex offender.

On July 27, 2006, Congress enacted the Adam Walsh Child Protection and Safety Act of 2006 ("Adam Walsh Act"). Title I of the Adam Walsh Act contains the Sex Offender Registration and Notification Act. SORNA establishes a national sex offender registry ....

The Act defines the term "sex offender" as "an individual who was convicted of a sex offense." Id. § 16911(1). Sex offenses include criminal offenses that have an element involving a sexual act or sexual contact with another and certain specified offenses against minors. Id. § 16911(5)(A). ...

SORNA requires states to incorporate its standards for sex offender registration and notification into their own laws and maintain a sex offender registry that conforms to certain statutory requirements. Id. § 16912. The Act also requires states to impose criminal penalties for a violation of its provisions. Id. § 16913 (requiring "criminal penalty that includes a maximum term of imprisonment that is greater than 1 year"). Any state that fails to implement SORNA's requirements within three years faces a ten percent reduction in federal justice funding. Id. §§ 16924, 16925(d). As of June 10, 2008, no state has fully complied with SORNA's requirements.

SORNA specifies when a sex offender must first register and then sets forth the sex offender's continuing obligation to keep his registration current. Id. § 16913. The statute states, in relevant part:

(a) In general

A sex offender shall register, and keep registration current, in each jurisdiction where the offender resides, where the offender is employed, and where the offender is a student. For initial registration purposes only, a sex offender shall also register in the jurisdiction in which convicted if such jurisdiction is different from the jurisdiction of residence.

...

SORNA also created a new federal offense for failing to register as a sex offender, with a maximum penalty of ten years imprisonment. 18 U.S.C. § 2250(a). The federal criminal statute provides:

Whoever-

(1) is required to register under the Sex Offender Registration and Notification Act;

(2)(A) is a sex offender as defined for the purposes of the Sex Offender Registration and Notification Act by reason of a conviction under Federal law (including the Uniform Code of Military Justice), the law of the District of Columbia, Indian

15

tribal law, or the law of any territory or possession of the United States; or

(B) travels in interstate or foreign commerce, or enters or leaves, or resides in, Indian country; and

(3) knowingly fails to register or update a registration as required by the Sex Offender Registration and Notification Act;

shall be fined under this title or imprisoned not more than 10 years, or both.

Id. § 2250(a).

B. Commerce Clause

Waybright argues Congress exceeded its power under the Commerce Clause by enacting two specific provisions of SORNA-18 U.S.C. § 2250(a) and 42 U.S.C. § 16913. Section 2250(a) creates a federal offense where an individual (1) is required to register under SORNA; (2) travels in interstate commerce; and (3) knowingly fails to register or update a registration as required by SORNA. Section 16913 imposes registration requirements on all sex offenders in the United States regardless of whether they travel in interstate commerce.

...

Waybright asserts, even if § 2250(a) is a valid exercise of Congress' Commerce Clause power, he cannot be convicted under the statute because he should not have been required to register under § 16913 in the first place. According to Waybright, the registration requirements found at § 16913 also exceed Congress' power under the Commerce Clause. Waybright contends § 16913 is unconstitutional because Congress lacks the power to force citizens who have been convicted of purely local offenses under state law to register as sex offenders.

A conviction for failure to register as a sex offender is predicated upon proof that the defendant was required to register under § 16913. 18 U.S.C. § 2250(a). Section 16913, in turn, requires all sex offenders in the United States to register. Unlike § 2250(a), its requirements are not limited to only those sex offenders who travel in interstate commerce. By its terms, § 16913 does not regulate the use of the channels of interstate commerce or the instrumentalities of interstate commerce.

16

Therefore, it cannot be upheld under either of the first two categories of activity subject to regulation under the Commerce Clause. Instead, if it is to be sustained under the Commerce Clause it must fall within the third Lopez category, i.e., regulation of "activities that substantially affect interstate commerce.".

Few courts have considered whether § 16913, as opposed to § 2250(a), is a valid exercise of Congress' power to regulate activities that substantially affect interstate commerce. Not surprisingly, the cases that have addressed the question rely heavily on two recent Supreme Court opinions striking down statutes under the Commerce Clause. See Lopez, 514 U.S. 549; United States v. Morrison, 529 U.S. 598 (2000).

...

The United States relies on United States v. Passaro, CR 07-2308-BEN (S.D.Cal. Dec. 17, 2007), in urging the Court to uphold § 16913. The Passaro court found § 16913 was a valid exercise of Congress' Commerce Clause power under the factors enumerated in Lopez and Morrison.. The court acknowledged § 16913 does not regulate commercial or economic activity and does not contain a jurisdictional element. Nevertheless, it concluded the statute regulated activity that substantially affects interstate commerce for two reasons. First, the statute is an essential part of a larger regulation of economic activity.. Specifically, § 16913 is part of the Adam Walsh Act, which also regulates interstate distribution of child pornography. According to the court, Congress' regulation of child pornography-an economic activity-could be undercut if sex offenders were not regulated. Second, the court found a connection between the regulation of sex offenders and interstate commerce. Relying on an argument similar to the "cost of crime" and "national productivity" arguments rejected in Lopez and Morrison, the court wrote:

Congress intended (in enacting SORNA) to protect public safety. It is rational to conclude that maintaining a comprehensive national registry of sex offenders affects interstate commerce. For individuals engaging in any commerce-related activity, personal safety and safety of their families is a prime concern. Economic development in certain areas may be encouraged or discouraged depending on the safety level. Requiring sex offenders to register within three days of a change in residence is a means reasonably adapted to achieving SORNA's purpose.

At oral argument on Waybright's motion to dismiss, the United States changed course and conceded § 16913 could not be upheld under the Commerce Clause alone. The concession is right. Section 16913 has nothing to do with commerce or any sort of economic enterprise; it regulates purely local, non-economic activity. While certain sex offenses may be commercial or economic in nature (e.g., child pornography), sex offenders themselves are not necessarily engaged in commercial or economic activity. Even though the Adam Walsh Act regulates some sex offenses that are commercial (e.g., the distribution of child pornography), its regulation of sex offenders is not indispensable to the success of its other provisions. Unlike § 2250(a), § 16913 has no express jurisdictional element to limit its reach to sex offenders connected with or affecting interstate commerce. SORNA's legislative history contains no express congressional findings regarding the effects of sex offender registration on interstate commerce. Tracking sex offenders may enhance public safety and may in turn promote a more productive economy as explained by the court in Passaro. But, any effect on interstate commerce from requiring sex offenders to register is too attenuated to survive scrutiny under the Commerce Clause. For these reasons, § 16913 is not a valid exercise of Congress' Commerce Clause power.

Because § 16913 cannot be sustained under the Commerce Clause, it is necessary to consider whether the statute is a valid exercise of any other power delegated to Congress in the Constitution. Several district courts have approved of Congress' enactment of § 16913 pursuant to powers other than the Commerce Clause power. In United States v. Thomas, 534 F.Supp.2d 912, 920-22 (N.D.Iowa 2008), for example, the court determined enactment of § 16913 was not within Congress' Commerce Clause power, but nevertheless upheld the statute as a valid exercise of Congress' power under the Necessary and Proper Clause. The Necessary and Proper Clause authorizes Congress to "make all Laws which shall be necessary and proper for carrying into Execution the [Congressional] Powers" enumerated in the Constitution. U.S. Const. art. I, § 8, cl. 18. Raich, 545 U.S. at 35 (Scalia, J., concurring). "The relevant question is simply whether the means chosen are reasonably adapted to the attainment of a legitimate end under the commerce power."

The Thomas court determined § 16913 was an appropriate and reasonably adapted means for Congress to attain the legitimate end of § 2250(a)-monitoring sex offenders who cross state lines. 534 F.Supp.2d at 921. The court reasoned as follows:

To be certain, § 16913's blanket-registration requirement is not narrowly tailored or absolutely necessary to [monitor sex offenders who cross state lines]. For example, Congress could have taken a less drastic step and only required sex offenders who have certain qualifying life events (e.g., a change in employment, school or residence) and actually travel in interstate commerce to register immediately after such travel takes place. Instead, § 16913 is over-inclusive and reaches those sex offenders who change jobs, schools or residences but never travel across state lines. Even so, the court concludes that § 16913 represents a reasonable, good-faith effort on the part of Congress to monitor sex offenders who cross state lines. It must be remembered that we live in a very mobile society. There can be no doubt that sex offenders, like other Americans, frequently change jobs, schools or residences. Congress may have determined that it was unworkable, as a practical matter, to devise and enforce a sex-offender registration system that could monitor only those sex offenders who traveled in interstate commerce. Recognizing the federalism concerns that the Supreme Court expressed in Lopez and Morrison, however, Congress limited federal criminal enforcement of § 16913 to instances in which the sex offender crosses state lines. Congress must be afforded the opportunity to use its discretion with respect to the means by which its powers are to be carried into execution ... in the manner most beneficial to the people.

At oral argument, the United States urged the Court to adopt the reasoning of Thomas to uphold § 16913. Thomas is not persuasive. Thomas ' analysis relies on Justice Scalia's characterization of the interplay between the Commerce Clause and the Necessary and Proper Clause in Raich....There is an established, and lucrative, interstate market for controlled substances. Prohibiting the intrastate possession or manufacture of controlled substances is a rational means of regulating that product. The Court specifically distinguished the statutes at issue in Lopez and Morrison from the CSA by acknowledging that the former statutes dealt with non-economic activities.. Like the statutes at issue in Lopez and Morrison, SORNA does not regulate any sort of economic or commercial activity. Sex offenders are not fungible commodities. There is no market for sex offenders. So, Congress does not need to regulate sex offenders who remain in a single state in order to effectively regulate sex offenders who travel in interstate commerce.

The Thomas court's reliance on Raich is also unpersuasive because § 16913 is not a means to an end; it is the end of SORNA. Raich recognized that Congress can regulate interstate trafficking in illicit drugs under the Commerce Clause. The issue considered was whether Congress could regulate activities beyond the scope of its Commerce Clause power in order to fill in gaps left in the CSA because of the limits of that power. The Court approved of such a practice in Raich, finding that the regulation of the intrastate cultivation of marijuana was "merely one of many essential part[s] of a larger regulation of economic activity, in which the regulatory scheme could be undercut unless the intrastate activity were regulated."

Unlike the intrastate regulation approved of in Raich, § 16913 is not one of many essential parts of a larger regulatory scheme. Nor is it intended to fill in the gaps in an otherwise valid exercise of Congress' power. The United States analogizes § 2250(a) to the CSA's regulation of interstate trafficking in illicit drugs. Unlike the regulation of interstate drug trafficking, the creation of a federal crime for sex offenders who travel in interstate commerce and fail to register is not the overriding purpose of SORNA. The purpose of the Act is to "establish[ ] a comprehensive national system for the registration of [sex offenders]." 42 U.S.C. § 16901. This primary purpose is accomplished by the enactment of § 16913. Unlike the CSA, which utilized the necessary and proper power to fill in the gaps of an overarching statutory scheme that was valid under the Commerce Clause power, SORNA attempts to utilize the necessary and proper power to enact an overarching statutory scheme based on the existence of Commerce Clause authority to enact a small part of that larger scheme. ...The Necessary and Proper Clause can come to the aid of validly exercised commerce power but the commerce power cannot come to the aid of the Necessary and Proper Clause. Because the regulation of sex offenders is not economic or commercial in nature and

§ 16913 is not merely a means to creating a federal crime for sex offenders who travel in interstate commerce and fail to register, Thomas' reliance on the Necessary and Proper Clause to uphold § 16913 is not persuasive.

...

Section 16913 is not a valid exercise of any of the congressional powers enumerated in the Constitution. As a consequence, Section 16913 is unconstitutional. To obtain a conviction under § 2250(a), the government must first prove ...Waybright was required to register under § 16913. Because § 16913 is unconstitutional, the government cannot satisfy its burden of proof with respect to § 2250(a). Accordingly, the Indictment must be dismissed

Page 65-66. *In connection with Scarborough v. United States, bottom paragraph, p. 65.*

See United States v. Patton, 451 F.3d 615 (10th Cir. 2006), applying Scarborough to a prosecution for possession by a convicted felon of body armor (a bullet proof vest) under 18 U.S.C.§ 931 (see the definition of body armor in § 921(a)(35)) and upholding the congressional authority to regulate its possession because the body armor "moved across state lines at some point in its existence."

Page 66. *In connection with the bottom paragraph.*

See United States v. Peters, 403 F.3d 12673 911th Cir. 2005), which held post-Lopez that the statute making it a federal crime to sell a firearm to a convicted felon, 18 U.S.C.§ 922(d)(1) is "a valid exercise of Congress' commerce power over the economic activity of distribution and sale of firearms." See also United States v. Haskins, 511 F.3d 688 (7th Cir. 2008).

Page 72. *Add to note 2.*

On remand of the Stewart case, 451 F.3d 1071 (9th Cir. 2006), Judge Kozinski wrote:

In our earlier opinion, we concluded that section 922(*o*) was quite similar to the statute at issue in *Lopez*. But *Raich* forces us to reconsider. Like the possession regulation in the Controlled Substances Act, the machinegun possession ban fits within a larger scheme for the regulation of interstate commerce in firearms. Guns, like drugs, are regulated by a detailed and comprehensive statutory regime designed to protect individual firearm ownership while supporting "Federal, State and local law enforcement officials in their fight against crime and violence." ... Just as the CSA classifies substances in five different categories, placing different controls on each class based on a combination of its legitimate uses, potential for abuse and effects on the body, the federal firearms statutory regime classifies weapons for differential treatment as well: Some firearms are freely transferrable, others must be registered and, still others (like machineguns) are largely banned.

Nevertheless, there is one major difference between the possession ban in the CSA and section 922(*o*): The machinegun ban was enacted almost twenty years after the statute establishing the current federal firearms regulatory regime. ...Nevertheless, we don't read *Raich* as requiring us to consider section 922(*o*) as stand alone legislation like that in *Morrison* and *Lopez*. *Raich* stands for the proposition that Congress can ban possession of an object where it has a rational basis for concluding that object might bleed into the interstate market and affect supply and demand, especially in an area where Congress regulates comprehensively. Neither the Gun-Free School Zones Act of 1990 nor the Violence Against Women Act of 1994 could be defended as plugging a hole in otherwise comprehensive regulation. Whether guns could be possessed in school zones was highly unlikely to affect the supply and demand for guns in the national market. And the Violence Against Women Act was at best tenuously related to interstate commerce. But section 922(*o*), like the marijuana possession ban in the CSA, is different-Congress could have rationally concluded that homemade machineguns would affect the national market. That Congress took a wait-and-see approach when it created the regime doesn't matter. The Commerce Clause does not prevent Congress from correcting deficiencies in its regulatory scheme in piecemeal fashion. To conclude otherwise would eliminate Congress's ability to regulate with a light touch in the first instance and tinker at the margins in light of experience. *Raich's* deferential review of comprehensive federal regulatory schemes ensures that Congress retains as much discretion to adjust the details of its regulatory scheme as it had when it created the regime. Therefore, the fact that section 922(*o*) was passed long after the Gun Control Act is not of constitutional significance.

Pages 75-77. Add to note 9.

In a landmark recent decision, District of Columbia v. Heller, —S.Ct.—, 2008 WL 2520816 (U.S.), Justice Scalia, writing for a five justice majority, applied the Second Amendment to protect the right to keep arms at home for self-defense, stating:

There seems to us no doubt, on the basis of both text and history, that the Second Amendment conferred an individual right to keep and bear arms. Of course the right was not unlimited, just as the First Amendment's right of free speech was not, see, e.g., United States v. Williams, 553 U. S. ___ (2008). Thus, we do not read the Second Amendment to protect the right of citizens to carry arms for any sort of confrontation, just as we do not read the First Amendment to protect the right of citizens to speak for any purpose....

...

Justice Stevens places overwhelming reliance upon this Court's decision in United States v. Miller, 307 U. S. 174 (1939). ...The most Justice Stevens can plausibly claim for Miller is that it declined to decide the nature of the Second Amendment right, despite the Solicitor General's argument (made in the alternative) that the right was collective, ...Miller stands only for the proposition that the Second Amendment right, whatever its nature, extends only to certain types of weapons.

It is particularly wrongheaded to read Miller for more than what it said, because the case did not even purport to be a thorough examination of the Second Amendment. ...The Government's Miller brief thus provided scant discussion of the history of the Second Amendment-and the Court was presented with no counterdiscussion. As for the text of the Court's opinion itself, that discusses none of the history of the Second Amendment. It assumes from the prologue that the Amendment was designed to preserve the militia, ...and then reviews some historical materials dealing with the nature of the militia, and in particular with the nature of the arms their members were expected to possess. Not a word (not a word) about the history of the Second Amendment. This is the mighty rock upon which the dissent rests its case.

We may as well consider at this point (for we will have to consider eventually) what types of weapons Miller permits. Read in isolation, Miller's phrase "part of ordinary military equipment" could mean that only those weapons useful in warfare are protected. That would be a startling reading of the opinion, since it would mean that the National Firearms Act's restrictions on machineguns (not challenged in Miller) might be unconstitutional, machineguns being useful in warfare in 1939. ...We ... read Miller to say only that the Second Amendment does not protect those weapons not typically possessed by law-abiding citizens for lawful purposes, such as short-barreled shotguns. That accords with the historical understanding of the scope of the right.

We conclude that nothing in our precedents forecloses our adoption of the original understanding of the Second Amendment. It should be unsurprising that such a significant matter has been for so long judicially unresolved. For most of our history, the Bill of Rights was not thought applicable to the States, and the Federal Government did not significantly regulate the possession of firearms by law-abiding citizens. Other provisions of the Bill of Rights have similarly remained unilluminated for lengthy periods. This Court first held a law to violate the First Amendment's guarantee of freedom of speech in 1931, almost 150 years after the Amendment was ratified, see Near v. Minnesota ex rel. Olson, 283 U. S. 697 (1931), and it was not until after World War II that we held a law invalid under the Establishment Clause, see Illinois ex rel. McCollum v. Board of Ed. of School Dist. No. 71, Champaign Cty., 333 U. S. 203 (1948). Even a question as basic as the scope of proscribable libel was not addressed by this Court until 1964, nearly two centuries after the founding. See New York Times Co. v. Sullivan, 376 U. S. 254 (1964). It is demonstrably not true that, as Justice Stevens claims, "for most of our history, the invalidity of Second-Amendment-based objections to firearms regulations has been well settled and uncontroversial." For most of our history the question did not present itself.

...

Like most rights, the right secured by the Second Amendment is not unlimited. From Blackstone through the 19th-century cases, commentators and courts routinely explained that the right was not a right to keep and carry any weapon whatsoever in any manner whatsoever and for whatever purpose.... For example, the majority of the 19th-century courts to consider the question held that prohibitions on carrying concealed weapons were lawful under the Second Amendment or state analogues....Although we do not undertake an exhaustive historical analysis today of the full scope of the Second Amendment, nothing in our opinion should be taken to cast doubt on longstanding prohibitions on the possession of firearms by felons and the mentally ill, or laws forbidding the carrying of firearms in sensitive places such as schools and government buildings, or laws imposing conditions and qualifications on the commercial sale of arms.

We also recognize another important limitation on the right to keep and carry arms. Miller said, as we have explained, that the sorts of weapons protected were those "in common use at the time." 307 U. S., at 179. We think that limitation is fairly supported by the historical tradition of prohibiting the carrying of "dangerous and unusual weapons." ...

It may be objected that if weapons that are most useful in military service-M-16 rifles and the like-may be banned, then the Second Amendment right is completely detached from the prefatory clause. But as we have said, the conception of the militia at the time of the Second Amendment's ratification was the body of all citizens capable of military service, who would bring the sorts of lawful weapons that they possessed at home to militia duty. It may well be true today that a militia, to be as effective as militias in the 18th century, would require sophisticated arms that are highly unusual in society at large. Indeed, it may be true that no amount of small arms could be useful against modern-day bombers and tanks. But the fact that modern developments have limited the degree of fit between the prefatory clause and the protected right cannot change our interpretation of the right.

We turn finally to the law at issue here. As we have said, the law totally bans handgun possession in the home. It also requires that any lawful firearm in the home be disassembled or bound by a trigger lock at all times, rendering it inoperable.

As the quotations earlier in this opinion demonstrate, the inherent right of self-defense has been central to the Second Amendment right. The handgun ban amounts to a prohibition of an entire class of "arms" that is overwhelmingly chosen by American society for that lawful purpose. The prohibition extends, moreover, to the home, where the need for defense of self, family, and property is most acute. Under any of the standards of scrutiny that we have applied to enumerated constitutional rights, banning from the home "the most preferred firearm in the nation to 'keep' and use for protection of one's home and family," would fail constitutional muster.

Few laws in the history of our Nation have come close to the severe restriction of the District's handgun ban. And some of those few have been struck down....

It is no answer to say, as petitioners do, that it is permissible to ban the possession of handguns so long as the possession of other firearms (i.e., long guns) is allowed. It is enough to note, as we have observed, that the American people have considered the handgun to be the quintessential self-defense weapon. There are many reasons that a citizen may prefer a handgun for home defense: It is easier to store in a location that is readily accessible in an emergency; it cannot easily be redirected or wrestled away by an attacker; it is easier to use for those without the upper-body strength to lift and aim a long gun; it can be pointed at a burglar with one hand while the other hand dials the police. Whatever the reason, handguns are the most popular weapon chosen by Americans for self-defense in the home, and a complete prohibition of their use is invalid.

We must also address the District's requirement (as applied to respondent's handgun) that firearms in the home be rendered and kept inoperable at all times. This makes it impossible for citizens to use them for the core lawful purpose of self-defense and is hence unconstitutional. The District argues that we should interpret this element of the statute to contain an exception for self-defense. But we think that is precluded by the unequivocal text, and by the presence of certain other enumerated exceptions: "Except for law enforcement personnel ... , each registrant shall keep any firearm in his possession unloaded and disassembled or bound by a trigger lock or similar device unless such firearm is kept at his place of business, or while being used for lawful recreational purposes within the District of Columbia." D. C. Code § 7-2507.02. The nonexistence of a self-defense exception is also suggested by the D. C. Court of Appeals' statement that the statute forbids residents to use firearms to stop intruders, see McIntosh v. Washington, 395 A. 2d 744, 755-756 (1978).

Apart from his challenge to the handgun ban and the trigger-lock requirement respondent asked the District Court to enjoin petitioners from enforcing the separate licensing requirement "in such a manner as to forbid the carrying of a firearm within one's home or possessed land without a license." The Court of Appeals did not invalidate the licensing requirement, but held only that the District "may not prevent [a handgun] from being moved throughout one's house." It then ordered the District Court to enter summary judgment "consistent with [respondent's] prayer for relief." Before this Court petitioners have stated that "if the handgun ban is struck down and respondent registers a handgun, he could obtain a license, assuming he is not otherwise disqualified," by which they apparently mean if he is not a felon and is not insane. Respondent conceded at oral argument that he does not "have a problem with ... licensing" and that the District's law is permissible so long as it is "not enforced in an arbitrary and capricious manner." We therefore assume that petitioners' issuance of a license will satisfy respondent's prayer for relief and do not address the licensing requirement.

...

Justice Breyer moves on to make a broad jurisprudential point: He criticizes us for declining to establish a level of scrutiny for evaluating Second Amendment restrictions. He proposes, explicitly at least, none of the traditionally expressed levels (strict scrutiny, intermediate scrutiny, rational basis), but rather a judge-empowering "interest-balancing inquiry" that "asks whether the statute burdens a protected interest in a way or to an extent that is out of proportion to the statute's salutary effects upon other important governmental interests." After an exhaustive discussion of the arguments for and against gun control, Justice Breyer arrives at his interest-balanced answer: because handgun violence is a problem, because the law is limited to an urban area, and because there were somewhat similar restrictions in the founding period (a false proposition that we have already discussed), the interest-balancing inquiry results in the constitutionality of the handgun ban. QED.

We know of no other enumerated constitutional right whose core protection has been subjected to a freestanding "interest-balancing" approach. The very enumeration of the right takes out of the hands of government-even the Third Branch of Government-the power to decide on a case-by-case basis whether the right is really worth insisting upon. A constitutional guarantee subject to future judges' assessments of its usefulness is no constitutional guarantee at all. Constitutional rights are enshrined with the scope they were understood to have when the people adopted them, whether or not future legislatures or (yes) even future judges think that scope too broad. We would not apply an "interest-balancing" approach to the prohibition of a peaceful neo-Nazi march through Skokie. See National Socialist Party of America v. Skokie, 432 U. S. 43 (1977) (per curiam). The First Amendment contains the freedom-of-speech guarantee that the people ratified, which included exceptions for obscenity, libel, and disclosure of state secrets, but not for the expression of extremely unpopular and wrong-headed views. The Second Amendment is no different. Like the First, it is the very product of an interest-balancing by the people-which Justice Breyer would now conduct for them anew. And whatever else it leaves to future evaluation, it surely elevates above all other interests the right of law-abiding, responsible citizens to use arms in defense of hearth and home.

Justice Breyer chides us for leaving so many applications of the right to keep and bear arms in doubt, and for not providing extensive historical justification for those regulations of the right that we describe as permissible. But since this case represents this Court's first in-depth examination of the Second Amendment, one should not expect it to clarify the entire field, .../. And there will be time enough to expound upon the historical justifications for the exceptions we have mentioned if and when those exceptions come before us.

In sum, we hold that the District's ban on handgun possession in the home violates the Second Amendment, as does its prohibition against rendering any lawful firearm in the home operable for the purpose of immediate self-defense. Assuming that Heller is not disqualified from the exercise of Second Amendment rights, the District must permit him to register his handgun and must issue him a license to carry it in the home.

We are aware of the problem of handgun violence in this country, and we take seriously the concerns raised by the many amici who believe that prohibition of handgun ownership is a solution. The Constitution leaves the District of Columbia a variety of tools for combating that problem, including some measures regulating handguns, ... But the enshrinement of constitutional rights necessarily takes certain policy choices off the table. These include the absolute prohibition of handguns held and used for self-defense in the home. Undoubtedly some think that the Second Amendment is outmoded in a society where our standing army is the pride of our Nation, where well-trained police forces provide personal security, and where gun violence is a serious problem. That is perhaps debatable, but what is not debatable is that it is not the role of this Court to pronounce the Second Amendment extinct.

We affirm the judgment of the Court of Appeals.

Page 77. *In connection with note 10.*

Compare United States v. Groves, 470 F.3d 31 (7th Cir. 2006) (proof of manufacture of the firearm outside of the state of Indiana held insufficient) with United States v. Dobbs, 449 F.3d 904 (8th Cir. 2006) (proof of manufacture outside of the state of Iowa held sufficient).

Note that Dobbs also sustained under the commerce power a Hobbs Act prosecution for armed robbery of a "mom and pop" convenience store in Dubuque Iowa. A concurring judge called attention to the fact that the assertion of federal jurisdiction in the case violates the United States Attorneys' written policy. See note 6, p. 275, main volume.

Page 108. Add as notes 14, 15 and 16.

14. In United States v. Giordano, 442 F.3d 30 (2d Cir. 2006), a former mayor was convicted, inter alia, of using a facility of interstate commerce for the purpose of enticing a person under the age of sixteen years to engage in sexual activity under 18 U.S.C. § 2425. (The convictions resulted from the defendant's actions, while still a mayor, in repeatedly sexually abusing the minor daughter and niece of a prostitute.) The jurisdictional clause of § 2425 provides: "Whoever, using the mail or any facility or means of interstate or foreign commerce...." On the jurisdictional issue posed, the court concluded: "...§ 2425... is satisfied by purely intrastate use of that facility.... The jurisdictional element of § 2425 is satisfied by intrastate use of a telephone capable of transmitting communications between states.

15. The use of computers and communications involving the use of the internet inevitably raises jurisdictional issues under the commerce power. See, e.g. United States v. MacEwan, 445 F.3d 237 (3rd Cir. 2006):

James MacEwan is a 71-year-old repeat offender of the federal laws prohibiting the distribution and receipt of child pornography. In 2001, prior to the present conviction for two counts of receiving child pornography in violation of § 2252A(a)(2)(B),[*] MacEwan had been arrested for and later pled guilty to possessing child pornography in violation of § 2252(a)(1)(B). On January 30, 2003, he was sentenced to five years probation. ...

---

[*] § 2252A(a)(2)(B) punishes "Any person who...knowingly receives or distributes...any material that contains child pornography that has been mailed, or shipped or transported in interstate or foreign commerce by any means, including by computer...."

Within little more than a year, MacEwan was found to have violated the terms of his probation three times, for which an indictment was returned on May 6, 2004. The indictment charged him with three counts of receiving materials containing child pornography in violation of 18 U.S.C. § 2252A(a)(2)(B).

...

At trial, MacEwan had stipulated to the number of images charged in Count ...Two, that they met the statutory definition of child pornography, and that the files had been knowingly downloaded from the Internet. He argued, however, that the government could not establish that, in compliance with the interstate commerce jurisdictional element of § 2252A(a)(2)(B), there was an interstate transmission of the pornographic images. He contended that, absent proof to the contrary, the images could just as easily have traveled intrastate and that such an activity was beyond the reach of Congress under the Commerce Clause.

To support its argument that the images had traveled in interstate commerce, the government had James Janco, the manager of Comcast's Network Abuse Department, testify. Comcast was MacEwan's Internet service provider from December 2002 to October 14, 2003. Janco chiefly summarized the flow of data over the Internet and the routing of subscribers' website connection requests.

He stated that when a Comcast subscriber accesses the Internet from his home computer and requests a connection with a website, the connection would first originate from the subscriber's computer, pass through the cable modem-both of which are located in the subscriber's house-and then be sent to a regional data center. For West Chester, Pennsylvania, where MacEwan resided, Comcast's regional data center was located within Pennsylvania. The regional data center takes the subscriber's request, transfers it through various routers within the regional data center, then sends the request to the Internet backbone, which is a series of leased, commercial and private lines. Janco then stated that those lines take the subscriber's specific request and connect it to the server containing the desired website.

Comcast calls this process of accessing a website "Shortest Path First" ("SPF"). Under SPF, when the signal travels from the regional data center it will be dynamically routed along the lines with the least volume of Internet traffic, rather than those covering the shortest geographical distance. In Janco's words: "[I]f the lines that [the request] would normally go within Pennsylvania are clogged or have a high amount of traffic on it, [the Internet backbone] would dynamically assign [the request] to another line connection and send it out of the shortest path first, what typically would be in the State of Pennsylvania in this case." Janco acknowledged, however, that if the Pennsylvania lines are full or too busy, the connection request could instead be routed through lines outside of Pennsylvania, even if the requested website were located on a server located within Pennsylvania. He stated that it was impossible to scientifically ascertain the exact path "any specific request, at a point in time would have done." Ultimately, however, the connection request would end up "wherever the server is physically located where [the subscriber] is trying to go." This server could be located in Pennsylvania or anywhere else within the United States.

Before the close of trial, MacEwan made a motion for acquittal pursuant to Rule 29(a) of the Federal Rules of Criminal Procedure. His motion contended that the government failed to prove the interstate commerce jurisdictional element of § 2252A(a)(2)(B) because there was no evidence presented at trial showing that the downloaded image files ever traveled outside of the state of Pennsylvania.

In its Memorandum Opinion dated December 29, 2004, the trial court rejected MacEwan's Rule 29(a) motion on Count Two and held that "the evidence which the government presented, that the images on the Defendant's computers were received through the internet, is sufficient to carry its burden of proof as to interstate commerce, and that it is not necessary to prove that the specific images were received from a source outside of Pennsylvania."

...

MacEwan presents a twofold challenge to the jurisdictional element of 18 U.S.C. § 2252A(a)(2)(B). He first contends that it must be strictly interpreted to require the government to prove that the child pornography images were transmitted interstate; otherwise, he contends, the jurisdictional element unconstitutionally expands Congress' power under the Commerce Clause to punish purely intrastate acts. Second, in what is essentially a sufficiency of the evidence challenge, MacEwan contends that the government failed to prove beyond a reasonable doubt that he met the jurisdictional element of § 2252A(a)(2)(B).

...

MacEwan is conflating "interstate commerce" with "interstate transmission" and confusing the nature of the jurisdictional basis for his charged offense. Nowhere in the statute does it state that the child pornography images must have crossed state lines; rather, it states solely that they must have been "transported in interstate ... commerce by any means, including by computer."

"The Internet is an international network of interconnected computers ... [and is comparable] to both a vast library including millions of readily available and indexed publications and a sprawling mall offering goods and services." *Reno v. ACLU,* 521 U.S. 844, 850-853, 117 S.Ct. 2329, 138 L.Ed.2d 874 (1997). Moreover, as is evident from the trial testimony of the government's expert, unless monitored by specific equipment, it is almost impossible to know the exact route taken by an Internet user's website connection request, such as MacEwan's requests to connect with various child pornography websites. Because of fluctuations in the volume of Internet traffic and determinations by the systems as to what line constitutes the "Shortest Path First," a website connection request can travel entirely intrastate or partially interstate.

Regardless of the route taken, however, we conclude that because of the very interstate nature of the Internet, once a user submits a connection request to a website server or an image is transmitted from the website server back to user, the data has traveled in interstate commerce. Here, once the images of child pornography left the website server and entered the complex global data transmission system that is the Internet, the images were being transmitted in interstate commerce. ...

That said, it is clear that Congress has the power to regulate the downloading of child pornography from the Internet. The Commerce Clause gives Congress power to regulate three types of activity: (1) "the use of channels of interstate commerce"; (2) "the instrumentalities of interstate commerce, or persons or things in interstate commerce, even though the threat may come only from intrastate activities"; and (3) "those activities having a substantial relation to interstate commerce, ... i.e., those activities that substantially affect interstate commerce." Ignoring the first

32

and second categories cited by *Lopez,* MacEwan proceeds to the third, and argues that because the government could not prove that the child pornography images traveled across state lines, the jurisdiction over his activity was only then created by his mere possession of child pornography. He then contends that, pursuant to *Lopez* and *Morrison,* Congress lacks the authority to regulate this activity because the mere *intrastate* possession of child pornography does not have a substantial impact on *interstate* commerce.

We disagree with this approach. In addressing the transmission of child pornography images over the Internet, we need not proceed to an analysis of *Lopez'* s third category when Congress clearly has the power to regulate such an activity under the first two....

Having concluded that the Internet is an instrumentality and channel of interstate commerce,[8] it therefore does not matter whether MacEwan downloaded the images from a server located within Pennsylvania or whether those images were transmitted across state lines. It is sufficient that MacEwan downloaded those images from the Internet, a system that is inexorably intertwined with interstate commerce. ...

16. For a decision contra to MacEwan, supra note 15, see United States v. Schaefer, 501 F.3d 1197 (10th Cir. 2007), which involved a prosecution under 18 U.S.C. § 2252 which contains jurisdictional language very similar to that used in § 2252A. The court stated:

We hold that the government did not present sufficient evidence to support the jurisdictional nexus of the § 2252(a) provisions at issue. They require a movement between states. The government did not present evidence of such movement;

---

[8] Because the Internet is a worldwide communications system composed of an interconnected network of computers, data lines, routers, servers, and electronic signals, it is difficult to discern when the instrumentality component of *Lopez'* s Category Two ends and the channel component of *Lopez'* s Category One begins. We find no need to make a distinction between the two categories, however, because the Internet is both a channel of interstate commerce, ...and, much like a bridge, railroad, highway, or airplane, it constitutes an instrumentality of interstate commerce, ...

instead, the government only showed that Mr. Schaefer used the Internet. We recognize in many, if not most, situations the use of the Internet will involve the movement of communications or materials between states. But this fact does not suspend the need for evidence of this interstate movement. The government offered insufficient proof of interstate movement in this case.

In a footnote, the court also stated:

We reach this conclusion understanding the likely interstate and international architecture and operation of the world wide web. ... But we cannot assume this intuitive fact (*i.e.,* a movement via the Internet of child-pornography images between states) on the record before us. Nor has the government asked us to take judicial notice of this fact under Federal Rule of Evidence 201. ...Although judicial notice may be taken *sua sponte,* Fed.R.Evid. 201(c), it would be particularly inappropriate for the court to make broad assumptions about the Internet absent notice to and comment by the parties.

The concurring judge stated:

I concur in the opinion but write separately to make two points. The first is about the Internet. The development and growth of the Internet over the past fifteen years complicates the statutory analysis in this case. We all know now that virtually every transmission over the Internet (especially web site access) crosses state boundaries, and quite often international borders. In this case, I have no doubt the images traveled across state and national borders.

Having said that, the statute of conviction, 18 U.S.C. § 2252(a)(2) and (a)(4), requires evidence of such a transmission. The government asserts that the record contained such evidence, but, as the opinion demonstrates, it did not. Nor has the government asked us to take judicial notice of the ubiquitous interstate nature of the Internet. Given the architecture of the Internet, it is vanishingly remote that an image did not cross state lines. Another case may well be a candidate for judicial notice of this issue....

CHAPTER 4

THE FEDERAL ROLE IN ENFORCEMENT AGAINST CRIME

Pages 129-130. Consider in connection with the material on these pages.

On March 2, 2006, Congress enacted the USA PATRIOT Improvement and Reauthorization Act of 2005. In addition to the addressing the sunsetting of 16 provisions of the original USA PATRIOT Act, the Act authorized a reorganization of the Department of Justice to function in rough parallel to the changes relating to anti-terrorism enforcement that had occurred at the FBI. The organization charts presenting the details of the change are reproduced in chapter 2 of this Supplement. The Department of Justice press release described the change as follows:

THE DEPARTMENT OF JUSTICE'S NATIONAL SECURITY DIVISION.

Since the attacks of September 11, 2001, the highest priority of the Department of Justice has been to prevent another terrorist attack on America. The reauthorizing legislation authorizes the Attorney General to reorganize the Department of Justice by placing the Department's primary national security elements under the leadership of a new Assistant Attorney General for National Security, fulfilling a recommendation of the Commission on the Intelligence Capabilities of the United States Regarding Weapons of Mass Destruction.

This reorganization would bring together under one umbrella the attorneys from the Criminal Division's Counterterrorism and Counterespionage Sections and the attorneys from the Office of Intelligence Policy and Review (OIPR), with their specialized expertise in the Foreign Intelligence Surveillance Act and other intelligence matters. The new Assistant Attorney General will thus have all three core national security components under his or her control. He or she will lead a dedicated team acting in concert to accomplish their shared mission of protecting the national security while simultaneously safeguarding Americans' civil liberties. The Assistant Attorney General will also serve as the Department's primary liaison to the new Director of National Intelligence, and the new Division will gather expertise from across the Department to create a focal point for providing advice on the numerous legal and policy issues raised by the Department's national security missions.

For a more detailed statement of the mission and functions of the new Division, see U.S. Department of Justice, National Security Division, Mission and Functions, http://www.usdoj.gov/nsd/mission_functions.htm.

Pages 126-142. Consider in connection with the material in this section.

Budgetary allocations, of course, affect the ability to pursue particular law enforcement missions. A report from the DOJ Inspector General titled, The Department of Justice's Internal Controls Over Terrorism Reporting, Audit Report 07-20, Feb. 2007, http://usdoj.gov/oig/reports/plus/a0720/index.htm indicated that departmental resources devoted to combating terrorism and promoting the nation's security increased from approximately $737 million in fiscal year 2001 to approximately $3.6 billion in fiscal year 2006, an increase of almost 400 percent, with the FBI receiving by far the biggest share of the increase. Further the President's Budget for fiscal year 2009 calls for $7.1 billion for the FBI to bolster its national security functions, and $84 million for DOJ's new National Security Division.

Page 158. Add as new subsections 3., 4., and 5. under g.

3. Early in 2007, there were reports that the Department of Justice had fired a number of U.S. Attorneys with sterling records in order to replace them with political loyalists. High ranking officials in the Department, including Attorney General Gonzales, denied the reports and insisted that in each case there had been appropriate grounds for the removal. Congress began to investigate and the matter was awash in controversy. For a news report and analysis based on an examination of emails provided by the Department, see David Johnson &Eric Lipton, 'Loyalty' to Bush and Gonzales Was Factor in Prosecutors' Firings, E-mail Shows, NY Time, Mar. 14, 2007 at A18. Also see Adam Liptak, For Federal Prosecutors,

Politics is Ever-present, NY Times, March 18, 2007 at 43, quoting Harvard Law School professor and former Solicitor General, Charles Fried, as advocating distinguishing between a failure to carry out the Administration's policies and priorities, which can appropriately be a subject of discipline and dismissal, and the targeting of political enemies for prosecution, which is "plainly out of bounds." The article suggests that drawing that line is not always easy.

4. The controversy described in note 3. above, brought attention to a previously unnoticed change in the law governing appointments of U.S. Attorneys that had been accomplished in March, 2006 by the USA PATRIOT Improvement and Reauthorization Act. It had eliminated the 120 day limit on interim appointments of U.S. Attorneys made by the Attorney General to fill vacancies. The Attorney General's interim appointments, of course, do not require Senate confirmation as do appointments of U.S. Attorneys by the President. The elimination of the 120 day limit only lasted until June 14, 2007 when S. 214, the Preserving United States Attorney Independence Act of 2007, having passed both houses of the Congress by overwhelming margins, was signed into law. This legislation restored the 120 limit on interim appointments of U.S. Attorneys.

5. On June 24, 2008, a Department of Justice report was released that indicated that highly credentialed young lawyers had been denied interviews for positions in the Department because of their political and ideological views and affiliations. The Justice Department was reported to have implemented new procedures last year to remove politics from the hiring process, and Attorney General Mukasey on the day the report was issued stated that additional reform measures would be implemented. Richard B. Schmitt, Probe Finds Illegal Hiring at Justice Department, LA Times, June 25, 2008, A9.

CHAPTER 5

MAIL FRAUD

Page 161-62.

In the wake of Hurricane Katrina, Congress enacted the Emergency and Disaster Assistance Fraud Penalty Enhancement Act of 2007. The act increases the maximum penalty for mail and wire fraud involving benefits connected to presidentially declared disasters or emergencies to 30 years. *See* Pub. L. No. 110-179, §§ 3-4, 121 Stat. 2556, 2557 (2008) (to be codified at 18 U.S.C. §§ 1341, 1343). The enhanced penalty, which was added by the Sarbanes Oxley Act of 2002, previously applied only to fraud affecting financial institutions.

Page 188. Add to note 4.

In *United States v. Sorich*, 523 F.3d 702 (7th Cir. 2008), federal prosecutors charged that an expansive patronage scheme in Chicago, involving the mayor's Office of Intergovernmental Affairs (IGA), constituted mail fraud as both a traditional deprivation of property and as a violation of honest services. The evidence showed that for many years the IGA had served as a conduit between political organizers and municipal departments, funneling the names of campaign workers to managers responsible for hiring in city departments including aviation, streets and sanitation, sewers, etc. The managers held sham interviews and falsified interview forms to select the politically favored applicants. Although some positions such as tree trimmer required merit tests, the test results were often ignored in favor of the politically connected candidates. Defendant Robert Sorich, Assistant to the IGA Director, was known as the "patronage chief." Although Sorich had attempted to delete incriminating files, investigators recovered a spreadsheet on his laptop computer containing 5,700 patronage applications.

The Seventh Circuit upheld both the honest services and traditional mail fraud theories of the case. The court reaffirmed its holding in *United States v. Bloom*, 149 F.3d 649, 655 (7th Cir. 1998), that § 1346 requires proof of misuse of office for private gain, which separates "'run-of-the-mill violations of state-law fiduciary duty . . . from federal crime.'" The court rejected the defendant's argument that the "gain" in question must flow to the defendant or one of his co-schemers. It held that a benefit that flows to a third party (such as the politically favored job applicants, who were not charged) can constitute the necessary private gain under the *Bloom* standard. The court explained:

> . . . By 'private gain' we simply mean illegitimate gain, which usually will go to the defendant, but need not.
>
> Imagine scenario (A) in which a mayor surreptitiously channels city contracts to his cronies in the business community; they get a windfall whereas he has merely helped his friends and takes no money. Or imagine scenario (B) in which an attorney bribes a court in order to obtain favorable results for his clients in their lawsuits. Or scenario (C) where a union boss sells union property to a senator even though the senator did not offer the highest price, and in exchange receives the senator's vote on a matter that concerns the union. In all three scenarios the public has been defrauded of the honest services of its public servants: the mayor, the court, and the senator. Moreover, in all three scenarios the defendant--the mayor, the attorney, and the union boss--was not the one who stood to gain financially. Certainly the defendants all received *something*: in (A), the mayor received the gratitude of his friends; in (B), the attorney could boast to future clients of a high success rate, which is good for business; and in (C) the union boss curried valuable favor with the senator. But the money went to another party. All three scenarios have played out in the federal courts and have resulted in convictions for mail fraud.
>
> These cases are the exception to a rule of human nature rather than of law: usually someone up to no good will be out to enrich himself, not others. It is thus with a hint of irony that we stated in *United States v. Spano*, 421 F.3d 599, 603 (7th Cir. 2005), that "[a] participant in a scheme to defraud is guilty even if he is an altruist and all the benefits of the fraud accrue to other participants."

Sorich is noteworthy because it compares the Seventh Circuit's position to that of other circuits (which have been critical of *Bloom*), and also because it provides an example of how § 1346 can be used to challenge the political culture of a city or state. The court also rejected a vagueness challenge to § 1346, noting that "[i]t is hard to take too seriously the contention that the defendants did not know that by creating a false hiring scheme that provided thousands of lucrative city jobs to political cronies, falsifying documents, and lying repeatedly about what they were doing, they were perpetrating a fraud."

Page 189. Add to note 4.

A recent honest services prosecution has become a poster child for claims that federal prosecutions have been politicized. In *United States v. Thompson*, 484 F.3d 877 (7th Cir. 2007), the appellate court not only reversed an honest services conviction, it took the highly unusual step of ordering Thompson released immediately after the oral argument, without waiting for a written opinion. From the bench Judge Diane Wood told the prosecutor that "Your evidence is beyond thin." Two weeks later the court followed up with an opinion explaining its action, finding the evidence insufficient to sustain the conviction and commenting on the breadth of honest services mail fraud.

Thompson, an official in Wisconsin's Bureau of Procurement, had deviated slightly from the procedures prescribed by the state's administrative code while managing the bidding process for a travel agent contract. The contract was then awarded to the low bidder. Although no one contended that Thompson had received a bribe, one of the owners of the winning travel agency had donated money to the Wisconsin governor's campaign, and Thompson reportedly made several statements to the effect that the winning agency had to receive the contract "for political reasons." A few months after the incident, Thompson received a $1,000 raise in salary. The court's opinion makes it clear that the evidence of a civil service raise after the award of a contract to the low bidder was not sufficient to justify a conviction for mail fraud (or for the other charge, federal program bribery). The court stressed the necessity of placing clear limitations on both statutes:

> Sections 666 and 1346 have an open-ended quality that makes it possible for prosecutors to believe, and public employees to deny, that a crime has occurred, and for both sides to act in good faith with support in the case law. Courts can curtail some effects of statutory ambiguity but cannot deal with the source. This prosecution, which led to the conviction and imprisonment of a civil servant for conduct that, as far as this record shows, was designed to pursue the public interest as the employee understood it, may well induce Congress to take another look at the wisdom of enacting ambulatory criminal prohibitions. Haziness designed to avoid loopholes through

41

which bad persons can wriggle can impose high costs on people the statute was not designed to catch.

Ms. Thompson's legal struggle has been linked to controversy regarding the alleged politicization of U.S. attorneys under the Bush administration. The U.S. attorney who prosecuted Thompson, Steven Biskupic, was nearly fired along with seven other U.S. attorneys in 2006, but managed to retain his job. Biskupic revealed the Thompson investigation to the media during the run up to the 2006 gubernatorial campaign, and her trial and conviction became a major issue during the campaign. The Republican candidate ran a barrage of ads linking Thompson to Governor Jim Doyle, the incumbent Democrat. (One ad showed Thompson's photo stamped "guilty," and another displayed her name on a jail cell slamming shut.) The state Democratic party chair said that the Thompson case became the number one issue in the governor's race. As the New York Times noted in an Op-Ed piece, Wisconsin is a swing state, which Bush lost narrowly in 2000 and 2004; Karl Rove was said to have identified it as the highest priority among the governor's races in 2006.

Do you think that the Thompson case demonstrates that honest services mail fraud can reach too far, allowing partisan prosecutors to pursue politically charged cases that may affect crucial elections? As you consider this issue, another facet of the case may be relevant: there is some indication that Thompson was not the prosecutor's target. According to Thompson's attorney, before and after charges were filed prosecutors offered generous plea bargains in exchange for information and testimony against Governor Doyle or other Democratic officials. Even after sentencing, prosecutors offered to file a motion to reduce Thompson's prison term if she helped build a case against more powerful state officials. In many different kinds of federal investigations, from drug trafficking to white collar crime, prosecutors use the strategy of prosecuting the little guys first, and then getting them to "flip," i.e., provide evidence against the big fish. (The sentencing guideline provisions that provide incentives for providing prosecutors with information incriminating others are discussed in the text in the notes on pages 887–89.) Perhaps that's what was going on here, and the investigation was aimed at more senior officials, up to and including the governor. If that is so, how would that affect your views on the propriety of the prosecution of Ms. Thompson? In our view, this would turn, to some degree at least, on how much other information prosecutors had to indicate that the senior officials had indeed been involved in criminal activity.

Additional material on the use of mail fraud, wire fraud, and other criminal statutes to prosecute state governors is included in Chapter 8, *infra* at 61.

Page 199. *Insert after note 3.*

The Department of Justice used honest services mail and wire fraud aggressively in prosecutions related to the Enron collapse, and the cases reflect two related points of interest. First, prosecutors pushed honest services in cases where it appeared that the employees furthered the corporation's own interests, as defined by the corporation or its management, raising the question whether this could be characterized as a breach of honest services. Second, despite the novelty of this theory and the fact that the prosecutions arose in the Fifth Circuit, which has typically read § 1346 narrowly, the government was initially successful in the district courts, where several defendants pled guilty without challenging the government's theory.

One case that finally made it to the Fifth Circuit on appeal arose out of a sham transaction, in which Enron offered to "sell" some Nigerian barges to Merrill Lynch, with Enron booking the "profit" and agreeing to repurchase the barges within six months if no third party purchaser could be found. Enron paid Merrill $250,000 plus the barges' rate of return over the six months. Merrill, which faced no risk, earned $775,000 on the deal, and by recording the transaction as a sale Enron inflated its earnings. Several Merrill employees were charged with wire fraud and conspiracy to commit wire fraud by depriving Enron of the honest services of its employees. Although the Enron employees did receive personal bonuses for helping Enron meet its earnings estimates, their conduct furthered a corporate goal. Is this a violation of the duty of honest services? On the one hand, it was obviously not in the corporation's long term interest: it was this sort of transaction that ultimately led to Enron's demise. On the other hand, their activity was inherently wrapped up in the well-being of Enron and, more importantly, in the way that Enron defined its own interests.

The court held that the employees' conduct did not constitute a violation of honest services, which applies only to cases where an employee is " 'conscious of the fact that his actions were something less than in the best interests of the employer.' " *United States v. Brown*, 459 F.3d 509 (5th Cir. 2006) The court explained:

Here, the private and personal benefit, i.e. increased personal bonuses, that allegedly diverged from the corporate interest was itself a promise of the corporation. According to the Government, Enron itself created an incentive structure tying employee compensation to the attainment of corporate earnings targets. In other words, this case presents a situation in which the employer itself created among its employees an understanding of its interest that, however benighted that understanding, was thought to be furthered by a scheme involving a fiduciary breach; in essence, all were driven by the concern that Enron would suffer absent the scheme. Given that the only personal benefit or incentive originated with Enron itself–not from a third party as in the case of bribery or kickbacks, nor from one's own business affairs outside the fiduciary relationship as in the case of self-dealing–Enron's legitimate interests were not so clearly distinguishable from the corporate goals communicated to the Defendants (via their compensation incentives) that the Defendants should have recognized, based on the nature of our past case law, that the "employee services" taken to achieve those corporate goals constituted a criminal breach of duty to Enron. We therefore conclude that the scheme as alleged falls outside the scope of honest-services fraud.

We do not presume that it is in a corporation's legitimate interests ever to misstate earnings–it is not. However, where an employer intentionally aligns the interests of the employee with a specified corporate goal, where the employee perceives his pursuit of that goal as mutually benefitting him and his employer, and where the employee's conduct is consistent with that perception of the mutual interest, such conduct is beyond the reach of the honest-services theory of fraud as it has hitherto been applied.

What do you think? Do you agree that these cases should not be treated as violations of honest services, even if it is agreed that the Enron employees breached a fiduciary duty? One way to think about this is to ask who should make the decision whether this kind of conduct should be regarded as criminal. In the case of prosecutions under the mail and wire fraud act, the judgment is not made by Congress, but rather after the fact, first by the prosecutors, and then by the jury and the reviewing courts. On the other hand, it seems in retrospect that the conduct inside Enron was beyond the pale, and a lot of people were hurt by the gross and repeated inflation of the earnings and share prices. Prosecutors saw the mail and wire fraud statutes as a way to reach this misconduct, punishing those who caused the problems, and perhaps deterring others in the future. These prosecutions reflect both the advantages and the disadvantages of the flexibility (and thus ambiguity) of the mail and wire fraud statutes. With that in mind, think again about the fact that several defendants pled guilty without challenging the government's theory. Some would argue that these guilty pleas are evidence of the fact that prosecutors are now wielding so much power that defendants can't afford to raise even strong defenses. This issue is considered in the note below.

Page 201. Insert after note 5.

After the collapse of Enron, Congress dramatically increased the statutory maximum sentences for mail and wire fraud from five years to twenty years, as part of the Sarbanes-Oxley Act of 2002. Additionally, the Department of Justice announced various steps to crack down on fraud and white collar offenses. And at the urging of the DOJ, the Sentencing Commission increased by one point the base offense level for fraud crimes with a maximum sentence of twenty or more years. It was widely expected that there would be more prosecutions, and higher sentences for those convicted.

But a recent article concludes that there have been fewer rather than more prosecutions for fraud and other white collar cases, and the sentences are virtually unchanged. *See* Lucian E. Dervan, *Plea Bargaining's Survival: Financial Crimes Plea Bargaining, a Continued Triumph in a Post-Enron World*, 60 Okla. L. Rev. 451 (2007). For example, between 2001 and 2006, the percentage of federal offenders who were charged with fraud as the primary offense fell from 11.4% to 9.7%. Dervan concludes that the net effect of all of the post-Enron reforms from Congress, the DOJ, and the Sentencing Commission was to increase sentences for economic crimes by less than one month in the years shortly after Enron. According to Dervan, however, the changes did have a different effect. They significantly strengthened prosecutors in plea bargain negotiations; longer potential sentences raise the stakes. Because the *potential* sentences that fraud and white collar defendants now face are longer, in some cases much longer, plea bargains have become even more appealing. He suggests that in some cases the discount is so enormous that it becomes an offer the defendant can't refuse. For example, Jamie Olis, a former executive at Dynergy, was initially sentenced to 292 months after trial. The CEO of Dynergy, who pled guilty and testified against Olis, was sentenced to about fifteen months imprisonment.

Even assuming that the CEO's sentence reflects reductions for his acceptance of responsibility and provision of substantial assistance to the government in Olis's case, the gap between 15 and 292 months is dramatic. It's a good question whether the cost of going to trial should ever be this high, but increasing the pressure to plead guilty may be especially problematic in mail and wire fraud cases. Given the amorphous nature of mail and wire fraud, should prosecutors have this much leverage in plea negotiations?

Pages 224-25. Insert at the end of note 2.

In *United States v. Lake*, 472 F.3d 1247 (10th Cir. 2007), the Tenth Circuit interpreted *Parr v. United States*, 363 U.S. 370 (1960), to hold that a legally compelled mailing or wire transmission is sufficient only if the transmission itself is false or fraudulent. The defendants, executives at Westar Energy, Inc., allegedly schemed to loot the corporation by initiating transactions and mergers that would result in large bonuses under their contracts. The wire fraud counts were premised on SEC filings that did not disclose the defendants' personal use of corporate aircraft. The court concluded that the SEC rules did not require the defendants to disclose their personal use of corporate aircraft. Since the required filings were neither false nor fraudulent, it reversed the wire fraud convictions.

Note that the prosecution failed solely because the government failed to prove the jurisdictional element. The court did not cast doubt on the government's allegations that the defendants had the intent to loot the corporation. If the allegations are true, isn't this a case where a federal prosecution is appropriate? On the other hand, if there is fraud in connection with SEC filings, shouldn't that be covered by some aspect of the federal securities laws, rather than mail and wire fraud?

CHAPTER 6

THE HOBBS ACT

<u>*Page 245. Add a new note after note 4.*</u>

In *Wilkie v. Robbins*, 127 S. Ct. 2588 (2007), a civil RICO case based on Hobbs Act predicate offenses, the Supreme Court considered whether the Hobbs Act applies when the federal government is the intended beneficiary of the alleged extortion. The plaintiff, a rancher, claimed that officials at the Bureau of Land Management waged a seven-year war of attrition against him. Their efforts to force the plaintiff to grant the government an easement over his property included trespasses, criminal charges, and cancellation of a right-of-way.

Reviewing the common law definition of extortion, which was the basis for the Hobbs Act's definition, the Court concluded that "the crime of extortion focused on the harm of public corruption, by the sale of public favors for private gain, not on the harm caused by overzealous efforts to obtain property on behalf of the Government." Since neither the text of the act nor the common law precedents supported a broader interpretation, the Court declined to extend the Hobbs Act to conduct undertaken by public officials that is intended to benefit the government. It explained:

> . . . without some other indication from Congress, it is not reasonable to assume that the Hobbs Act (let alone RICO) was intended to expose all federal employees, whether in the Bureau of Land Management, the Internal Revenue Service, the Office of the Comptroller of the Currency (OCC), or any other agency, to extortion charges whenever they stretch in trying to enforce Government property claims . . . . Robbins does not face up to the real problem when he says that requiring proof of a wrongful intent to extort would shield well-intentioned Government employees from liability. It is not just final judgments, but the fear of criminal charges or civil claims for treble damages that could well take the starch out of regulators who are supposed to bargain and press demands vigorously on behalf of the Government and the public. This is the reason we

would want to see some text in the Hobbs Act before we could say that Congress meant to go beyond the common law preoccupation with official corruption, to embrace the expansive notion of extortion Robbins urges on us.

The Court also rejected the plaintiff's other cause of action, the claim of a constitutional tort under *Bivens v. Six Unknown Fed. Narcotics Agents*, 403 U.S. 388 (1971). Although all members of the Court joined the majority opinion concerning the Hobbs Act, several justices filed concurring and dissenting opinions discussing the *Bivens* claim.

Page 245. Insert at end of note 4.

Scheidler II said the Hobbs Act applies only if the defendant "obtains" property, but it did not define what property means for this purpose or exactly what it means to obtain property by extortion. Those were the questions in *United States v. Gotti*, 459 F.3d 296 (2d Cir. 2006). Various members of the Gambino Organized Crime Family appealed their convictions of Hobbs Act violations, which were charged as separate offenses and RICO predicate offenses. The extortionate conduct involved in this case varied from controlling the internal politics and health plan coverage of the International Longshoremen's Association (ILA) to using threats in an attempt to force Steven Seagal to work with a Gambino associate.

The 68-count indictment charged, inter alia, that the Gambino family took control of the affairs of the ILA, determining who filled various union positions, ensuring that organized crime associates were in those positions, and then directing the activities of the office holders. The prosecution argued that the defendants had wrongfully obtained the following property of union members:

"(1) ILA labor union positions, money paid as wages and employee benefits, and other economic benefits that such ILA union members would have obtained but for the defendants' corrupt influence over such union; (2) the right of ILA union members to free speech and democratic participation in the affairs of their labor organization as guaranteed by [Sections 411 and 481 of the Labor-Management Reporting Disclosure Act ('LMRDA'), 29 U.S.C. § 401 *et seq.*]; and (3) the right of ILA union members to have the officers, agents, delegates, employees and other representatives of their labor organization manage the money, property and financial affairs of the organization in accordance with [Section 501(a) of the LMRDA]."

Is the right of a union member to free speech and democratic participation in union affairs a property right? Did the defendants who took over the union by force and violence obtain these rights from the members by extortion?

The court of appeals noted that in *Schiedler II*, the anti-abortion protesters' activity was not extortion because they had not "'pursued [or] received something of value from [victims] that they could exercise, transfer, or sell.'" (quoting *Schiedler II*, 537 U.S. at 405). Accordingly, the court held:

> . . . in evaluating an extortion count's conformity with *Scheidler II* – *i.e.,* whether it adequately alleges the "obtaining of property" for purposes of the Hobbs Act's definition of extortion – the key inquiry is whether the defendant is (1) alleged to have carried out (or, in the case of attempted extortion, attempted to carry out) the deprivation of a property right from another, with (2) the intent to exercise, sell, transfer, or take some other analogous action with respect to that right. A motive ultimately to profit by cashing out the value of the property right will generally serve as powerful evidence that the defendant's goal was to obtain the right for himself, rather than merely to deprive the victim of that right.

Applying this test, the court found that the defendants in *Gotti* did seek to obtain the ILA members' rights to free speech and democratic participation, and to exercise those rights themselves by telling various delegates for whom to vote, and by controlling the elected officials' performance of their union duties, in a way that would benefit them financially. The court applied a similar analysis to the other Hobbs Act charges, upholding them all.

Are you surprised at the decision in the *Gotti* case? The court begins by saying that the case concerns intangible property rights, but it seems clear that these were not the more traditional forms of intangible property, such as a contract or a patent. (Do you think that this would be treated as property for purposes of the mail fraud act? See text at 202 et seq.)

Page 259. Insert new note before note 4.

Does the quid pro quo test, by its nature, require that when the "quid" is received the parties have identified a specific act or acts that will be performed in return? What if there is an ongoing stream of benefits and official acts done in return, as issues arise?

In *United States v. Ganim*, 510 F.3d 134 (2d Cir. 2007), the mayor of Bridgeport used his official power to help two friends obtain city contracts. In return, they were to give Ganim what he wanted, when he wanted it – cash, meals, clothes, jewelry, and more. Ganim was convicted of racketeering, racketeering conspiracy, Hobbs Act extortion, honest services mail fraud, program bribery, conspiracy to commit bribery, and filing false income tax returns.

On appeal, Ganim challenged the jury instructions for the Hobbs Act charge because they did not require a finding that the benefits he received were connected to a specific act. The court rejected this argument, holding that "so long as the jury finds that an official accepted gifts in exchange for a promise to perform official acts for the giver, it need not find that the specific act to be performed was identified at the time of the promise, nor need it link each specific benefit to a single official act." It distinguished language from the Supreme Court's decision in *Sun Diamond*, text at 279, noting that the prosecution in that case was under a different statute, 18 U.S.C. § 201, which distinguishes between bribery and the lesser offense of illegal gratuities. As noted in Chapter 8, *infra* at 50, some members of Congress have suggested that the *Ganim* rule should be extended to Section 201.

CHAPTER 7

OFFICIAL BRIBERY AND GRATUITIES

Page 289. Add to note 3.

In some cases, the quid pro quo and corrupt intent are blatant. In 2005, Randy "Duke" Cunningham (R-CA) pled guilty to conspiracy and tax evasion charges in connection with accepting $2.4 million in bribes of many forms and evading over $1 million in taxes. Cunningham served as a Navy fighter pilot in Vietnam and represented California's 50th district for over a decade. A member of the powerful House Appropriations Committee from 1998 to 2005, he solicited and accepted bribes from defense contractors in exchange for government contracts. Cunningham pled guilty to one count each of tax evasion and conspiracy to commit bribery, honest services wire and mail fraud, and tax evasion. He was sentenced to eight years and four months in prison, the longest sentence ever given to a congressman.

Cunningham gave Mitchell Wade, founder and former President of MZM Inc., a "bribe menu" (pictured below) indicating that a boat worth $140,000 ("140 BT") would buy $16 million (16) in defense contracts. The note, scrawled below the Congressional seal, further delineated what each additional million dollars in government contracts would cost in payments to Cunningham.

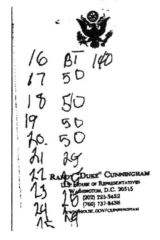

In exchange for approximately $160 million in Pentagon contracts, MZM gave Cunningham more than $1 million in payments and gifts, including money to pay off his mortgage and an extensive array of services, including travel on a charter jet, and luxury items including a Rolls-Royce, antique furnishings, and Persian-style rugs. Cunningham even charged the bill for his daughter's graduation party to the company credit card. The former congressman also received more than $700,000 in cash, checks, meals, and luxury items and services from another defense contractor, which received $90 million in contracts.

A number of other members of Congress, executive branch officials, and lobbyists have also been prosecuted in recent years for bribery and influence peddling, though not all of the cases have been based upon § 201. In 2006, former Ohio Congressman Robert Ney pled guilty to corruption charges in connection with his dealings with former lobbyist Jack Abramoff. In exchange for pushing legislation favorable to Abramoff's clients, Ney enjoyed a stream of benefits including trips valued at over $170,000, tickets to sporting events, expensive meals, and campaign contributions. Ney's official favors included sponsoring legislation, attaching amendments to a 2002 election reform bill, inserting comments in the Congressional Record, and helping a client win a contract to provide wireless communication services to the U.S. Capitol. Ney pled guilty to one count of making false statements and one count of conspiracy to violate the following federal laws: honest services wire and mail fraud, in violation of 18 U.S.C. §§ 1341, 1343, and 1346; making false statements, in violation of 18 U.S.C. § 1001; and post employment restrictions for former Congressional staffers, in violation of 18 U.S.C § 207(e). A federal judge sentenced Ney to 30 months in prison, which is more than what the government requested. He was released in February of 2008 and moved to a halfway house after serving a little under a year.

The Ney/Abramoff investigation has claimed several other victims, and it is still continuing. Abramoff pled guilty to fraud charges unrelated to Ney's case, and he agreed to cooperate in the ongoing federal bribery investigation. The now-infamous lobbyist's team included Ney's former chief of staff, Neil Volz, and two of former House Majority Leader Tom Delay's former aides. Volz, who assisted in the investigation of Ney, was sentenced to probation after pleading guilty to a charge of conspiracy to violate his one year lobbying ban and to commit honest services mail and wire fraud. DeLay's former aides pled guilty to public corruption charges including conspiracy to commit bribery, mail and wire fraud, and honest services fraud. The same federal task force prosecuted Bush administration officials David Safavian, former chief of staff at the General Services Administration, and Roger Stillwell, an Interior Department official. Safavian was sentenced to 18 months in prison after he was found guilty of lying to federal officials about an Abramoff-sponsored golfing trip in Scotland (of which Ney was also a part). Stillwell pled guilty to giving Abramoff copies of internal agency documents and accepting hundreds of dollars worth of football and concert tickets without reporting them. The task force has also examined Abramoff's dealings with the Congressional offices of Senator Conrad Burns (R-Mont.) and Representative John Doolittle (R-Calif.). Burns, who narrowly lost re-election amid the scandal back in 2006, is no longer under investigation. However, federal officials are still looking closely at Abramoff's relationship with Doolittle, who announced he would not seek re-election in 2008. In the wake of the Cunningham and Abramoff scandals, the House and Senate passed ethics reforms prohibiting lawmakers from accepting gifts, meals, and travel from lobbyists or making anonymous earmarks.

Page 290. Add to note 5.

The D.C. Circuit read the official act requirement very narrowly in *Valdes v. United States*, 475 F.3d 1319 (D.C. Cir. 2007) (en banc), reversing the jury conviction of a D.C. police officer indicted for bribery and found guilty of the lesser-included offense of receiving illegal gratuities. The appellate panel held that the illegal gratuities statute did not apply because the officer's actions–searching a law enforcement database to obtain vehicle-registration and arrest-warrant information–lacked a sufficiently "formal" relationship to his official duties. The dissent warned that such a narrow conception of official action would "undermine the prosecution of public corruption." *Id.* at 1346 (Garland, J., dissenting). Valdes conducted the searches in exchange for secret cash payments from an FBI informant posing as a judge seeking information on individuals who owed him money. It seems highly unlikely that Congress intended the official act requirement to exempt this type of conduct from prosecution under § 201. Indeed, pending legislation, see *infra* page 60, would clarify that any action in the range of a public official's duties qualifies as an official act.

Page 290. Add to note 6.

A recent case highlighted the special problems that can arise in connection with the prosecution of members of Congress. In 2007, federal prosecutors charged Congressman William Jefferson (D-La.) with sixteen counts of wrongdoing including soliciting bribes, violating the Foreign Corrupt Practices Act, obstructing justice, honest services wire fraud, money laundering, and racketeering. Jefferson's indictment details seven different bribery schemes involving telecommunications deals and other business ventures in Africa. The Congressman allegedly received hundreds of thousands of dollars worth of bribes from companies seeking to benefit from his connections. In exchange, Jefferson led official delegations to Africa, communicated with foreign and domestic government officials, and utilized the resources of his staff and office to advance the companies' business interests.

In 2006, FBI officials seized $90,000 from the freezer in Jefferson's Washington home. The cash had been provided to Jefferson by a wealthy businesswoman with whom he had secretly been working to launch a business venture in Africa. The plan was to use the money to bribe a high-ranking Nigerian official to secure a favorable deal with a government-controlled telecommunications service provider. In exchange for making the bribe, Jefferson's family members would receive a financial stake in the businesswoman's fledgling Nigerian company.

Following the seizure of the cash from Jefferson's home, the FBI obtained a warrant and searched Jefferson's Congressional office. A federal appeals court held that, under the Speech or Debate Clause, the FBI is barred from searching a location containing legislative materials without the Member's consent. *United States v. Rayburn House Office Bldg.*, 497 F.3d 654 (D.C. Cir. 2007). The Supreme Court denied the Justice Department's petition for certiorari. *United States v. Rayburn House Office Bldg.*, 128 S.Ct. 1738 (2008). Opponents of the search of the Congressional office saw the search as an assault on the separation of powers. Proponents of the search noted that the ruling casts too broad a protective shield. It suggests that if missing Congressional intern Chandra Levy's body had been dismembered and stored in a Congressional office there would have been no way to legally seize it.

Jefferson's case is demonstrative of the procedural thicket that federal officials face when investigating and prosecuting a member of Congress. Jefferson invoked the Speech or Debate Clause again when he moved to dismiss his indictment on grounds that it was based on privileged information. The Court upheld the indictment on the ground that it alleges criminal conduct beyond the protection of the Speech or Debate Clause, which applies only to legislative acts. *United States v. Jefferson*, 534 F. Supp. 2d 645, 652 (E.D. Va. 2008).

Page 304. Add to Note 4.

Recent prosecutions suggest that federal prosecutors are pushing the envelope, using § 666 to reach state judges and members of the state legislature, without any special showing that the state official in question was responsible for federal programs or funds.

Trial lawyer Richard "Dickie" Scruggs made millions in class-action suits against the tobacco and asbestos industries and is famous for helping negotiate the $200 billion dollar tobacco settlement. He was played by actor Com Feore in the 1999 film, "The Insider," which tells the story of the scientist who exposed Big Tobacco's shady practices. Scruggs starred in his own legal drama in 2007, when he was caught attempting to buy a favorable ruling in a dispute over the distribution of $26.5 million in legal fees generated by a mass settlement of Hurricane Katrina-related claims. The judge reported the bribe overture to the FBI, and Scruggs, along with four co-conspirators, was indicted for violating 18 U.S.C. §§ 666, 1343, and 1346. The indictment alleges that Scruggs not only instructed lawyer Anthony Balducci to make bribe payments but also manufactured documents showing that Balducci was hired to do jury selection work.

This case raises two interesting questions. The first concerns the applicability of the federal program bribery statute to state judges. Scruggs was charged with violating § 666 despite the absence of a demonstrable nexus between federal funds received by the state of Mississippi and the object of the bribe, a favorable ruling. Since all states receive at least $10,000 in federal funds, does this case establish that federal prosecutors can charge a violation of § 666 whenever a state judge is bribed? Perhaps, but note that Scruggs pled guilty, so the issue of the outer boundary of § 666 was not fully litigated. Second, why did the state judge report the bribe overture to the FBI as opposed to state prosecutors? Perhaps he feared that Scruggs' political connections would shield him within the state system; Scruggs' brother-in-law is former U.S. Senator Trent Lott. If that were the case, would it affect your view on the propriety of giving § 666 such a broad interpretation?

The prosecution of North Carolina House Speaker Jim Black (who has since resigned) shows the applicability of§ 666 to state legislators. Black pled guilty to corruptly accepting payments totaling $29,000 from three chiropractors in violation of§ 666. In exchange, Black promised to push legislation favorable to the chiropractic profession through the North Carolina General Assembly. On several occasions, Black met chiropractors in restaurant bathrooms and accepted payments that he later deposited in his personal bank account. Although Black neither reported the payments to the North Carolina State Board of Elections nor placed them in his campaign account, he initially claimed they were campaign contributions. Eventually, however, Black pled guilty to violating§ 666 and was sentenced to five years and three months in prison and a $50,000 fine.

The factual basis for Black's plea agreement does not map very easily onto the structure of§ 666, which requires that a thing of value be given in connection with "any business, transaction, or series of transactions ... involving anything of value of $5,000 or more." Federal program bribery typically involves government contracts valued at $5,000 or more. In Black's case, however, the chiropractors were seeking advancement of legislation benefitting their profession, and, presumably, their pocketbooks. How should the value of the transaction be determined when the goal of the bribe is favorable legislation, and not monetary contracts? Would the value of the transaction be the expected value of the legislation to the chiropractors? If so, is the amount of money paid in the bribes ($29,000) an indication that the legislation had a value to the givers of the bribe of much more than $5,000? Or, would you actually have to figure out how much chiropractors stood to earn by changing the law?

The factual basis statement filed with the plea agreement is also vague with regard to the requirement of§ 666 that the organization, government, or agency receives over $10,000 in federal money:

> During every one-year period while Jim Black was Speaker, the State of North Carolina received millions of dollars in benefits under scores of Federal programs involving various forms of Federal assistance. Among such programs receiving such Federal assistance are many that impact health care services, including Medicaid.

If you were a federal judge, would you find the facts in the Black case legally sufficient to bring the payments within§ 666? If so, does that mean that any bribe to any state official in North Carolina is subject to§ 666? If not, what more would be necessary? There was a loose connection between favorable legislation related to insurance and the federal Medicaid program. Is that enough? Should it be?

CHAPTER 8

AN OVERVIEW OF FEDERAL CRIMES DEALING WITH POLITICAL CORRUPTION

Several developments that affect public corruption in general, as well as specific crimes, have generated concern in Congress, particularly in the Senate, in which there is now wide support for legislative action. The principal vehicle in the Senate has been S. 1946, the Public Corruption Prosecution Improvement Act of 2007, sponsored by Senator Leahy, the Democratic chairman of the Judiciary Committee, and co-sponsored by Senators Cornyn and Sessions, Republican members of the Committee. The Judiciary Committee passed the bill, which as of this writing has been placed on the Senate Legislative Calendar. Because so little time remains before the end of the legislative session, unanimous consent is being sought, and would probably be required to pass the bill in this session. Even if the bill passes in the Senate, it is unlikely that it would pass the House before adjournment. Nevertheless, S. 1946 provides significant insight into perceptions in Congress of the directions in which legislative reforms may go. The following information is taken from the Judiciary Committee's report on S. 1946, S. Rep. 110-239 (2007).

In describing the rationale for the bill, the Committee first stressed the serious danger presented by public corruption, and the need for legislative action. The report states:

> . . . Public corruption victimizes all Americans by quietly chipping away at the foundations of our democracy. Americans' faith in their elected leaders and their Government has been tested in recent years as several high-ranking public officials have pleaded guilty or been convicted of serious and corrosive public corruption offenses. The stain of corruption has spread to all levels of Government and affected both major political parties.

> The American people have taken notice. Exit polls following the 2006 mid-term elections revealed that 42 percent of voters identified 'corruption and ethics' as 'extremely

important to their vote,' trumping terrorism, the economy and Iraq. They rightly expect Congress to do all it can to not only police itself, but also to insure that corruption is stamped out at all levels of government.

* * * * *

Notwithstanding several recent prosecutions of high-profile public officials, public corruption enforcement generally has waned since 9/11, because scarce FBI resources have been shifted away from the pursuit of white collar crime to counterterrorism. A September 2005 report by Department of Justice Inspector General Glenn Fine found that, from 2000 to 2004, there was an overall reduction in public corruption matters handled by the FBI. More recently, a study by the nonpartisan research group Transactional Records Access Clearinghouse (TRAC) found that the prosecution of all kinds of white collar crimes is down 27 percent since 2000, and official corruption cases have dropped in the same period by 14 percent.

Man-power and funding shortages have contributed to these declines, and this trend has real-world consequences: the Wall Street Journal reported recently that the investigation of a federal elected official stalled for six months because the investigating U.S. Attorney's Office could not afford to replace the prosecutor who was handling the case.

Funding shortfalls in this area of criminal enforcement should be of particular concern to lawmakers. Public corruption cases are time and resource intensive, because they often involve complex schemes hatched by sophisticated criminals who know how to cover their tracks. Their investigation and prosecution frequently requires teams of federal agents, multiple prosecutors, financial analysts, and paralegals, among other specialists. They often include the use of time-consuming investigative techniques such as forensic analysis as well as the execution of search warrants and wiretaps. Efforts to fully fund anti-corruption units to ensure that investigators and prosecutors have enough time to put cases together are imperative because without adequate time and resources, these cases simply will not be brought.

Even absent the diversion of resources since 9/11, public corruption enforcement must be a national law enforcement priority for this Congress, because corrupt public officials can compromise our national security in alarming ways. Indeed, the FBI's own web site notes that 'public corruption can have a direct impact on national security,' and it is not difficult to understand this relationship. A bribed customs official who allows a terrorist to smuggle a dirty bomb into the country could cause grave harm to our national security, as could a corrupt consular officer who illegally supplies U.S. entry visas to would-be terrorists. This link between public corruption and national security must be addressed if Congress is serious about doing all it can to protect national security.

Corruption cases are also very difficult to prove, so Congress must speak with absolute clarity in those statutes that criminalize corrupt conduct by Government employees and officials. Those who agree to sell their office for personal gain through a bribery scheme, or to use their office to extort money from private citizens, know how to recognize and exploit ambiguities in the law that have been created by unexpected court decisions or by creative end-runs around the anti-corruption laws unforeseen by the policy makers who originally passed those laws. Just as Congress recently shored up its ethics rules to leave no doubt as to the obvious impropriety of taking excessive gifts from outside interests, it is crucial that Congress shore up the criminal law to close loopholes and resolve legal ambiguities that may allow corrupt actors to evade or defeat prosecution.

With this background in mind, the bill proposed by the Committee contains (1) additional resources of $25 million per year for FY 2008-2011 for FBI and Department of Justice efforts to combat official corruption, and (2) a variety of reforms to strengthen and clarify existing corruption laws. Several of the most significant changes are:

- amending the mail and wire fraud statutes to reach schemes involving intangible interests such as "contract rights, licenses, permits, trade secrets, franchises, and government grants." This is intended to reverse the Supreme Court's decision in *Cleveland*, text at 206, by extending the reach of the statutes to schemes to defraud states and local governments of unissued licenses.

- amending 18 U.S.C.§ 666 (the federal program bribery statute, text at 296) by reducing the $5,000 requirement to $1,000 for section 666 bribery offenses, increasing the maximum penalty for all offenses under this section from 10 years to 15 years, and clarifying that a 'thing' of value can refer to a single item or more than one item.

- increasing the maximum term of imprisonment for bribery violations under 18 U.S.C. § 201(b) (text at 278) from 15 years to 20 years.

- amending the gratutity provisions (18 U.S.C. § 201(c)(1)(A) & (B), text at 279) to clarify that things of value, given to a public official 'for or because of' that official's position and not otherwise permitted by law or regulation, are illegal under the federal gratuities statute. This would effectively overrule the Supreme Court's decision in *Sun Diamond*, text at 279.

- expanding the definition of 'official act' (18 U.S.C. § 201(a)(3), text at 278) to include any conduct that falls within the range of official duty of the public official. This change counters the D.C. Circuit's narrow reading of the official act requirement in *Valdes*, *supra* page 53.

- clarifying that an 'official act' can be a single act, more than one act, or a course of conduct, and that a corrupt payment or series of such payments can be made to influence a government official to perform an official act or a series of such acts. These changes would, inter alia, endorse the decision in *Ganim*, *supra* page 50, which dealt with the Hobbs Act and federal program bribery under§ 666, and extend its reasoning to bribery under § 201. The purpose of the clarification is to close a potential loophole where bribery is a course of conduct rather than a one-to-one quid pro quo by confirming that the government is not required to tie payments to specific acts.

In its consideration of the bill, the Senate Committee on the Judiciary rejected two amendments offered by Ranking Member, Arlen Specter (R-Pa.), aimed at limiting the potential sweep of the federal gratuities statute, 18 U.S.C. § 201(c). One amendment would have precluded campaign contributions from being charged as gratuities. The other would have added a new element to the offense: that it be committed "knowingly and corruptly." Proponents of the amendments expressed concern that the federal gratuities statute creates a potential trap for the unwary and gives federal prosecutors too much power, problems to which the Supreme Court alluded in *Sun Diamond*, text at 279. Opponents of the amendments argued that prosecutors need a means to go after corruption not rising to the level of bribery, and that the government's interest in preventing the appearance of corruption is just as strong as the interest in preventing blatant quid pro quos. The bill does, however, address Justice Scalia's concern in *Sun Diamond* that broadly reading § 201(c)(1)(A) would criminalize token gifts like the replica jerseys traditionally given by championship sports teams to the President. A new safe harbor provision would prevent this by exempting benefits accepted by public officials that are permitted by rules or regulations from prosecution for gratuities.

Although the breadth of federal anti-corruption statutes creates the potential for abuse and political manipulation, federal prosecutors may be the only check on pervasive state corruption that has serious or even tragic consequences. In 2003, former Illinois Republican Governor George Ryan became the sixty-sixth individual charged in *Operation Safe Road*, which was initiated in 1998 after a federal investigation into an accident that killed six children revealed that bribes were being paid to obtain truck-driving licenses in Illinois. Many of those who obtained their licenses in this fashion were totally unqualified. When the investigation implicated some of his closest aides, Governor Ryan announced that he would not seek re-election in 2002. The election of a Democratic governor in 2002 ended twenty-five years of Republican control of the Illinois governorship. Federal prosecutors in Ryan's case described public corruption in the state of Illinois as a "mutating virus." A total of seventy-nine former state officials, lobbyists, and truck drivers have been charged in the ongoing federal probe, and practically all of them have been convicted. Ryan was indicted on racketeering conspiracy, mail and tax fraud, and false statement charges. The indictment alleged that during Ryan's terms as Secretary of State and Governor he engaged in a pattern of corruption that involved steering lucrative state business to friends and performing official favors in exchange for payments, vacations, and services worth at least $167,000. A jury convicted Ryan of all charges brought against him, though the trial judge threw out two of the counts for lack of proof. Ryan fought the remaining racketeering and fraud charges all the way up to the Supreme Court, which recently declined to hear his case. The former governor, who began serving a six and a half year prison sentence in 2007, is scheduled to be released at age 79.

Although the Illinois prosecutions seem like a success story, other public corruption prosecutions have been plagued by plausible claims of political tampering. The prosecution of former Alabama Governor Don Siegelman has become a national controversy, with its effects spilling over into the House Judiciary Committee and even the Federal Communications Commission. After a long investigation, Siegelman was indicted in 2005 on multiple charges, including federal funds bribery, aiding and abetting honest services mail fraud, obstruction of justice, and Hobbs Act extortion. Most of the charges were based on large contributions made by Richard Scrushy, the former CEO of HealthSouth, to the campaign for an Alabama state lottery system, one of Siegelman's pet issues which was on the ballot in 1999. Siegelman appointed Scrushy to the Alabama Certificate of Need Review Board, allegedly in exchange for the contributions. Siegelman was convicted on multiple counts and in 2007 was sentenced to more than seven years imprisonment.

The Siegelman prosecution became controversial due in part to the political connections of U.S. Attorney Leura Canary's husband. William Canary worked on the campaign of Bob Riley, who defeated Siegelman in the 2002 gubernatorial election. In a conference call concerning a threatened election recount after Riley's victory, William Canary said " 'his girls' would take care of" Siegelman, according to an affidavit from a participant in the call. It is also alleged in the affidavit that Canary mentioned the involvement of Karl Rove, telling supporters "not to worry–that he had already gotten it worked out with Karl and Karl had spoken with the Department of Justice and the Department of Justice was already pursuing Don Siegelman."

In 2008 Siegelman was released pending appeal of his conviction to the Eleventh Circuit. In an odd twist, an Alabama CBS affiliate suffered a blackout during the airing of a 60 Minutes episode about the Siegelman prosecution. The intense controversy surrounding the case led to inquiries from an FCC commissioner, despite the station's claim that technical difficulties caused the blackout. Karl Rove is scheduled to testify before the House Judiciary Committee on July 10, 2008 about his potential involvement in the Siegelman prosecution and U.S. Attorney firings. At the time this supplement is being written, however, it is uncertain whether Rove will comply with the subpoena.

Several other governors have recently been involved in public corruption scandals, leading to federal charges in some–but not all–cases. In 2004, former Connecticut governor John Rowland pled guilty to conspiracy to commit honest services mail fraud and tax fraud. Rowland, who was elected to three terms as governor, accepted inappropriate gifts related to state business, amounting to more than $100,000 in value. Also in 2004, federal prosecutors indicted a fundraiser for then New Jersey governor James McGreevey, connecting McGreevey to the alleged corruption scheme without charging him. Shortly thereafter, McGreevey resigned after admitting to an affair with a male aide. And in 2008, New York governor Eliot Spitzer resigned in disgrace after suspicious money transfers led to a federal investigation that linked him to a pricey prostitution ring.

What do these cases indicate? One possible interpretation is that corruption at the highest levels in the states is so pervasive that federal intervention is necessary. According to this view, it's to be expected that political opponents seek to discredit such prosecutions. But one can also argue that the breadth of the federal public corruption statutes allows prosecutors to use them as partisan weapons, and that the general breadth of other federal criminal laws (such as the law making it a crime to transport prostitutes across state lines) just makes the problem worse.

The malleable nature of these public corruption statutes may be especially problematic if the Department of Justice is highly politicized, as it allegedly was during much of the Bush presidency. Nine U.S. Attorneys were fired in 2006, a number unprecedented in recent administrations. Critics allege that the firings were linked to the attorneys' decisions in politically motivated corruption and election fraud prosecutions. *See* John McKay, *Train Wreck at the Justice Department: An Eyewitness Account*, 31 Seattle U. L. Rev. 265 (2008); *Continuing Investigation into the US Attorneys Controversy and Related Matters (Part I): Hearing Before the H. Comm. On the Judiciary*, 110th Cong. 56 (2007); Majority Staff of H. Comm. On the Judiciary, 110th Cong., Allegations of Selective Prosecution in our Federal Criminal Justice System (2008) (prepared for Rep. John Conyers, Chairman, H.Comm. on the Judiciary).

The U. S. Attorney firings provide an important perspective not only on the consequences of the breadth (and arguably vagueness) of the federal statutes used to prosecute political corruption, but also on issues concerning the decision-making process in corruption cases. In many contexts requiring review or approval in Main Justice has been seen as a mechanism for enhancing fairness and consistency. The U.S. Attorney firings, however, suggest that centralization might have its own perils, potentially increasing the likelihood that partisan motivations will affect prosecutorial decisions. One could locate the discretion for such prosecutions exclusively in the individual U.S. Attorneys Offices, but that would give all of the power to local actors who may have close ties to some or all of the potential defendants, and also increases the possibility that a rogue U.S. Attorney might go after her political enemies. Moreover, vesting exclusive discretion farther down within the federal system inevitably means that various offices will adopt conflicting interpretations of the statutes in question. For an excellent discussion of the many issues that should be considered in allocating prosecutorial power in the federal system, see Bruce A. Green & Fred C. Zacharias, *The U.S. Attorneys Scandal" and the Allocation of Prosecutorial Power*, 69 Ohio St. L. J. (forthcoming 2008).

CHAPTER 9

DRUG OFFENSE ENFORCEMENT

Page 338. Insert after first paragraph.

Following *Raich*, the government deployed the big gun of the continuing criminal enterprise statute (discussed in the text at 389-403) to convict two leaders of the California Healthcare Collective. The Collective, which was licensed and paid taxes, claimed to be operating in conformity with the California laws allowing marijuana use in some medical circumstances. The business was highly profitable, with estimated revenues of $9 million in two years. Federal prosecutors argued that California law does not allow for-profit medical marijuana distributors, but even if the Collective was operating legally under state law, it was still violating the federal laws regulating marijuana. The district court made a number of rulings that greatly restricted the defenses available at trial. It excluded evidence concerning the legality of medical marijuana under California law and its medical value, held that the defendant could not raise the defenses of necessity or entrapment by estoppel, and barred evidence intended to promote jury nullification. *United States v. Scarmazzo*, 2008 W.L. 1946523 (E.D. Cal. 2008).

Insert at page 345

The Adam Walsh Child Protection and Safety Act of 2006 amended § 841 to reflect risks posed by date rape drugs and the Internet. *See* Pub. L. No. 109-248, § 201, 120 Stat. 587, 611-12 (2006). The act adds subsection (g), which states:

> (1) Whoever knowingly uses the Internet to distribute a date rape drug to any person, knowing or with reasonable cause to believe that–
>
>> (A) the drug would be used in the commission of criminal sexual conduct; or
>>
>> (B) the person is not an authorized purchaser . . . .

The statute provides a detailed definition of the term "authorized purchaser."

Page 368. Substitute for note 3.

The Sentencing Commission, the courts and Congress have all been active in dealing with the problem of crack sentencing, which is discussed in the casebook on pages 357-69. Note that the sentences in each case are controlled by (1) the statute defining the offense and applicable penalty, and (2) the Guidelines. Almost all of the action has focused on the Guidelines, which are part–but by no means all–of the problem.

The Commission

The Commission acted first, renewing its efforts to reduce the disparity in treatment between crack and powder cocaine. In the 2007 amendment cycle it proposed an amendment that Congress failed to block from taking effect as of December 1, 2007. The amendment reduces by two levels the base offense level associated with each quantity of crack. *See* Amendments to the Sentencing Guidelines for United States Courts, 72 Fed. Reg. 28571-28572 (2007). In effect, the Guidelines now incorporate a crack/powder ratio that varies (at different offense levels) between 25 to 1 and 80 to 1. The amendment yields sentences for crack offenses between two and five times longer than sentences for equal amounts of powder. Describing the amendment as "only . . . a partial remedy" for the problems generated by the crack/powder disparity, the Commission noted that "[a]ny comprehensive solution requires appropriate legislative action by Congress."

The Supreme Court

The Supreme Court acted next, responding to an issue set in motion by its decision in *Booker v. United States*, 543 U.S. 220 (2005) (text at 854), which made the Sentencing Guidelines advisory, rather than mandatory. Some district courts used this new freedom in sentencing to grant defendants convicted of crack offenses below-Guidelines sentences, often by using ratios less than 100 to 1. But other judges disagreed, seeing this as a legislative judgment. As the court explained in *United States v. Tabor*, 365 F. Supp. 2d 1052, 1060-61 (D. Neb. 2005):

> Simply stated, unlike Congress or the Commission, we judges lack the institutional capacity (and, frankly, the personal competence) to set and then enforce one new, well-chosen, theoretically coherent, national standard. As opposed to a uniform, albeit flawed, Guideline, it would make things far worse to have a bunch of different standards for crack sentencing. For that reason alone, we should sit on our

collective hands and give the crack Guidelines substantial or heavy weight until Congress decides otherwise.

In *Kimbrough v. United States,* 128 S. Ct. 558 (2007), the Court settled the issue, holding that the district courts do have the authority to sentence individual defendants to a below-Guideline sentence based, in part, on the court's conclusion that the guideline for crack would impose an unduly harsh sentence. This decision relied on the Sentencing Commission's own series of reports (most described in the casebook) finding that the crack penalties were unjustifiably high. The Court noted that prior Commission reports identified three problems with the 100-to-1 crack to powder ratio:

(1) the ratio rested on erroneous assumptions about the relative harmfulness of the two drugs and the relative prevalence of harmful conduct associated with their use and distribution;

(2) the ratio does not achieve the objective of punishing major drug traffickers most harshly, and instead can lead to the "anomalous" result that "retail crack dealers get longer sentences than the wholesale drug distributors who supply them the powder cocaine from which their crack is produced;" and

(3) the crack/powder sentencing differential fosters disrespect for the criminal justice system and a perception that it promotes unwarranted disparity based on race because 85% of the defendants receiving harsher sentences for crack offenses are black.

After reviewing its blockbuster *Booker* decision holding the Sentencing Guidelines advisory, the Court stated that the district courts must ordinarily treat the Guidelines as the "starting point and the initial benchmark." This reflects the Commission's role of formulating and refining national sentencing standards based upon empirical data and national experience, guided by a professional staff with appropriate expertise. But that model, the majority held, does not apply to the crack Guideline. Writing for the Court, Justice Ginsburg explained:

The crack cocaine Guidelines, however, present no occasion for elaborative discussion of this matter because those Guidelines do not exemplify the Commission's exercise of its characteristic institutional role. In formulating Guidelines ranges for crack cocaine offenses, as we earlier noted, the Commission looked to the mandatory minimum sentences set in the 1986 Act, and did not take account of "empirical data and national experience."

Indeed, the Commission itself has reported that the crack/powder disparity produces disproportionately harsh sanctions, *i.e.*, sentences for crack cocaine offenses "greater than necessary" in light of the purposes of sentencing set forth in § 3553(a). *Given all this, it would not be an abuse of discretion for a district court to conclude when sentencing a particular defendant that the crack/powder disparity yields a sentence "greater than necessary" to achieve § 3553(a)'s purposes, even in a mine-run case.* (emphasis added).

Accordingly, the Court upheld the below-Guidelines sentence of a first-time offender who had served in Operation Desert Storm, received an honorable discharge from the Marine Corps, and had a steady history of employment. The 180 month (15 year) sentence imposed by the District Court was four and a half years less than the lowest Guideline sentence. The Court held:

> . . . in determining that 15 years was the appropriate prison term, the District Court properly homed in on the particular circumstances of Kimbrough's case and accorded weight to the Sentencing Commission's consistent and emphatic position that the crack/powder disparity is at odds with § 3553(a). Indeed, aside from its claim that the 100-to-1 ratio is mandatory, the Government did not attack the District Court's downward variance as unsupported by § 3553(a). Giving due respect to the District Court's reasoned appraisal, a reviewing court could not rationally conclude that the 4.5-year sentence reduction Kimbrough received qualified as an abuse of discretion.

Justices Alito and Thomas dissented. Justice Alito warned that the ruling would increase sentencing disparity.

The ball is now back in the lower courts. Appellate courts are beginning to reverse and remand some cases in which district courts did not consider whether to reduce crack sentences, because they felt they lacked the authority to do so. The Supreme Court vacated the sentence in the *Tabor* case, quoted earlier in this note, and remanded it for reconsideration in light of *Kimbrough*. On resentencing, the amended crack guidelines will be applicable. For further discussion of the implications of *Kimbrough*, see *infra* at 67.

The Commission (part 2)

The day after the Supreme Court's decision in *Kimbrough*, the Sentencing Commission voted to make the change in the crack Guideline retroactive, meaning that defendants whose sentences would have been shorter under the new Guidelines could apply for resentencing and early release. The amendment could, however, be blocked by Congress.

Congress

The Department of Justice strongly–though unsuccessfully–opposed making the change in the crack Guideline retroactive, arguing that it would allow the early release of thousands of dangerous offenders. Supporters of the retroactive change emphasized that it would be implemented on a case-by-case basis, with judges reducing the sentences of only those inmates identified as appropriate candidates for early release. According to the Washington Post, Sentencing Commission officials circulated a report on the Hill concluding that most of the 1,500 crack offenders who would be immediately eligible for release under the retroactive Guideline were not career criminals, but rather small time dealers or addicts whose charges involved neither firearms *nor* violence. Congress failed to block the amendment, which became effective March 3, 2008.

The Commission has consistently urged Congress to reduce the statutory minimum sentences that use the 100-to-1 ratio. Without legislative change, the mitigating effects of the actions by the Sentencing Commission and the courts will be limited. In most crack cases, the statute will still require a lengthy mandatory prison term based on the 100-to-1 ratio. Despite considerable interest on the part of both the public and many members of Congress, no viable legislation has emerged. According to some insiders, a compromise measure making the ratio to 20-to-1 might have been possible this term. But liberals held out for an even lower ratio, and it now appears that change is not likely until after the 2008 elections.

The issue of crack sentencing has received a fairly high degree of attention from the media. For example, a 2008 editorial in the New York Times criticized Attorney General Mukasey's efforts "to try to scare the House Judiciary Committee ... into blocking a responsible plan ... to address the gross disparity in penalties for possession or sale of crack cocaine and those for powder cocaine." It concluded that "[i]nstead of brandishing overblown fears to try to defeat a limited reform, Mr. Mukasey should be working with Congress to finally end the damaging 100-to-1 rule."

Implementing the New Crack Guideline

Resentencing under the retroactive Guideline seems to be proceeding smoothly. Preliminary data from cases the Sentencing

Commission received by May 13, 2008 indicated that 5,796 reduction requests have been made so far in the federal courts. Of these, 80.5% were granted and 19.5% were denied. In 23.1% of denials, the statutory mandatory minimum barred the reduction; in 8.1%, the offender's conviction did not even involve crack. The average reduction granted was 22 months, or 17.5% percent of the original sentence.

Page 402. *Insert after first full paragraph.*

Some federal prosecutors have found a new use for CCE, using it to prosecute online pharmacies as continuing criminal enterprises.

In *United States v. Fuchs*, 467 F.3d 889 (5th Cir. 2006), the defendant was a pharmacist who opened an Internet business called Friendly Pharmacy. Fuchs enlisted a doctor to provide prescriptions for online patients. The Pharmacy offered great convenience to Internet drug purchasers, who simply filled out an information form and placed their order. Customers received their medications after a doctor reviewed the electronic forms and wrote a prescription (for which the site paid him $100 a pop.) A year after opening, the pharmacy was filling 150 to 200 orders a day. Then the Texas State Board of Pharmacy informed Fuchs that his online prescriptions were illegal.

Fuchs closed Friendly and shortly thereafter opened Main Street Pharmacy, with the same employees, across the state line in Oklahoma. By the time Fuchs was indicted, Main Street was receiving 300 to 500 orders a day, mostly for hydrocodone (Vicodin).

Prosecutors charged Fuchs with three counts of dispensing a controlled substance not in the usual course of professional practice under 21 U.S.C. § 841(a)(1), as well as conspiracy to distribute a controlled substance under 21 U.S.C. § 846, engaging in a continuing criminal enterprise under 21 U.S.C. § 848, and conspiracy to commit money laundering. The continuing criminal enterprise count was premised on the § 841(a)(1) charges. Note that § 841(a)(1), text at 343, makes it illegal to "dispense" controlled substances (as well as to "manufacture" or "distribute" them). As the Supreme Court explained in *United States v. Moore*, 423 U.S. 122, 124 (1975), medical professionals "can be prosecuted under § 841 when their activities fall outside the usual course of professional practice."

A CCE trial in Baltimore (ongoing as this supplement is being prepared) involves the participants in an online pharmacy that bought 6.1 million doses of hydrocodone in less than 10 months during 2006. (In contrast, American pharmacies purchased an average of 71,632 doses during that time, according to a press release from the Maryland U.S. Attorney's Office.) The prescriptions from these online pharmacies could be deadly. Prosecutors said that at least two people who purchased drugs from the Baltimore pharmacy died from overdosing, and the parents of a teenager who overdosed on hydrocodone have brought civil suits against Fuchs and doctors involved in his pharmacy.

Page 411. Insert as a new note at the end of note 3.

The USA Patriot Improvement and Reauthorization Act of 2005 expanded extraterritorial jurisdiction to reach acts of "narco-terrorism." Pub. L. No. 109-177, § 122, 120 Stat. 192, 225 (2006). Conduct prohibited by 21 U.S.C. § 841(a) that is performed with knowledge or intent to provide "anything of pecuniary value" to persons or organizations involved in terrorism falls under 21 U.S.C. § 960a, which includes the following provision for extraterritorial jurisdiction:

(b) Jurisdiction. There is jurisdiction over an offense under this section if–

(1) the prohibited drug activity or the terrorist offense is in violation of the criminal laws of the United States;

(2) the offense, the prohibited drug activity, or the terrorist offense occurs in or affects interstate or foreign commerce;

(3) an offender provides anything of pecuniary value for a terrorist offense that causes or is designed to cause death or serious bodily injury to a national of the United States while that national is outside the United States, or substantial damage to the property of a legal entity organized under the laws of the United States (including any of its States, districts, commonwealths, territories, or possessions) while that property is outside of the United States;

(4) the offense or the prohibited drug activity occurs in whole or in part outside of the United States (including on the high seas), and a perpetrator of the offense or the prohibited drug activity is a national of the United States or a legal entity organized under the laws of the United States (including any of its States, districts, commonwealths, territories, or possessions); or

(5) after the conduct required for the offense occurs an offender is brought into or found in the United States, even if the conduct required for the offense occurs outside the United States.

Review note 1, text pages 409-10. What principles of jurisdiction does the new statute rely upon? Does it meet the standards set by the cases in note 3, pages 410-11?

CHAPTER 10

CURRENCY REPORTING OFFENSES AND MONEY LAUNDERING

Pages 430-31.

Eliot Spitzer first gained national prominence as a result of his aggressive pursuit of corporate wrongdoing as the Attorney General of New York. Ironically, not long after he took office as governor the man once dubbed the "Sheriff of Wall Street" was implicated in the investigation of a prostitution ring that had been triggered by SARs. Spitzer resigned and admitted to being a client, but as of this writing he has not been charged in connection with the investigation. Organizers of the ring were charged with conspiring to violate the Travel Act, 18 U.S.C. § 1952(a)(3), and the Mann Act, 18 U.S.C. " 2421 and 2422(a).

The Spitzer case raises again the question how SARs are used, and specifically how investigators sift through the large numbers of SARs that are filed each year. As far as we can determine, there is no rule on how many SARs must be filed on a bank customer before an investigation is opened. Rather, the decision is based on a combination of objective and subjective factors including the type and frequency of the activity reported, whether the activity can be connected to an existing investigation, and the prosecutive threshold in that federal judicial district. Spitzer's transactions were all below $10,000, suggesting that they might have been structured to avoid federal reporting requirements. Moreover, the SARs filed on Eliot Spitzer identified him as a politically exposed person (PEP). SARs regarding PEPs tend to receive heightened scrutiny, because transactions may be structured to conceal bribery or official corruption.

Technology is helping banks and law enforcement identify cases of interest. Banks have software that identifies potentially suspicious activity, but there still must be an investigative process by the bank to make a final decision. The FBI has developed data mining capabilities that enable SARs to be linked once they are filed in the central system. These technologies are essential to take advantage of the millions of SARs that have been filed since 1996.

According to a 2005 U.S. Government-wide money laundering threat assessment, the most complex money laundering efforts often involve the use of international trade to disguise the transfer of funds. Trade-based money laundering includes such forms as the Black Market Peso Exchange (BMPE), a scheme in which drug dealers give illicit U.S. dollars to professional money launderers who make clean pesos available in Colombia. The assessment also identified "stored value cards," like prepaid cash or phone service cards, as a means to store and access cash value that is easy for money launderers to abuse and difficult for law enforcement to monitor. These cards enable holders to obtain cash from an ATM without having an individual bank account (card management firms use "pooled" accounts held in the name of the firm) and without verification of cardholder identity (banks are required to conduct such procedures on the card management firm only).

U.S. intelligence officials are also worried that popular online communities, such as Second Life, may provide terrorists and criminals with new ways to either launder illicit funds or support unlawful activities. In addition to socializing and exploring fantasies within these virtual worlds, people are also earning and spending money. Corporations and organizations even hold meetings online. However, the features that have made these communities so popular among Internet users are also a cause for concern. The ability to make anonymous, borderless financial transactions outside of the normal channels is attractive to terrorists and criminals and difficult for the government to monitor.

Page 449-50. Add to Note 1

The Supreme Court's decision in *Cuellar v. United States*, 128 S. Ct. 1994 (2008), explored the complex mens rea structure of § 1956. Police found approximately $81,000 in a secret compartment under the rear floorboards of a vehicle Humberto Cuellar was driving south towards the border between Texas and Mexico. A jury convicted Cuellar of attempting to transport illicit funds across the border, knowing the transportation was "designed . . . to conceal or disguise the nature, the location, the source, the ownership, or the control of the proceeds of specified unlawful activity," in violation of 18 U.S.C. § 1956(a)(1)(B)(i).

The Supreme Court reversed Cuellar's conviction, taking a middle position between the Government, which argued that the statute covers merely hiding the money during transportation, and Cuellar, who argued that the statute requires proof that the transportation was meant to create the "appearance of legitimate wealth." The Court interpreted "design" to require that the defendant know the *purpose* of transporting the funds is to conceal or disguise the attributes specified in § 1956(a)(1)(B)(i) (the nature, location, source, ownership, or control of the proceeds of specified unlawful activity). There was no evidence that the defendant knew about or intended such an effect, and indeed the Government's own witness had testified that the purpose of transporting the funds was to compensate the Mexican leaders of the operation. Accordingly, the evidence was sufficient to prove that "the secretive aspects of the transportation were employed to *facilitate* the transportation, but not necessarily that secrecy was the *purpose* of the transportation"(emphasis in original).

While requiring the government to prove "purpose" seems like a high bar, Justice Alito's concurring opinion suggests that the jury may be able to infer the requisite intent from readily available circumstantial evidence:

> [A] criminal defendant's intent is often inferred. Here, proof of . . . the intent of the person or persons who "designed" the transportation would have been sufficient if the prosecution had introduced evidence showing, not only that taking "dirty" money across the border has one or more of the effects noted above, but that it is commonly known in the relevant circles . . . that taking dirty money into Mexico has one of the effects noted [in § 1956(a)(1)(B)(I)].

Page 450. *Add to Note 3*

Another issue raised by the defendant in *Cuellar v. United States*, 128 S. Ct. 1994 (2008) was the relationship between § 1956's money laundering transportation provisions and the bulk cash smuggling statute. The defendant argued that the secretive transportation of illicit funds is the core offense defined by the bulk cash smuggling statute, and therefore § 1956 should be interpreted to require something more. The Supreme Court rejected this argument, reasoning that the two statutes target distinct activities despite the fact that certain conduct may fall under both statutes: only the money laundering statute is violated in the absence of intent to evade a currency reporting requirement, and only the bulk cash smuggling statute is violated where the transported funds are lawfully derived.

Section 1956(a)(1)(a) (text at 440) makes it a crime to launder the "proceeds" of crime by engaging in a transaction with the intent to promote specified unlawful activity. In *United States v. Santos*, 128 S. Ct. 2020 (2008), the defendant was convicted of running an illegal gambling business and of laundering the "proceeds" by making payments to runners, winners, and collectors. But what does "proceeds" mean in this context? Gross receipts, or profits?

The Supreme Court vacated Santos' conviction, but the government may have won more than it lost. Four members of the Court concluded that for purposes of § 1956 the term "proceeds" means profits, and four members disagreed, arguing that the term proceeds refers to "the total amount brought in." Justice Stevens, who held the deciding vote, disagreed with both the plurality and the dissent, concluding that "this Court need not pick a single definition of 'proceeds.'" As noted below, his interpretation may be favorable to the Government in other types of money laundering prosecutions.

What made this such a hard issue? All of the opinions grapple with the issue of merger, i.e., the question whether the money laundering statute criminalizes the very same conduct as the predicate specified unlawful activity. The defendant (and the dissenters) argued that Congress did not intend to treat each payment of a winner as money laundering, since every gambling business pays winners as an integral part of its illegal gambling operation. Shouldn't the money laundering statute be interpreted to require more than a garden variety violation of the predicate statute?

Writing for the plurality, Justice Scalia found the meaning of "proceeds" to be ambiguous, and accordingly he turned to the rule of lenity to break the tie in the defendant's favor. Interpreting "proceeds" as profits avoids the merger problem (payments to winners are not profits) and "ensure[s] that the severe money-laundering penalties will be imposed only for the removal of profits from criminal activity, which permit the leveraging of one criminal activity to the next." Justice Scalia found no inconsistency between this interpretation and the purpose of the statute:

> To be sure, if "proceeds" meant "receipts," one could say that the statute was aimed at the dangers of concealment and promotion. But whether "proceeds" means "receipts" is the very issue in the case. If "proceeds" means "profits," one could say

that the statute is aimed at the distinctive danger that arises from leaving in criminal hands the yield of a crime. A rational Congress could surely have decided that the risk of leveraging one criminal activity into the next poses a greater threat to society than the mere payment of crime-related expenses and justifies the money laundering statute's harsh penalties.

The four dissenters, in opinions written by Justices Alito and Breyer, disagreed, arguing that the term "proceeds" refers to "the total amount brought in." Justice Alito's opinion, joined by Justices Roberts, Kennedy, and Breyer, rejects the plurality's assumption that the term "proceeds" is ambiguous in the context of § 1956, emphasizing that a variety of state and international money laundering provisions define the term to include criminal receipts. In addition, defining "proceeds" as receipts better serves the general purposes of money laundering provisions, both preventing drug traffickers and other criminals from enjoying the fruits of their crimes and preventing the use of dirty money to promote the enterprise's growth. In the dissenters's view, narrowing a money laundering statute to reach only profits also introduces pointless and difficult problems of proof.

Justice Stevens, who wielded the swing vote, did not agree with either of these opposing interpretations. He disagreed with the plurality's complete reliance on the rule of lenity, reasoning that "[w]hen Congress fails to define potentially ambiguous terms, it delegates to federal judges the task of filling gaps in the statute." In Justice Stevens' view, the appropriate way to fill in the gap in the *Santos* case was to limit the term "proceeds" to profits. He agreed with the plurality that "there is 'no explanation for why Congress would have wanted a transaction that is a normal part of a crime it had duly considered and appropriately punished elsewhere in the Criminal Code, to radically increase the sentence for that crime.' " This conclusion, he noted, "dovetails with what common sense and the rule of lenity would require." The dissent's interpretation, in contrast, runs squarely into the merger problem:

> Allowing the government to treat the mere payment of the expense of operating an illegal gambling business as a separate offense is in practical effect tantamount to double jeopardy, which is particularly unfair in this case because the penalties for money laundering are substantially more severe than those for the underlying offense of operating a gambling business.

On the other hand, Justice Stevens seems to have agreed with the dissenters that "proceeds" should be read as gross receipts in other kinds of money laundering prosecutions. He wrote:

As Justice Alito rightly argues, the legislative history of § 1956 makes it clear that Congress intended the term "proceeds" to include gross revenues from the sale of contraband and the operation of organized crime syndicates involving such sales.

What is the legal effect of Justice Stevens' split-the-baby interpretation? The plurality and dissent both reject Justice Stevens' argument that the meaning of "proceeds" can vary in § 1956 cases depending on the nature of the predicate offense. The plurality also characterizes these comments as "speculation," and the "purest of dicta." The dissent, however, notes pointedly that "five justices agree with the position taken by Justice Stevens" that Congress intended "proceeds" to include gross revenues in the specific context noted above. Even if we assume that a majority did clearly indicate gross receipts are "proceeds" in money laundering prosecutions involving the sale of contraband, what about all of the other offenses that qualify as "specified unlawful offenses" under § 1956? The list, pages 442-44, is a long one.

CHAPTER 11

RICO—THE RACKETEER INFLUENCED AND CORRUPT ORGANIZATIONS STATUTE

Page 491. Add to note 9.

The RICO statute has been used with increasing frequency to prosecute members of street gangs. See, e.g., U.S. v. Nascimento, 491 F.3d 25 (1st Cir. 2007); United States v. Smith, 413 F.3d 1253 (10th Cir. 2005). In Smith, there was significant evidence that defendant's gang had an existence as an entity separate and apart from the pattern of racketeering activity in which it engaged. The evidence indicated that defendant committed certain rules to writing in a "bible" that set forth gang's structure and bylaws, that defendant adopted certain symbols for the gang, that new members were brought into the gang by a formalized process, that gang held weekly meetings at which attendance was mandatory, that meetings were conducted according to established rules, and that defendant remained leader of gang, even while incarcerated.

Other cases, however, have emphasized the same type of factors identified in the main volume:

a. See, e.g., United States. v. Gross, 199 Fed. Appx. 219 (4th Cir. 2006), cert. denied, 127 S. Ct. 534 (U.S. 2006) where the evidence showed that organization in which defendant participated had continuity, unity, shared purpose and identifiable structure, namely, the organization was headed by the same person or persons for at least four years, the organization's activities were coordinated and operated through various businesses created by its members, the members shared the purpose of making money by illicit means, including drug dealing and fraud, and the organization had an identifiable structure in that it was headed by identified individuals who carried out activities through street level operatives.

b. See also United States v. Johnson, 430 F.3d 383 (6th Cir. 2005) which emphasized the division of labor within the organization—one member of the alleged enterprise orchestrated activities of enterprise by deciding what crimes were to be committed, offering payment for their commission, and selling any stolen property; other members performed "work" of committing crimes but had no decision-making power; and the common purpose of enterprise was to make money--the members of alleged enterprise considered themselves to be part of a business, and numerous crimes were committed during the two-and-a-half year duration of enterprise.

Page 495. Add to note 14.

The courts of appeal continue to develop the concept of a RICO enterprise based on an association in fact. In some of the recent cases, attention has been paid to factors in addition to common purpose, ascertainable structure and similar factors identified in the main volume. For example, the stability of the membership, control over territory and adherence to rules are mentioned. See, e.g., United States v. Dixon, 167 Fed. Appx. 841 (2d Cir. 2006): Evidence was sufficient to support finding that association was a Racketeer Influenced and Corrupt Organizations Act (RICO) enterprise, including the fact that the association had a core membership that remained constant over a 12-year period, established and protected a territory in which only they, or people to whom they gave permission, could sell cocaine and crack cocaine, and adhered to certain rules, including prohibiting cooperation with the police and dealing violently with those who did. See also United States v. Edwards, 214 F. Appx. 57 (2d Cir. 2007); United States v. Nascimento, supra; and United States v. Smith, supra.

The Supreme Court has never ruled on whether a particular organizational structure is required for an association in fact enterprise, though during its last term an opportunity to address the issue was presented. The Court declined to review Odom v. Microsoft Corp., 486 F.3d 541 (9th Cir. 2007), cert. denied, 2007 WL 2982493 (U.S. 2007). One of the issues raised by the petition for certiorari had asked: whether an association-in-fact "enterprise" under the RICO statute must be an organization with an ascertainable structure separate and apart from that inherent in the alleged pattern of racketeering activity.

Page 498. Add to note 3.

In United States v. Warner, 498 F. 3d 666 (7th Cir. 2007), the State of Illinois was alleged as the RICO enterprise based on the actions of a former governor, George H. Ryan, and one of his associates. Affirming the conviction, the U.S. court of appeals stated:

> In this case, the prosecution thought that it had identified an ongoing scheme to defraud the State of Illinois through the illegal use of two of the most significant executive branch offices of the state and of the state's electoral processes during Ryan's campaign for Governor in 1998. The scheme revolved around an elected official [ed. Ryan] throughout his tenure in these two offices-Secretary of State and Governor-and during the time he was a candidate for the latter office. No legal rule prohibited the prosecution from concluding that there was no single entity or office that it could have identified, short of the state as a whole, that would have encompassed the enterprise that was used by the defendants. In these unusual circumstances, comity interests do not override the broad language of RICO, as interpreted in Turkette. The district court did not err by allowing the state to be the RICO enterprise in this RICO conspiracy prosecution.

The Supreme Court denied certiorari on May 27, 2008, Warner v. United States.--- S.Ct. ----, 2008 WL 219182.

Page 496. Add as note 16.

16. In Lockheed Martin Corp. v. The Boeing Co., 357 F. Supp. 2d 1350, 1359-60 (M.D. Fla. 2005), the court delved into what it means to associate together and to have a common purpose:

> Lockheed Martin has alleged the existence of four RICO enterprises: 1) a legitimate association-in-fact comprised of the Air Force, Lockheed Martin, Boeing, McDonnell Douglas, BLS, and Alliant, joined together for the common purpose of designing, proposing, and building the most innovative EELV systems for the Government at the best value; 2) a legitimate association-in-fact comprised of the Air Force, Lockheed Martin, Boeing, McDonnell Douglas, BLS, and Alliant, as well as NASA, Matthew Jew, General Dynamics, and Martin Marietta, also joined together for the purpose of designing, proposing, and building the most innovative EELV systems for the Government at the best value; 3) a criminal association-in-fact consisting of Erskine, Satchell, Branch, and other Boeing employees, including Tom Alexiou, joined together for the common purpose of stealing the confidential and proprietary information of the Boeing's competitors; and 4) a criminal association-in-fact consisting of McDonnell Douglas, Launch

Services Subsidiary, Boeing, Hughes, Allen Cantu, Branch, Erskine, Satchell, Alexiou, Black, Hora, and others known and unknown, also joined together for the purpose of stealing the confidential and proprietary information of Boeing's competitors....

...

The Boeing Defendants primarily argue that Lockheed Martin's allegations of legitimate association-in-fact enterprises fail because the entities which comprise the alleged enterprises do not satisfy the requirement that associations-in-fact be "associated together for the common purpose of engaging in a course of conduct." The Boeing Defendants contend that, quite apart from "working together for any common purpose," the entities comprising both alleged legitimate enterprises were "vigorous competitors." Thus, the Boeing Defendants conclude, "the mere fact that the alleged 'associates' were involved in government-sponsored programs cannot establish a 'common purpose' among the alleged associates."

In response to the Boeing Defendants' argument, Lockheed Martin focuses on two issues. First, Lockheed Martin emphasizes that a RICO enterprise can be either criminal or legitimate. Second, Lockheed Martin contends that an association-in-fact can include entities with conflicting interests. Neither of these arguments, however, addresses the core issue raised by the Boeing Defendants, which is whether the entities alleged to constitute the claimed legitimate enterprises "associated together for the common purpose of engaging in a course of conduct."

For the purposes of addressing the Boeing Defendants' argument, it is accepted as true that Boeing and its competitors each sought to provide the government with quality satellite launch services at the best possible value.[7] Yet, while this fact

---

[7] ....[T]here is a question as to whether there is, or should be, a requirement that the purpose binding together an association-in-fact

would be sufficient to establish that there was a purpose commonly shared by Boeing and its competitors, it does not follow that Lockheed Martin has succeeded in satisfying the "common purpose" requirement for pleading a RICO enterprise. Rather, to meet this requirement, Lockheed Martin must allege, not only that there was some commonly shared purpose among Boeing and its competitors, but also that they *associated together* for that purpose.

To decide whether Boeing and its competitors associated together, it is critical to determine, first, what it means to "associate" or to be "associated." RICO does not define these terms, and a search has failed to yield any cases which directly endeavor to define them insofar as they relate to an association-in-fact. As such, the only resort is to accord the terms their "ordinary meaning" consistent with a reasonable interpretation of RICO. ...

---

be an illegitimate or criminal one. The Supreme Court in *Turkette* held that a RICO enterprise could be an "exclusively criminal" association-in-fact but did not decide whether an association-in-fact *had* to be comprised of criminals (or at least be formed for an illegitimate purpose). Later statements of *Turkette* 's holding, however, suggested that RICO may require that enterprises be comprised of either " *legal entities* " or " *illegitimate associations-in-fact.*" *See, e.g., Russello v. U.S.,* 464 U.S. 16, 24, 104 S.Ct. 296 ...It is unclear whether some rationale, consistent with RICO's purpose, exists for using the statute to reach an association-in-fact with a legitimate purpose. Because the Court rejects Lockheed Martin's claims of legitimate associations-in-fact on a separate basis, it need not decide this difficult issue today. The Court notes, however, that Lockheed Martin's allegations appear to fall outside the categories of concern described by the court in *Turkette.* That is, it would seem that targeting entities bound together by a legitimate purpose would neither: (1) "cope with the infiltration of legitimate businesses"; nor (2) deal with the problem of organized crime "at its very source." 452 U.S. at 591, 101 S.Ct. 2524 ("Accepting that the primary purpose of RICO is to cope with the infiltration of legitimate businesses, applying the statute in accordance with its terms, so as to reach criminal enterprises, would seek to deal with the problem at its very source.").

According to Webster's, "associate" means "to come together as partners" or "to combine or join together." Merriam-Webster's Collegiate Dictionary (10th ed.1999) (intransitive form). If the parties' own pleadings are any indication, this definition is consonant with the ordinary meaning and usage of "associate." While Lockheed Martin alleges that Boeing and its competitors *joined together* for a common purpose, the Boeing Defendants contend that they "never *worked together* for any common purpose." The point, of course, is not the parties' disagreement but their use of nearly identical terminology in contexts in which they might have just as readily employed "associated together." Similarly, although the Court can find no case which squarely confronts the definition of "associate," some courts have used the phrases "worked together" or "joined together" synonymously with "associated together." ...

As Lockheed Martin's claims illustrate, the concern for clarity is more than merely academic. In essence, Lockheed Martin argues for an interpretation of "associate" that would effectively negate the enterprise requirement in any case in which competitors are alleged to comprise an association-in-fact. First, given that the relationship between Boeing and its competitors consisted of only their participation in bidding competitions for government contracts, the first logical implication of Lockheed Martin's approach is that competitors in any given bidding competition are presumptively "associated." However, the breadth of Lockheed Martin's approach does not, as a matter of logic, end there. Rather, absent any principled means of distinguishing between participation in a bidding competition and other forms of market participation (and Lockheed has proffered none), competitors in *any* market would be deemed "associated." To take the final step of alleging that the competitors were not only "associated" but "associated together for [a] common purpose" would demand only that plaintiffs, *a la* Lockheed Martin, plead the obvious-that competitors in a given market seek to produce a certain product or satisfy a common class of consumers. There is simply no cause to invite such an expansive application of RICO. Requiring instead that there be a joining together of alleged associated-in-fact entities comports with the plain definition of "associate" at the same time that it guards against overreaching by creative plaintiffs. Moreover, this requirement stops well short of adopting anything like a formal structure requirement. Rather, associated-in-fact entities may be "joined together" formally or informally, so long as their association "furnishes a vehicle for the commission of two or more predicate crimes."

Under the standard now adopted, Lockheed Martin's claims of legitimate enterprises clearly fail. Far from joining or working together in contests for government contracts, Boeing and its competitors were *competing* for contracts. ... If anything, then, the relationship between Boeing and its competitors present a paradigmatic case of what is *not* an association-in-fact under RICO.

Page 497. Add to note 2.

In Lockheed Martin Corp. v. The Boeing Co., 357 F. Supp. 2d 1350, 1359-60 (M.D. Fla. 2005), supra, the court also addressed the following issue:

A secondary argument raised by the Boeing Defendants is that Lockheed Martin's allegations of legitimate enterprises fail because corporations and government agencies cannot be associated in fact under RICO. Relying in part on language in United States v. Hartley, the Boeing Defendants contend, as a matter of statutory interpretation, that the use of "individual" in RICO's definition of "enterprise" refers only to a living person. 678 F.2d 961, 989 (11th Cir.1982) ("Section 1961(3) defines 'person' as 'any individual or entity capable of holding a legal or beneficial interest in property.' It is clear from the definition that 'individual' is used differently from 'person' in the act to connote a living person."), *rev'd on other grounds, United States v. Goldin Industries, Inc.,* 219 F.3d 1268, 1271 (11th Cir.2000)

Since *Hartley,* the trend has clearly been in favor of permitting associations-in-fact to include corporations. *United States v. Navarro-Ordas,* 770 F.2d 959 (11th Cir.1985) (three-judge panel rejected defendant's argument that the indictment against him "failed to describe a RICO 'enterprise' " because "it only alleged that the enterprise consisted of a group of corporate entities rather than living persons" and found that "a group of corporations can be a 'group of individuals associated in fact' within the meaning of the 'enterprise' definition of 18 U.S.C. § 1961(4)"); ... However, despite the weight of authority favoring the view that associations-in-fact may be comprised of corporations, *Hartley* controls under the Eleventh Circuit's prior precedent rule. That rule holds that, where there is intra-circuit conflict, "the earliest panel opinion resolving the issue in question binds the circuit until the court resolves the issue *en banc.*" While *Hartley* was overruled by an *en banc* court in *Goldin I,* the court did not address the issue of whether associations-in-fact may be comprised of corporations or other non-living entities. ... Thus, *Hartley* remains good law at least to the extent that it held that an association-in-fact may not be comprised of non-living persons. Accordingly, Lockheed Martin's claims of legitimate associations-in-fact fail for the additional reason that they are alleged to include corporations and government agencies.

Page 506. Add to note 5.

The need for separateness between the RICO "person" and the "enterprise" continues to be a stumbling block for civil RICO plaintiffs. See, e.g., Nordberg v. Trilegiant Corp., 445 F. Supp. 2d 1082 (N.D. Cal. 2006); Prunte v. Universal Music Group, 484 F. Supp. 2d 32 (D.D.C. 2007). **In** German Free State of Bavaria v. Toyobo Co., Ltd., 480 F. Supp. 2d 958 (W.D. Mich. 2007), the court cited Ingraham v. IRS Bonus Partners, 2006 WL 89868 (W.D.Mich. 2006) for the proposition that a RICO enterprise cannot merely consist of the named defendants. And see again Lockheed Martin Corp. v. The Boeing Co., 357 F. Supp. 2d 1350, 1365-67 (M.D. Fla. 2005):

> Determining whether a RICO defendant is sufficiently distinct from an alleged RICO enterprise is a fact-intensive inquiry that is not driven solely by formal legal relationships among the alleged associates-in-fact; the crucial factor is whether each entity alleged to be part of the association-in-fact is free to act independently and advance its own interests contrary to those of the other entities.

Page 524. Add to note 5.

In Lockheed Martin Corp. v. The Boeing Co., 357 F. Supp. 2d 1350, 1359-60 (M.D. Fla. 2005), the court also addressed the outsider-management or control issue in a context where the entity allegedly controlled was a U.S. government agency :

> The Boeing Defendants contend that, at most, they merely *influenced* the alleged legitimate enterprises to make certain decisions in Boeing's favor. Lockheed Martin, however, submits that, "by stealing and using Lockheed Martin ... confidential and proprietary information," the Boeing Defendants exerted *control* over the bidding processes for

satellite launch contracts with the Government, and thereby caused the Government to grant contracts to Boeing.

In *Castro,* the Eleventh Circuit found that a group of lawyers " 'agreed' to affect the operation or management" of a state circuit court by paying kickbacks to judges who appointed the lawyers as special assistant public defenders. 89 F.3d at 1447-48. The lawyers were "outsiders" in the sense that they did not work for the court and had no formal decision-making authority over which lawyers received the public defender appointments. Nevertheless, the court deemed the lawyers' kickbacks to the judges sufficient to satisfy the *Reves* "operation or management" test.

Lockheed Martin's allegations of "control" bear a strong resemblance to the facts in *Castro.* In this case, the Boeing Defendants were not primarily responsible for determining which companies received launch contracts. Yet, like the defendants in *Castro,* they are alleged to have engaged in illegal activity which substantially impacted the decisions of those who did have principal decision-making authority. The only difference in this case is that the decision-makers were neither aware of, nor complicit in, the alleged scheme. This is a distinction, however, that is irrelevant to the question of whether the Boeing Defendants controlled the alleged legitimate enterprises through their illegal conduct.

In *Castro,* the Eleventh Circuit, in support of its determination that "[o]utsiders may exert control over an enterprise's affairs," cited *Aetna Casualty Surety Co. v. P & B Autobody,* 43 F.3d 1546, 1559-60 (1st Cir.1991), for its finding that "claimants who submitted fraudulent claims to [an] insurance company [and] caused the insurance company to pay out large sums of money ... exerted sufficient control over [the] affairs of the insurance company to satisfy the dictates of *Reves.*" Considering the Eleventh Circuit's approval of *Aetna,* it seems unlikely that the court would have altered its conclusion in *Castro* had it found that the lawyers had deceived, rather than bribed, the judges in order to obtain the public defender appointments.

Similarly, the issue here is not the means that the Boeing Defendants employed to impact the Government's decisions or whether the Government was aware of the Boeing Defendants' illegal conduct, but whether it can reasonably be inferred from the facts alleged in Lockheed Martin's Amended Complaint that the Boeing Defendants exercised some measure of control over the awarding of launch contracts. Lockheed Martin has satisfied that burden. Much as there was a cause and effect relationship between the kickbacks and public defender appointments in *Castro,* the Boeing Defendants' illegal activity, as alleged in this case, enabled Boeing to secure contracts that it would not have otherwise obtained. In this way, the Boeing Defendants controlled the outcome of the bidding competitions for launch contracts. Accordingly, Lockheed Martin's claims of legitimate associations-in-fact satisfy the "operation or management" test.

Page 543. Add to note 5.

Recent cases have added to the body of law on open and closed-end continuity. See, e.g., U.S. v. Browne, 505 F.3d 1229 (11th Cir. 2007): Evidence presented by government in RICO prosecution of former union officer was sufficient to establish continuity of predicate violations of the Taft-Hartley Act and acts of mail fraud on either an open-ended or closed-ended theory, where government proved at least three related predicates that extended over period of roughly five years, and also established sufficient threat of repetition on theory that these predicate acts were part of defendants' regular way of doing business. Gotfredson v. Larsen LP, 432 F. Supp. 2d 1163 (D. Colo. 2006): Contractors' allegations that property owners engaged in a single scheme over period of 17 months by pursing false or fraudulent claims and a sham arbitration to garner a large sum of money from contractors were insufficient to establish open-ended continuity, for purposes of proving a pattern under RICO provision prohibiting conduct of enterprise's affairs through a pattern of racketeering activity; complaint alleged a single scheme to accomplish a discrete goal, alleged scheme only extended to contractors, and contractors did not allege that scheme was owners' regular way of conducting business.

Page 544. Add to note 7,

Also consider U.S. v. Daidone, 471 F.3d 371, 375 (2d Cir. 2006): "This Court has further developed this requirement of "relatedness," holding that predicate acts "must be related to each other ('horizontal' relatedness), and they must be related to the enterprise ('vertical' relatedness)."

Page 568. Add to note 2.

The type of allegations that are sometimes made in some of the more creative RICO civil suits--that an association in fact has been formed between various persons and entities to accomplish a particular purpose--has in a number of cases been held not to be sufficient because the association lacked sufficient continuity.

a. See, e.g., Milgrom v. Burstein, 374 F. Supp.2d 523 (E.D.Ky. 2005): Plaintiff's ex-wife, her divorce attorney, and others involved in her divorce proceedings did not constitute "enterprise," despite plaintiff's contention that they conspired to obtain an disproportionate and unfair settlement of cash and property.

b. See also, Kearney v. Dimanna, 195 Fed. Appx. 717 (10th Cir. 2006): Private investigator's allegation that police officers, law firm, and police association had filed a defamation suit against him to punish him for accusing officers of covering up shooting failed to properly plead an "enterprise," where there was no indication that the alleged enterprise had any existence or purpose outside of alleged malicious prosecution and intimidation of investigator to prevent him from continuing to expose supposed illegal activity and cover-up.

c. And see Burkett v. City of El Paso, 513 F.Supp. 2d 800 (W.D. Tex. 2007)--City, county, city police officers and district attorneys were not an enterprise for purposes of arrestee's RICO claim in action alleging denial of his right to be taken before a magistrate judge for probable cause hearing; arrestee failed to allege that any of the defendants were associated in any manner with one another apart from their responsibilities at the district attorney's office. Note that in Burkett the plaintiff alleged that government agencies along with individual government officials formed an association in fact.

Page 568. Add to note 5.

For cases ruling that the RICO injury under § 1962(a) must be caused by reason of the investment of the racketeering proceeds, not from the underlying racketeering activity itself, see Fuller v. Home Depot Services, LLC, 512 F.Supp.2d 1289, 1294 (N.D.Ga. 2007); Lockheed Martin Corp. v. The Boeing Co., 357 F. Supp. 2d 1350, 1368-71 (M.D. Fla. 2005); Decatur Ventures, LLC v. Stapleton Ventures, Inc., 373 F. Supp. 2d 829 (S.D. Ind. 2005).

The Supreme Court took the opportunity to apply the doctrine of Holmes in Anza v. Ideal Steel Supply Corp., 547 U.S. 451, 126 S.Ct. 1991 (2006):

> Justice Kennedy delivered the opinion of the court:
>
> …
>
> In *Holmes v. Securities Investor Protection Corporation*, 503 U.S. 258, 268, 112 S.Ct. 1311, 117 L.Ed.2d 532 (1992), this Court held that a plaintiff may sue under § 1964(c) only if the alleged RICO violation was the proximate cause of the plaintiff's injury. The instant case requires us to apply the principles discussed in *Holmes* to a dispute between two competing businesses.
>
> Because this case arises from a motion to dismiss, we accept as true the factual allegations in the amended complaint....
>
> Respondent Ideal Steel Supply Corporation (Ideal) sells steel mill products along with related supplies and services. It operates two store locations in New York, one in Queens and the other in the Bronx. Petitioner National Steel SupplyInc. (National), owned by petitioners Joseph and Vincent Anza, is Ideal's principal competitor. National offers a similar array of products and services, and it, too, operates one store in Queens and one in the Bronx.
>
> Ideal sued petitioners in the United States District Court for the Southern District of New York. It claimed petitioners were engaged in an unlawful racketeering scheme aimed at "gain[ing] sales and market share at Ideal's expense." According to Ideal, National adopted a practice of failing to charge the requisite New York sales tax to cash-paying customers, even when conducting transactions that were not exempt from sales tax under state law. This practice allowed National to reduce its prices without affecting its profit margin. Petitioners allegedly submitted fraudulent tax returns to the New York State Department of Taxation and Finance in an effort to conceal their conduct.
>
> Ideal's amended complaint contains, as relevant here, two RICO claims. The claims assert that petitioners, by submitting the fraudulent tax returns, committed various acts of mail fraud

(when they sent the returns by mail) and wire fraud (when they sent them electronically). Petitioners' conduct allegedly constituted a "pattern of racketeering activity," because the fraudulent returns were submitted on an ongoing and regular basis.

Ideal asserts in its first cause of action that Joseph and Vincent Anza violated § 1962(c), which makes it unlawful for "any person employed by or associated with any enterprise engaged in, or the activities of which affect, interstate or foreign commerce, to conduct or participate, directly or indirectly, in the conduct of such enterprise's affairs through a pattern of racketeering activity or collection of unlawful debt." The complaint states that the Anzas' goal, which they achieved, was to give National a competitive advantage over Ideal.

...

Applying the principles of *Holmes* to the present case, we conclude Ideal cannot maintain its claim based on § 1962(c). Section 1962(c), as noted above, forbids conducting or participating in the conduct of an enterprise's affairs through a pattern of racketeering activity. The Court has indicated the compensable injury flowing from a violation of that provision "necessarily is the harm caused by predicate acts sufficiently related to constitute a pattern, for the essence of the violation is the commission of those acts in connection with the conduct of an enterprise." *Sedima, S.P.R.L. v. Imrex Co.,* 473 U.S. 479, 497, 105 S.Ct. 3275, 87 L.Ed.2d 346 (1985).

Ideal's theory is that Joseph and Vincent Anza harmed it by defrauding the New York tax authority and using the proceeds from the fraud to offer lower prices designed to attract more customers. The RICO violation alleged by Ideal is that the Anzas conducted National's affairs through a pattern of mail fraud and wire fraud. The direct victim of this conduct was the State of New York, not Ideal. It was the State that was being defrauded and the State that lost tax revenue as a result.

The proper referent of the proximate-cause analysis is an alleged practice of conducting National's business through a pattern of defrauding the State. To be sure, Ideal asserts it suffered its own harms when the Anzas failed to charge customers for the applicable sales tax. The cause of Ideal's asserted harms, however, is a set of actions (offering lower prices) entirely distinct from the alleged RICO violation

91

(defrauding the State). The attenuation between the plaintiff's harms and the claimed RICO violation arises from a different source in this case than in *Holmes,* where the alleged violations were linked to the asserted harms only through the broker-dealers' inability to meet their financial obligations. Nevertheless, the absence of proximate causation is equally clear in both cases.

This conclusion is confirmed by considering the directness requirement's underlying premises. One motivating principle is the difficulty that can arise when a court attempts to ascertain the damages caused by some remote action. ("[T]he less direct an injury is, the more difficult it becomes to ascertain the amount of a plaintiff's damages attributable to the violation, as distinct from other, independent, factors"). The instant case is illustrative. The injury Ideal alleges is its own loss of sales resulting from National's decreased prices for cash-paying customers. National, however, could have lowered its prices for any number of reasons unconnected to the asserted pattern of fraud. It may have received a cash inflow from some other source or concluded that the additional sales would justify a smaller profit margin. Its lowering of prices in no sense required it to defraud the state tax authority. Likewise, the fact that a company commits tax fraud does not mean the company will lower its prices; the additional cash could go anywhere from asset acquisition to research and development to dividend payouts. ...

There is, in addition, a second discontinuity between the RICO violation and the asserted injury. Ideal's lost sales could have resulted from factors other than petitioners' alleged acts of fraud. Businesses lose and gain customers for many reasons, and it would require a complex assessment to establish what portion of Ideal's lost sales were the product of National's decreased prices. ...

The attenuated connection between Ideal's injury and the Anzas' injurious conduct thus implicates fundamental concerns expressed in *Holmes.* Notwithstanding the lack of any appreciable risk of duplicative recoveries, which is another consideration relevant to the proximate-cause inquiry, these concerns help to illustrate why Ideal's alleged injury was not the direct result of a RICO violation. Further illustrating this

92

point is the speculative nature of the proceedings that would follow if Ideal were permitted to maintain its claim. A court considering the claim would need to begin by calculating the portion of National's price drop attributable to the alleged pattern of racketeering activity. It next would have to calculate the portion of Ideal's lost sales attributable to the relevant part of the price drop. The element of proximate causation recognized in *Holmes* is meant to prevent these types of intricate, uncertain inquiries from overrunning RICO litigation. It has particular resonance when applied to claims brought by economic competitors, which, if left unchecked, could blur the line between RICO and the antitrust laws.

The requirement of a direct causal connection is especially warranted where the immediate victims of an alleged RICO violation can be expected to vindicate the laws by pursuing their own claims. ... Again, the instant case is instructive. Ideal accuses the Anzas of defrauding the State of New York out of a substantial amount of money. If the allegations are true, the State can be expected to pursue appropriate remedies. The adjudication of the State's claims, moreover, would be relatively straightforward; while it may be difficult to determine facts such as the number of sales Ideal lost due to National's tax practices, it is considerably easier to make the initial calculation of how much tax revenue the Anzas withheld from the State. There is no need to broaden the universe of actionable harms to permit RICO suits by parties who have been injured only indirectly.

The Court of Appeals reached a contrary conclusion, apparently reasoning that because the Anzas allegedly sought to gain a competitive advantage over Ideal, it is immaterial whether they took an indirect route to accomplish their goal. This rationale does not accord with *Holmes*. A RICO plaintiff cannot circumvent the proximate-cause requirement simply by claiming that the defendant's aim was to increase market share at a competitor's expense. ...When a court evaluates a RICO claim for proximate causation, the central question it must ask is whether the alleged violation led directly to the plaintiff's injuries. In the instant case, the answer is no. We hold that Ideal's § 1962(c) claim does not satisfy the requirement of proximate causation.

In Bridge v. Phoenix Bond & Indem. Co. --- S.Ct. ----, 2008 WL 2329761 (U.S), Justice Thomas, writing for a unanimous court, addressed question of whether RICO civil plaintiffs who allege mail fraud as the RICO racketeering activity must allege that they relied on the misrepresentations used as the basis for the fraud:

> ...The question presented in this case is whether a plaintiff asserting a RICO claim predicated on mail fraud must plead and prove that it relied on the defendant's alleged misrepresentations. Because we agree with the Court of Appeals that a showing of first-party reliance is not required, we affirm.

> Each year the Cook County, Illinois, Treasurer's Office holds a public auction at which it sells tax liens it has acquired on the property of delinquent taxpayers. Prospective buyers bid on the liens, but not in cash amounts. Instead, the bids are stated as percentage penalties the property owner must pay the winning bidder in order to clear the lien. The bidder willing to accept the lowest penalty wins the auction and obtains the right to purchase the lien in exchange for paying the outstanding taxes on the property. The property owner may then redeem the property by paying the lienholder the delinquent taxes, plus the penalty established at the auction and an additional 12% penalty on any taxes subsequently paid by the lienholder. If the property owner does not redeem the property within the statutory redemption period, the lienholder may obtain a tax deed for the property, thereby in effect purchasing the property for the value of the delinquent taxes.

> Because property acquired in this manner can often be sold at a significant profit over the amount paid for the lien, the auctions are marked by stiff competition. As a result, most parcels attract multiple bidders willing to accept the lowest penalty permissible-0%, that is to say, no penalty at all. (Perhaps to prevent the perverse incentive taxpayers would have if they could redeem their property from a winning bidder for less than the amount of their unpaid taxes, the county does not accept negative bids.) The lower limit of 0% creates a problem: Who wins when the bidding results in a tie? The county's solution is to allocate parcels "on a rotational basis" in order to ensure that liens are apportioned fairly among 0% bidders.

But this creates a perverse incentive of its own: Bidders who, in addition to bidding themselves, send agents to bid on their behalf will obtain a disproportionate share of liens. To prevent this kind of manipulation, the county adopted the "Single, Simultaneous Bidder Rule," which requires each "tax buying entity" to submit bids in its own name and prohibits it from using "apparent agents, employees, or related entities" to submit simultaneous bids for the same parcel. Upon registering for an auction, each bidder must submit a sworn affidavit affirming that it complies with the Single, Simultaneous Bidder Rule.

Petitioners and respondents are regular participants in Cook County's tax sales. In July 2005, respondents filed a complaint in the United States District Court for the Northern District of Illinois, contending that petitioners had fraudulently obtained a disproportionate share of liens by violating the Single, Simultaneous Bidder Rule at the auctions held from 2002 to 2005. According to respondents, petitioner Sabre Group, LLC, and its principal Barrett Rochman arranged for related firms to bid on Sabre Group's behalf and directed them to file false attestations that they complied with the Single, Simultaneous Bidder Rule. Having thus fraudulently obtained the opportunity to participate in the auction, the related firms collusively bid on the same properties at a 0% rate. As a result, when the county allocated liens on a rotating basis, it treated the related firms as independent entities, allowing them collectively to acquire a greater number of liens than would have been granted to a single bidder acting alone. The related firms then purchased the liens and transferred the certificates of purchase to Sabre Group. In this way, respondents allege, petitioners deprived them and other bidders of their fair share of liens and the attendant financial benefits.

Respondents' complaint contains five counts. Counts I-IV allege that petitioners violated and conspired to violate RICO by conducting their affairs through a pattern of racketeering activity involving numerous acts of mail fraud. In support of their allegations of mail fraud, respondents assert that petitioners "mailed or caused to be mailed hundreds of mailings in furtherance of the scheme," when they sent property owners various notices required by Illinois law. Count V alleges a state-law claim of tortious interference with prospective business advantage.

On petitioners' motion, the District Court dismissed respondents' RICO claims for lack of standing. It observed that "[o]nly [respondents] and other competing buyers, as opposed to the Treasurer or the property owners, would suffer a financial loss from a scheme to violate the Single, Simultaneous Bidder Rule." But it concluded that respondents "are not in the class of individuals protected by the mail fraud statute, and therefore are not within the 'zone of interests' that the RICO statute protects," because they "were not recipients of the alleged misrepresentations and, at best were indirect victims of the alleged fraud." The District Court declined to exercise supplemental jurisdiction over respondents' tortious-interference claim and dismissed it without prejudice.

The Court of Appeals for the Seventh Circuit reversed. …

We granted certiorari, to resolve the conflict among the Courts of Appeals on "the substantial question," Anza, 547 U.S., at 461, 126 S.Ct. 1991, whether first-party reliance is an element of a civil RICO claim predicated on mail fraud.

…

…RICO provides a private right of action for treble damages to any person injured in his business or property by reason of the conduct of a qualifying enterprise's affairs through a pattern of acts indictable as mail fraud. Mail fraud, in turn, occurs whenever a person, "having devised or intending to devise any scheme or artifice to defraud," uses the mail "for the purpose of executing such scheme or artifice or attempting so to do." § 1341. The gravamen of the offense is the scheme to defraud, and any "mailing that is incident to an essential part of the scheme satisfies the mailing element," …even if the mailing itself "contain[s] no false information,"

Once the relationship among these statutory provisions is understood, respondents' theory of the case is straightforward. They allege that petitioners devised a scheme to defraud when they agreed to submit false attestations of compliance with the Single, Simultaneous Bidder Rule to the county. In furtherance of this scheme, petitioners used the mail on numerous occasions to send the requisite notices to property owners. Each of these mailings was an "act which is indictable" as mail fraud, and together they constituted a "pattern of racketeering activity."

By conducting the affairs of their enterprise through this pattern of racketeering activity, petitioners violated § 1962(c). As a result, respondents lost the opportunity to acquire valuable liens. Accordingly, respondents were injured in their business or property by reason of petitioners' violation of § 1962(c), and RICO's plain terms give them a private right of action for treble damages.

Petitioners argue, however, that because the alleged pattern of racketeering activity consisted of acts of mail fraud, respondents must show that they relied on petitioners' fraudulent misrepresentations. This they cannot do, because the alleged misrepresentations-petitioners' attestations of compliance with the Single, Simultaneous Bidder Rule-were made to the county, not respondents. The county may well have relied on petitioners' misrepresentations when it permitted them to participate in the auction, but respondents, never having received the misrepresentations, could not have done so. Indeed, respondents do not even allege that they relied on petitioners' false attestations. Thus, petitioners submit, they fail to state a claim under RICO.

If petitioners' proposed requirement of first-party reliance seems to come out of nowhere, there is a reason: Nothing on the face of the relevant statutory provisions imposes such a requirement. Using the mail to execute or attempt to execute a scheme to defraud is indictable as mail fraud, and hence a predicate act of racketeering under RICO, even if no one relied on any misrepresentation. And one can conduct the affairs of a qualifying enterprise through a pattern of such acts without anyone relying on a fraudulent misrepresentation.

It thus seems plain-and indeed petitioners do not dispute-that no showing of reliance is required to establish that a person has violated § 1962(c) by conducting the affairs of an enterprise through a pattern of racketeering activity consisting of acts of mail fraud. See Anza, 547 U.S., at 476, 126 S.Ct. 1991 (THOMAS, J., concurring in part and dissenting in part) ("Because an individual can commit an indictable act of mail or wire fraud even if no one relies on his fraud, he can engage in a pattern of racketeering activity, in violation of § 1962, without proof of reliance"). If reliance is required, then, it must be by virtue of § 1964(c), which provides the right of action. But it is difficult to derive a first-party reliance requirement from § 1964(c), which states simply that "[a]ny person injured in his business or property by reason of a violation of section 1962" may sue for treble damages. The statute provides a right of action to "[a]ny person" injured by the violation, suggesting a breadth of coverage not easily reconciled with an implicit requirement that the plaintiff show reliance in addition to injury in his business or property.

Moreover, a person can be injured "by reason of" a pattern of mail fraud even if he has not relied on any misrepresentations. This is a case in point. Accepting their allegations as true, respondents clearly were injured by petitioners' scheme: As a result of petitioners' fraud, respondents lost valuable liens they otherwise would have been awarded. And this is true even though they did not rely on petitioners' false attestations of compliance with the county's rules. Or, to take another example, suppose an enterprise that wants to get rid of rival businesses mails misrepresentations about them to their customers and suppliers, but not to the rivals themselves. If the rival businesses lose money as a result of the misrepresentations, it would certainly seem that they were injured in their business "by reason of" a pattern of mail fraud, even though they never received, and therefore never relied on, the fraudulent mailings. Yet petitioners concede that, on their reading of § 1964(c), the rival businesses would have no cause of action under RICO, even though they were the primary and intended victims of the scheme to defraud.

Lacking textual support for this counterintuitive position, petitioners rely instead on a combination of common-law rules and policy arguments in an effort to show that Congress should be presumed to have made first-party reliance an element of a civil RICO claim based on mail fraud. None of petitioners' arguments persuades us to read a first-party reliance requirement into a statute that by its terms suggests none.

Petitioners first argue that RICO should be read to incorporate a first-party reliance requirement in fraud cases "under the rule that Congress intends to incorporate the well-settled meaning of the common-law terms it uses." It has long been settled, they contend, that only the recipient of a fraudulent misrepresentation may recover for common-law fraud, and that he may do so "if, but only if ... he relies on the misrepresentation in acting or refraining from action."

Restatement (Second) of Torts § 537 (1977). Given this background rule of common law, petitioners maintain, Congress should be presumed to have adopted a first-party reliance requirement when it created a civil cause of action under RICO for victims of mail fraud.

In support of this argument, petitioners point to our decision in Beck v. Prupis, 529 U.S. 494, 120 S.Ct. 1608, 146 L.Ed.2d 561 (2000). There, we considered the scope of RICO's private right of action for violations of § 1962(d), which makes it "unlawful for any person to conspire to violate" RICO's criminal prohibitions. The question presented was "whether a person injured by an overt act in furtherance of a conspiracy may assert a civil RICO conspiracy claim under § 1964(c) for a violation of § 1962(d) even if the overt act does not constitute 'racketeering activity.' " . Answering this question in the negative, we held that "injury caused by an overt act that is not an act of racketeering or otherwise wrongful under RICO is not sufficient to give rise to a cause of action under § 1964(c) for a violation of § 1962(d)." In so doing, we "turn[ed] to the well-established common law of civil conspiracy." Because it was "widely accepted" by the time of RICO's enactment "that a plaintiff could bring suit for civil conspiracy only if he had been injured by an act that was itself tortious," we presumed "that when Congress established in RICO a civil cause of action for a person 'injured ... by reason of' a 'conspir [acy],' it meant to adopt these well-established common-law civil conspiracy principles." We specifically declined to rely on the law of criminal conspiracy, relying instead on the law of civil conspiracy:

"We have turned to the common law of criminal conspiracy to define what constitutes a violation of § 1962(d), see Salinas v. United States, 522 U.S. 52, 63-65[, 118 S.Ct. 469, 139 L.Ed.2d 352] (1997), a mere violation being all that is necessary for criminal liability. This case, however, does not present simply the question of what constitutes a violation of § 1962(d), but rather the meaning of a civil cause of action for private injury by reason of such a violation. In other words, our task is to interpret §§ 1964(c) and 1962(d) in conjunction, rather than § 1962(d) standing alone. The obvious source in the common law for the combined meaning of these provisions is the law of civil conspiracy."

Petitioners argue that, as in Beck, we should look to the common-law meaning of civil fraud in order to give content to the civil cause of action § 1964(c) provides for private injury by reason of a violation of § 1962(c) based on a pattern of mail fraud. The analogy to Beck, however, is misplaced. The critical difference between Beck and this case is that in § 1962(d) Congress used a term-"conspir[acy]"-that had a settled common-law meaning, whereas Congress included no such term in § 1962(c). Section 1962(c) does not use the term "fraud"; nor does the operative language of § 1961(1)(B), which defines "racketeering activity" to include "any act which is indictable under ... section 1341." And the indictable act under § 1341 is not the fraudulent misrepresentation, but rather the use of the mails with the purpose of executing or attempting to execute a scheme to defraud. In short, the key term in § 1962(c)-"racketeering activity"-is a defined term, and Congress defined the predicate act not as fraud simpliciter, but mail fraud-a statutory offense unknown to the common law. In these circumstances, the presumption that Congress intends to adopt the settled meaning of common-law terms has little pull. ..."There is simply no "reason to believe that Congress would have defined 'racketeering activity' to include acts indictable under the mail and wire fraud statutes, if it intended fraud-related acts to be predicate acts under RICO only when those acts would have been actionable under the common law." Anza, 547 U.S., at 477-478, 126 S.Ct. 1991 (THOMAS, J., concurring in part and dissenting in part).

Nor does it help petitioners' cause that here, as in Beck, the question is not simply "what constitutes a violation of § 1962[(c)], but rather the meaning of a civil cause of action for private injury by reason of such a violation." To be sure, Beck held that a plaintiff cannot state a civil claim for conspiracy under § 1964(c) merely by showing a violation of § 1962(d) and a resulting injury. But in so doing, Beck relied not only on the fact that the term "conspiracy" had a settled common-law meaning, but also on the well-established common-law understanding of what it means to be injured by a conspiracy for purposes of bringing a civil claim for damages. No comparable understanding exists with respect to injury caused by an enterprise conducting its affairs through a pattern of acts indictable as mail fraud. And even the common-law understanding of injury caused by fraud does not support petitioners' argument. ...[T]he common law has long recognized that plaintiffs can recover in a variety of circumstances where, as here, their injuries result directly from the defendant's fraudulent misrepresentations to a third party.

For these reasons, we reject petitioners' contention that the "common-law meaning" rule dictates that reliance by the plaintiff is an element of a civil RICO claim predicated on a violation of the mail fraud statute. Congress chose to make mail fraud, not common-law fraud, the predicate act for a RICO violation. And "the mere fact that the predicate acts underlying a particular RICO violation happen to be fraud offenses does not mean that reliance, an element of common-law fraud, is also incorporated as an element of a civil RICO claim." Anza, supra, at 476, 126 S.Ct. 1991 (THOMAS, J., concurring in part and dissenting in part).

Petitioners next argue that even if Congress did not make first-party reliance an element of a RICO claim predicated on mail fraud, a plaintiff who brings such a claim must show that it relied on the defendant's misrepresentations in order to establish the requisite element of causation. ...

...

Pointing to our reliance on common-law proximate-causation principles in Holmes and Anza, petitioners argue that "[u]nder well-settled common-law principles, proximate cause is established for fraud claims only where the plaintiff can demonstrate that he relied on the misrepresentation." In support of this argument, petitioners cite Restatement (Second) of Torts § 548A, which provides that "[a] fraudulent misrepresentation is a legal cause of a pecuniary loss resulting from action or inaction in reliance upon it if, but only if, the loss might reasonably be expected to result from the reliance." Thus, petitioners conclude, "a plaintiff asserting a civil RICO claim predicated on mail fraud cannot satisfy the proximate cause requirement unless he can establish that his injuries resulted from his reliance on the defendant's fraudulent misrepresentation."

Petitioners' argument is twice flawed. First, as explained above, the predicate act here is not common-law fraud, but mail fraud. Having rejected petitioners' argument that reliance is an element of a civil RICO claim based on mail fraud, we see no reason to let that argument in through the back door by holding that the proximate-cause analysis under RICO must precisely track the proximate-cause analysis of a common-law fraud claim....

Second, while it may be that first-party reliance is an element of a common-law fraud claim, there is no general common-law principle holding that a fraudulent misrepresentation can cause legal injury only to those who rely on it. ...

...

Nor is first-party reliance necessary to ensure that there is a sufficiently direct relationship between the defendant's wrongful conduct and the plaintiff's injury to satisfy the proximate-cause principles articulated in Holmes and Anza. Again, this is a case in point. Respondents' alleged injury-the loss of valuable liens-is the direct result of petitioners' fraud. It was a foreseeable and natural consequence of petitioners' scheme to obtain more liens for themselves that other bidders would obtain fewer liens. And here, unlike in Holmes and Anza, there are no independent factors that account for respondents' injury, there is no risk of duplicative recoveries by plaintiffs removed at different levels of injury from the violation, and no more immediate victim is better situated to sue. Indeed, both the District Court and the Court of Appeals concluded that respondents and other losing bidders were the only parties injured by petitioners' misrepresentations. Petitioners quibble with that conclusion, asserting that the county would be injured too if the taint of fraud deterred potential bidders from participating in the auction. But that eventuality, in contrast to respondents' direct financial injury, seems speculative and remote.

Of course, none of this is to say that a RICO plaintiff who alleges injury "by reason of" a pattern of mail fraud can prevail without showing that someone relied on the defendant's misrepresentations. ...In most cases, the plaintiff will not be able to establish even but-for causation if no one relied on the misrepresentation. If, for example, the county had not accepted petitioners' false attestations of compliance with the Single, Simultaneous Bidder Rule, and as a result had not permitted petitioners to participate in the auction, respondents' injury would never have materialized. In addition, the complete absence of reliance may prevent the plaintiff from establishing proximate cause. Thus, for example, if the county knew petitioners' attestations were false but nonetheless permitted them to participate in the auction, then arguably the county's actions would constitute an intervening cause breaking the chain of causation between petitioners' misrepresentations and respondents' injury.

Accordingly, it may well be that a RICO plaintiff alleging injury by reason of a pattern of mail fraud must establish at least third-party reliance in order to prove causation. "But the fact that proof of reliance is often used to prove an element of the plaintiff's cause of action, such as the element of causation, does not transform reliance itself into an element of the cause of action." ...Nor does it transform first-party reliance into an indispensable requisite of proximate causation. Proof that the plaintiff relied on the defendant's misrepresentations may in some cases be sufficient to establish proximate cause, but there is no sound reason to conclude that such proof is always necessary. By the same token, the absence of first-party reliance may in some cases tend to show that an injury was not sufficiently direct to satisfy § 1964(c)'s proximate-cause requirement, but it is not in and of itself dispositive. A contrary holding would ignore Holmes ' instruction that proximate cause is generally not amenable to bright-line rules.

As a last resort, petitioners contend that we should interpret RICO to require first-party reliance for fraud-based claims in order to avoid the "over-federalization" of traditional state-law claims. ...

Whatever the merits of petitioners' arguments as a policy matter, we are not at liberty to rewrite RICO to reflect their-or our-views of good policy. We have repeatedly refused to adopt narrowing constructions of RICO in order to make it conform to a preconceived notion of what Congress intended to proscribe....

We see no reason to change course here. RICO's text provides no basis for imposing a first-party reliance requirement. If the absence of such a requirement leads to the undue proliferation of RICO suits, the "correction must lie with Congress."

In an unusual step, a RICO civil lawsuit has been filed in a Moscow, Russia arbitration court. The Russian customs service has filed a RICO suit against the Bank of New York/Mellon claiming 22.5 billion dollars in treble damages. The suit is unusual in that it has been filed in a foreign court. Compare and contrast, Tafflin v. Levitt, 493 U.S. 455 (1990) holding that "state courts retain their presumptive authority to adjudicate" civil claims arising under the laws of the United States.

The Russian lawsuit is based on allegations that bank employees had illegally transferred Russian money into off-shore accounts. Professors Robert Blakey and Alan Dershowitz are involved in the case on behalf of the Russian plaintiffs. Former Attorney General and former Governor of New York, Richard Thornburgh is involved on behalf of the defendant bank. The suit is pending. For updates, see http://russianbanksuit.com.

What kind of issues are raised by this lawsuit? How are they different from the civil RICO issues we have already seen?

After the decision in United States v. Philip Morris, supra, the Supreme Court denied certiorari, U.S. v. Philip Morris USA Inc., 546 U.S. 960 (2005). Subsequently, the district court, ruled: 1) that the defendants were not entitled to clarification of order which permanently enjoined them from committing any act of racketeering relating in any way to the manufacturing, marketing, promotion, health consequences, or sale of cigarettes in the United States, where defendants had more than sufficient notice of the illegal conduct that was prohibited under the injunction; and 2) a stay of the injunction pending appeal was not warranted following judgment for government in its RICO suit against cigarette manufacturers and tobacco-related trade organizations alleging conspiracy to deceive public about, inter alia, health effects of smoking and health benefits from low-tar cigarettes, and culminating in order for corrective statements; it was likely that young people exposed to defendants' advertising, and others, would be directly harmed in event of stay, and manufacturers' anticipated loss of market share did not constitute irreparable harm warranting stay. See respectively, United States v. Philip Morris USA, Inc., 477 F.Supp.2d 191 (D.D.C. 2007) and United States v. Philip Morris USA, Inc., 449 F.Supp.2d 988 (D.D.C. 2006). The Department of Justice maintains a website that provides information on the course of the government's litigation against the Tobacco   Companies. http://www.usdoj.gov/civil/cases/tobacco2/index.htm. The website indicates that the both the defendants and the United States filed notices of appeal from the court of appeals decision.

Page 577. Substitute the following for note 5.

5. The latest stage in the government's civil suit addressing corruption at the docks is United States v. International Longshoremen's Ass'n, 518 F.Supp.2d 422 (E.D.N.Y. 2007). In this lawsuit, the district court ruled that the government's RICO complaint against a labor union, its officers, and various members of crime families failed to plead a cognizable association-in-fact enterprise operating on the New York/New Jersey waterfront and the Port of Miami. The court stated:

> This action is the latest episode in a decades-long effort by the United States to curtail the influence of the La Cosa Nostra organized crime families over the vehicles of interstate commerce operating along the waterfront areas in the Port of New York and New Jersey and the Port of Miami. The Government's prolix, 85-page Amended Complaint, with its hundreds of pages of attached exhibits, alleges in essence that from 1995 onward, the Genovese and Gambino crime families conspired with their associates occupying high-ranking positions in legitimate Waterfront operations, particularly the ILA and several associated labor organizations, to extend and maintain the influence of organized crime through a pattern of racketeering activity including extortion, money laundering, and mail and wire fraud. The Amended Complaint is burdened with lengthy discussions of the history and operations of La Cosa Nostra generally, as well as discussions of Government investigations and prosecutions of organized crime activity on the Waterfront going back several decades. While the Government argues that all of this historical material is necessary to place the allegations regarding the charged conspiracies in their proper context, the Court shall ignore much of this material and focus its discussion of the relevant facts on the allegations comprising the charged offenses as well as the relatively recent related civil and criminal litigation that directly preceded this action.

> ...

1. The Waterfront Enterprise

At the heart of the Government's theory of this case is the "Waterfront Enterprise," an alleged association-in-fact RICO enterprise that is comprised of the members of the Gambino and Genovese families operating on the Waterfront and their associates and co-conspirators in the ILA and other legitimate Waterfront organizations. The Amended Complaint defines the Waterfront Enterprise as an aggregation of the ILA and certain of its subordinate components, namely, the Atlantic Coast District, the South Atlantic & Gulf Coast District, Locals 1, 824, 1235, 1588, 1804-1, 1814, 1922, 1922-1, and 2062; certain current and former ILA officials; certain welfare benefit and pension benefit funds managed for the benefit of ILA members, namely, MILA, the METRO-ILA Funds, the ILA Local 1922 Health and Welfare Fund, the ILA-Employers Southeast Florida Ports Welfare Fund; certain businesses operating on or about the Waterfront; an "employer association" operating on or about the Waterfront, namely METRO; certain members and associates of the Genovese and Gambino crime families; and certain businesses operating in the Port of Miami. . . . The Government alleges that each of the Racketeering Defendants "were leaders of the Enterprise who directed other members of the Enterprise in carrying out unlawful and other activities in furtherance of the conduct of the Enterprise's affairs." In a section captioned "Purpose of the Enterprise," the Government alleges that

> [t]he Defendants' common purpose was to exercise corrupt control and influence over labor unions and businesses operating on the Waterfront, the Port of Miami and elsewhere in order to enrich themselves and their associates. In order to achieve this objective, the Defendants have established and maintained control and influence over labor unions and businesses. To ensure the continued effectiveness of this corrupt system and as part of the overall plan and pattern of control, the Gambino and Genovese families have generally maintained and recognized their respective areas of control and domination on the Waterfront, the Port of Miami and elsewhere.

. . .

The Court concludes that the ILA is correct, and that the Amended Complaint fails to plead a cognizable association-in-fact enterprise. The Amended Complaint contains virtually no allegations regarding the structure and organization of the alleged Waterfront Enterprise, and leaves a plethora of unanswered questions regarding the membership, purpose, and structure of that entity. For example, who are the unnamed "current and former ILA officials" and "certain businesses operating on or about the Waterfront" that are members of the Waterfront Enterprise? What criteria distinguish a Waterfront entity that is a member of the Waterfront Enterprise from one that is not? What is the organizational structure of the Waterfront Enterprise? Who is in charge of it? How are instructions conveyed between its members? How does one become a member of, or terminate membership in, the Waterfront Enterprise? As discussed further below, what common purpose unites the members of the Waterfront Enterprise, and what is the purpose of the enterprise itself? ... At best, the Amended Complaint depicts the Waterfront Enterprise as a quasi-discrete commercial ecosystem, populated by various entities interconnected in a web of personal and commercial relationships that evolves organically as each entity pursues its own interests, some of which coincide with those of other denizens of the Waterfront commercial habitat and others being quite adversely aligned. The same could be said of virtually any commercial or geographic sector of this District, and simply does not rise to the level of an organized, unitary enterprise as is required under RICO.

It should further be noted that, by the Government's own admission at oral argument, the Amended Complaint fails to allege any common purpose uniting the Waterfront Enterprise as an entity, as is required to plead a valid association-in-fact enterprise. ... Paragraph 68 of the Amended Complaint, captioned "Purpose of the Enterprise," states in relevant part that "[t]he Defendants' common purpose was to exercise corrupt control and influence over labor unions and businesses operating on the Waterfront, the Port of Miami and elsewhere in order to enrich themselves and their associates." When asked by the Court at oral argument to identify the common purpose of the Waterfront Enterprise, counsel for the Government directed the Court to the quoted language in paragraph 68. However, the Government subsequently clarified that the "common purpose" identified in paragraph 68 is not intended to be attributed to the nominal defendants in this action, nor, presumably, to the non-parties that are identified as members of the Waterfront Enterprise. In other words, the "common purpose" alleged in paragraph 68 is only the Racketeering Defendants' common purpose, not the common purpose of the Waterfront Enterprise. While the corrupt purposes of certain members of the enterprise may be relevant to the Government's allegations of RICO conspiracy, they are insufficient to establish the existence of a cohesive association-in-fact enterprise that is a necessary component of a RICO violation.

As this Court suggested at oral argument, what the Government is really alleging in this case is an enterprise comprised of the Gambino and Genovese families, certain members and associates of those families, and a handful of co-conspirators placed in key positions in the ILA and associated labor unions who together have allegedly conspired to corrupt and control interstate commerce on the New York/New Jersey Waterfront and the Port of Miami through a pattern of racketeering activity involving the infiltration and control of labor unions and businesses operating on the Waterfront. While limiting the alleged enterprise to that relatively narrow group might create potentially insurmountable obstacles to the Government's efforts to impose equitable relief on some of the nominal defendants in this action, this Court will not abet the Government's effort to stretch the concept of a racketeering enterprise beyond all recognition in order to bring various otherwise disinterested parties within its scope, even for the worthwhile purpose of combating the influence of organized crime on the Waterfront. The Court therefore holds that the Amended Complaint fails to allege a cognizable association-in-fact enterprise.

CHAPTER 12

ANTI-TERRORISM ENFORCEMENT

Page 579. Add as a new paragraph before the last paragraph.

Three additional specific subject matter anti-terrorism statutes have been enacted since the publication of the main volume, the Detainee Treatment Act of 2005 (DTA), the Military Commissions Act of 2006 (MCA) and the Protect America Act of 2007(PAA). The PAA, which amended the Foreign Intelligence Surveillance Act, addressed the issue of the government's electronic eavesdropping on persons abroad as well as conversations between persons abroad and individuals in the United States. The legislation had a short sunset period and eventually lapsed in early Spring, 2008. Among the issues which made proposed replacement legislation controversial was the question of whether to give immunity to telephone companies that cooperated with requests from the government for telephonic data bank records in connection with a government data mining program (which reportedly did not intrude on the contents of conversations). Negotiations on legislation to replace the PAA have been taking place in the Congress, and in June, 2008, at the time of this writing, it was widely reported that a deal had been struck on new legislation on this subject. The DTA and MCA are treated infra, insofar as relevant to the casebook materials.

Page 580. Replace the reference at the end of the first paragraph.

Norman Abrams, Anti-terrorism and Criminal Enforcement, 3rd Edition (Thomson-West, 2008).

Page 592. Add to note 1.

In October, 2006, Lynne Stewart was sentenced to 28 months in prison on each of the counts, the sentences to run concurrently, to be followed by two years of supervised release. She was disbarred on conviction. In February, 2008, the United States Court of Appeals for the Second Circuit heard arguments in the appeal of the case. At the time of this writing, the court has not yet handed down its decision.

Page 604. Add to note 1.

Padilla's petition for certiorari was denied. 547 U.S. 1062 (2006). Justice Kennedy, joined by The Chief Justice and Justice Stevens, wrote an opinion concurring in the denial in which he wrote, "...Padilla, ... has a continuing concern that his status might be altered again [ed. that is, back again to military custody since he had been shifted originally from civilian to military custody and now was being shifted back to civilian custody]... Were the Government to seek to change the status or conditions of Padilla's custody, that court would be in a position to rule quickly....Padilla, moreover, retains the option of seeking a writ of habeas corpus in this Court."

Padilla was subsequently tried in the United States district court in Florida on the indicated civilian criminal charges. In August, 2007, he was convicted and sentenced to 17 years and four months. The judge was reported to have said that she took into consideration the treatment he had received while detained as an enemy combatant in military custody. Wash. Post Jan. 23, 2008, AO3

Page 605. Add to note 2.

A second instance of a person arrested in the United States, declared to be an enemy combatant and detained in military custody is the case of Ali Saleh Kahlah al-Marri. Al-Marri, who has been detained since 2003, is not a U.S. citizen. His habeas corpus suit reached the U.S. Court of Appeals for the Fourth Circuit, and a panel of the court ruled, 2-1, in favor of al-Marri. A motion to rehear the matter en banc was granted, and the case was argued en banc on October 31, 2007. At the time of this writing, the en banc opinion has not yet been handed down. It may be that the court was waiting for the Supreme Court's decision in Boumediene v. Bush, which has recently been handed and is treated infra. The panel opinion in the al-Marri case, al-Marri v. Wright, 487 F.3d 160 (4th Cir. 2007), reads as follows:

DIANA GRIBBON MOTZ, Circuit Judge.

For over two centuries of growth and struggle, peace and war, the Constitution has secured our freedom through the guarantee that, in the United States, no one will be deprived of liberty without due process of law. Yet more than four years ago military authorities seized an alien lawfully residing here. He has been held by the military ever since-without criminal charge or process. He has been so held despite the fact that he was initially taken from his home in Peoria, Illinois by civilian authorities, and indicted for purported domestic crimes. He has been so held although the Government has never alleged that he is a member of any nation's military, has fought alongside any nation's armed forces, or has borne arms against the United States anywhere in the world. And he has been so held, without acknowledgment of the protection afforded by the Constitution, solely because the Executive believes that his military detention is proper.

While criminal proceedings were underway against Ali Saleh Kahlah al-Marri, the President ordered the military to seize and detain him indefinitely as an enemy combatant. Since that order, issued in June of 2003, al-Marri has been imprisoned without charge in a military jail in South Carolina. Al-Marri petitions for a writ of habeas corpus to secure his release from military imprisonment. The Government defends this detention, asserting that al-Marri associated with al Qaeda and "prepar[ed] for acts of international terrorism." It maintains that the President has both statutory and inherent constitutional authority to subject al-Marri to indefinite military detention and, in any event, that a new statute-enacted years after al-Marri's seizure-strips federal courts of jurisdiction even to consider this habeas petition.

We hold that the new statute does not apply to al-Marri, and so we retain jurisdiction to consider his petition. Furthermore, we conclude that we must grant al-Marri habeas relief. Even assuming the truth of the Government's allegations, the President lacks power to order the military to seize and indefinitely detain al-Marri. If the Government accurately describes al-Marri's conduct, he has committed grave crimes. But we have found no authority for holding that the evidence offered by the Government affords a basis for treating al-Marri as an enemy combatant, or as anything other than a civilian.

This does not mean that al-Marri must be set free. Like others accused of terrorist activity in this country, from the Oklahoma City bombers to the surviving conspirator of the September 11th attacks, al-Marri can be returned to civilian prosecutors, tried on criminal charges, and, if convicted, punished severely. But the Government cannot subject al-Marri to indefinite military detention. For in the United States, the military cannot seize and imprison civilians-let alone imprison them indefinite-ly.

Al-Marri, a citizen of Qatar, lawfully entered the United States with his wife and children on September 10, 2001, to pursue a master's degree at Bradley University in Peoria, Illinois, where he had obtained a bachelor's degree in 1991. The following day, terrorists hijacked four commercial airliners and used them to kill and inflict grievous injury on thousands of Americans. Three months later, on December 12, 2001, FBI agents arrested al-Marri at his home in Peoria as a material witness in the Government's investigation of the September 11th attacks. Al-Marri was imprisoned in civilian jails in Peoria and then New York City.

In February 2002, al-Marri was charged in the Southern District of New York with the possession of unauthorized or counterfeit credit-card numbers with the intent to defraud. A year later, in January 2003, he was charged in a second, six-count indictment, with two counts of making a false statement to the FBI, three counts of making a false statement on a bank application, and one count of using another person's identification for the purpose of influencing the action of a federally insured financial institution. Al-Marri pleaded not guilty to all of these charges. In May 2003, a federal district court in New York dismissed the charges against al-Marri for lack of venue.

The Government then returned al-Marri to Peoria and he was re-indicted in the Central District of Illinois on the same seven counts, to which he again pleaded not guilty. The district court set a July 21, 2003 trial date. On Friday, June 20, 2003, the court scheduled a hearing on pre-trial motions, including a motion to suppress evidence against al-Marri assertedly obtained by torture. On the following Monday, June 23, before that hearing could be held, the Government moved ex parte to dismiss the indictment based on an order signed that morning by the President.

In the order, President George W. Bush stated that he "DETERMINE[D] for the United States of America that" al-Marri: (1) is an enemy combatant; (2) is closely associated with al Qaeda; (3) "engaged in conduct that constituted hostile and war-like acts, including conduct in preparation for acts of international terrorism;" (4) "possesses intelligence ... that ... would aid U.S. efforts to prevent attacks by al Qaeda;" and (5) "represents a continuing, present, and grave danger to the national security of the United States." The President determined that al-Marri's detention by the military was "necessary to prevent him from aiding al Qaeda" and thus ordered the Attorney General to surrender al-Marri to the Secretary of Defense, and the Secretary of Defense to "detain him as an enemy combatant."

The federal district court in Illinois granted the Government's motion to dismiss the criminal indictment against al-Marri. In accordance with the President's order, al-Marri was then transferred to military custody and brought to the Naval Consolidated Brig in South Carolina.

Since that time (that is, for four years) the military has held al-Marri as an enemy combatant, without charge and without any indication when this confinement will end. For the first sixteen months of his military confinement, the Government did not permit al-Marri any communication with the outside world, including his attorneys, his wife, or his children. He alleges that he was denied basic necessities, interrogated through measures creating extreme sensory deprivation, and threatened with violence. A pending civil action challenges the "inhuman, degrading" and "abusive" conditions of his confinement. …

… On July 8, 2004, al-Marri's counsel filed the present habeas petition on al-Marri's behalf in the District of South Carolina. On September 9, 2004, the Government answered al-Marri's petition, citing the Declaration of Jeffrey N. Rapp, Director of the Joint Intelligence Task Force for Combating Terrorism, as support for the President's order to detain al-Marri as an enemy combatant.

The Rapp Declaration asserts that al-Marri: (1) is "closely associated with al Qaeda, an international terrorist organization with which the United States is at war"; (2) trained at an al Qaeda terrorist training camp in Afghanistan sometime between 1996 and 1998; (3) in the summer of 2001, was introduced to Osama Bin Laden by Khalid Shaykh Muhammed; (4) at that time, volunteered for a "martyr mission" on behalf of al Qaeda; (5) was ordered to enter the United States sometime before September 11, 2001, to serve as a "sleeper agent" to facilitate terrorist activities and explore disrupting this country's financial system through computer hacking; (6) in the summer of 2001, met with terrorist financier Mustafa Ahmed Al-Hawsawi, who gave al-Marri money, including funds to buy a laptop; (7) gathered technical information about poisonous chemicals on his laptop; (8) undertook efforts to

113

obtain false identification, credit cards, and banking information, including stolen credit card numbers; (9) communicated with known terrorists, including Khalid Shaykh Muhammed and Al-Hawsawi, by phone and e-mail; and (10) saved information about jihad, the September 11th attacks, and Bin Laden on his laptop computer.

The Rapp Declaration does not assert that al-Marri: (1) is a citizen, or affiliate of the armed forces, of any nation at war with the United States; (2) was seized on or near a battlefield on which the armed forces of the United States or its allies were engaged in combat; (3) was ever in Afghanistan during the armed conflict between the United States and the Taliban there; or (4) directly participated in any hostilities against United States or allied armed forces.

On October 14, 2004, the Government permitted al-Marri access to his counsel for the first time since his initial confinement as an enemy combatant sixteen months before. ...

On November 13, 2006, three months after al-Marri noted his appeal, the Government moved to dismiss this case for lack of jurisdiction, citing section 7 of the recently enacted Military Commissions Act of 2006 (MCA), Pub.L. No. 109-366, 120 Stat. 2600.

[Judge Motz in this part of her opinion addressed the jurisdiction argument raised by the government citing the Military Commissions Act. Judge Motz's opinion then proceeded to address the merits of al-Marri's habeas claim.]

...

Al-Marri premises his habeas claim on the Fifth Amendment's guarantee that no person living in this country can be deprived of liberty without due process of law. He maintains that even if he has committed the acts the Government alleges, he is not a combatant but a civilian protected by our Constitution, and thus is not subject to military detention. Al-Marri acknowledges that the Government can deport him or charge him with a crime, and if he is convicted in a civilian court, imprison him. But he insists that neither the Constitution nor any law permits the Government, on the basis of the evidence it has proffered to date-even assuming all of that evidence is true-to treat him as an enemy combatant and subject him to indefinite military detention, without criminal charge or process.

The Government contends that the district court properly denied habeas relief to al-Marri because the Constitution allows detention of enemy combatants by the military without criminal process, and according to the Government it has proffered evidence that al-Marri is a combatant. The Government argues that the Authorization for Use of Military Force (AUMF), Pub.L. No. 107-40, 115 Stat. 224 (2001), as construed by precedent and considered in conjunction with the "legal background against which [it] was enacted," empowers the President on the basis of that proffered evidence to order al-Marri's indefinite military detention as an enemy combatant. Alternatively, the Government contends that even if the AUMF does not authorize the President to order al-Marri's military detention, the President has "inherent constitutional power" to do so.

Each party grounds its case on well established legal doctrine. Moreover, important principles guiding our analysis seem undisputed.

...

The act of depriving a person of the liberty protected by our Constitution is a momentous one; thus, recognized exceptions to criminal process are narrow in scope, and generally permit only limited periods of detention. ... In Hamdi, the plurality explained that precisely the same principles apply when the Government seeks to detain a person as an enemy combatant. Under the habeas procedure prescribed in Hamdi, if the Government asserts an exception to the usual criminal process by detaining as an enemy combatant an individual with constitutional rights, it must proffer evidence to demonstrate that the individual "qualif[ies]" for this exceptional treatment. 542 U.S. at 516, 534, 124 S.Ct. 2633. Only after the Government has "put[ ] forth credible evidence that" an individual "meets the enemy-combatant criteria" does "the onus" shift to the individual to demonstrate "that he falls outside the [enemy combatant] criteria." Id. at 534, 124 S.Ct. 2633. For in this country, the military cannot seize and indefinitely detain an individual-particularly when the sole process leading to his detention is a determination by the Executive that the detention is necessary.

...

Moreover, when the Government contends, as it does here, that an individual with constitutional rights is an enemy combatant, whose exclusive opportunity to escape indefinite military

115

detention rests on overcoming presumptively accurate hearsay, courts must take particular care that the Government's allegations demonstrate that the detained individual is not a civilian, but instead, as the Supreme Court has explained, "meets the enemy-combatant criteria." Id. at 534, 124 S.Ct. 2633. ...

These principles thus form the legal framework for consideration of the issues before us. Both parties recognize that it does not violate the Due Process Clause for the President to order the military to seize and detain individuals who "qualify" as enemy combatants for the duration of a war. They disagree, however, as to whether the evidence the Government has proffered, even assuming its accuracy, establishes that al-Marri fits within the "legal category" of enemy combatants. The Government principally contends that its evidence establishes this and therefore the AUMF grants the President statutory authority to detain al-Marri as an enemy combatant. Alternatively, the Government asserts that the President has inherent constitutional authority to order al-Marri's indefinite military detention. Al-Marri maintains that the proffered evidence does not establish that he fits within the "legal category" of enemy combatant and so the AUMF does not authorize the President to order the military to seize and detain him, and that the President has no inherent constitutional authority to order this detention. We now turn to these contentions.

The Government's primary argument is that the AUMF, as construed by precedent and considered against "the legal background against which [it] was enacted," i.e. constitutional and law-of-war principles, empowers the President to order the military to seize and detain al-Marri as an enemy combatant. ...

Tellingly, the Government does not argue that the broad language of the AUMF authorizes the President to subject to indefinite military detention anyone he believes to have aided any "nation[ ], organization[ ], or person[ ]" related to the September 11th attacks. Such an interpretation would lead to absurd results that Congress could not have intended. Under that reading of the AUMF, the President would be able to subject to indefinite military detention anyone, including an American citizen, whom the President believed was associated with any organization that the President believed in some way "planned, authorized, committed, or aided" the September 11th attacks, so long as the President believed this to be "necessary and appropriate" to prevent future acts of terrorism.

Under such an interpretation of the AUMF, if some money from a nonprofit charity that feeds Afghan orphans made its way to al Qaeda, the President could subject to indefinite military detention any donor to that charity. Similarly, this interpretation of the AUMF would allow the President to detain indefinitely any employee or shareholder of an American corporation that built equipment used by the September 11th terrorists; or allow the President to order the military seizure and detention of an American-citizen physician who treated a member of al Qaeda.

To read the AUMF to provide the President with such unlimited power would present serious constitutional questions....

We need not here deal with the absurd results, nor reach the constitutional concerns, raised by an interpretation of the AUMF that authorizes the President to detain indefinitely-without criminal charge or process-anyone he believes to have aided any "nation[ ], organization[ ], or person[ ]" related to the September 11th terrorists. For the Government wisely limits its argument. It relies only on the scope of the AUMF as construed by precedent and considered in light of "the legal background against which [it] was enacted." Specifically, the Government contends that "[t]he Supreme Court's and this Court's prior construction of the AUMF govern this case and compel the conclusion that the President is authorized to detain al-Marri as an enemy combatant."

The precedent interpreting the AUMF on which the Government relies for this argument consists of two cases: the Supreme Court's opinion in Hamdi, 542 U.S. 507, 124 S.Ct. 2633, 159 L.Ed.2d 578, and our opinion in Padilla v. Hanft, 423 F.3d 386 (4th Cir.2005). The "legal background" for the AUMF, which it cites, consists of two cases from earlier conflicts, Ex Parte Quirin, 317 U.S. 1, 63 S.Ct. 2, 87 L.Ed. 3 (1942) (World War II), and Ex parte Milligan, 71 U.S. (4 Wall.) 2, 18 L.Ed. 281 (1866) (U.S. Civil War), as well as constitutional and law-of-war principles.

...

In the case at hand, the Government asserts that the construction given the AUMF in Hamdi and Padilla-based on ... law-of-war principles-"compel [s] the conclusion that the

117

President is authorized [by the AUMF] to detain al-Marri as an enemy combatant." In other words, the Government contends that al-Marri fits within the "legal category" of persons that the Supreme Court in Hamdi, and this court in Padilla, held the AUMF authorized the President to detain as enemy combatants. Thus, we examine those cases to determine whether the interpretation of the AUMF they adopt does indeed empower the President to treat al-Marri as an enemy combatant.

In Hamdi, the Supreme Court looked to precedent and the law of war to determine whether the AUMF authorized the President to detain as an enemy combatant an American citizen captured while engaging in battle against American and allied armed forces in Afghanistan as part of the Taliban. See Hamdi, 542 U.S. at 518-22, 124 S.Ct. 2633. In support of that detention, the Government offered evidence that Yaser Esam Hamdi "affiliated with a Taliban military unit and received weapons training," "took up arms with the Taliban," "engaged in armed conflict against the United States" in Afghanistan, and when captured on the battlefield "surrender [ed] his Kalishnikov assault rifle." Hamdi, 542 U.S. at 510, 513, 516, 124 S.Ct. 2633 (internal quotation marks omitted). Hamdi's detention was upheld because in fighting against the United States on the battlefield in Afghanistan with the Taliban, the de facto government of Afghanistan at the time, Hamdi bore arms with the army of an enemy nation and so, under the law of war, was an enemy combatant. Hamdi, 542 U.S. at 518-20, 124 S.Ct. 2633.

The Hamdi Court expressly recognized that the AUMF did not explicitly provide for detention. Id. at 519, 124 S.Ct. 2633; see also id. at 547, 124 S.Ct. 2633 (Souter, J., concurring). It concluded, however, "in light of" the law-of-war principles applicable to Hamdi's battlefield capture, that this was "of no moment" in the case before it. Id. at 519, 124 S.Ct. 2633 (plurality). As the plurality explained, "[b]ecause detention to prevent a combatant's return to the battlefield is a fundamental incident of waging war, in permitting the use of 'necessary and appropriate force,' Congress has clearly and unmistakably authorized detention in the narrow circumstances considered here." Id. (emphasis added). Thus, the Hamdi Court reached the following limited holding: "the AUMF is explicit congressional authorization for the detention of individuals in the narrow category we describe," that is, individuals who were "part of or supporting forces hostile to the United States or coalition partners in Afghanistan and who engaged in an armed conflict against the United States there."...

In Padilla, we similarly held that the AUMF authorized the President to detain as an enemy combatant an American citizen who "was armed and present in a combat zone" in Afghanistan as part of Taliban forces during the conflict there with the United States. 423 F.3d at 390-91 (internal quotation marks omitted). The Government had not been able to capture Jose Padilla until he came to the border of the United States, but because the Government presented evidence that Padilla "took up arms against United States forces in [Afghanistan] in the same way and to the same extent as did Hamdi" we concluded that he "unquestionably qualifies as an 'enemy combatant' as that term was defined for the purposes of the controlling opinion in Hamdi." 423 F.3d at 391...[1]

---

[1] Although our opinion discussed Padilla's association with al Qaeda, we held that Padilla was an enemy combatant because of his association with Taliban forces, i.e. Afghanistan government forces, on the battlefield in Afghanistan during the time of the conflict between the United States and Afghanistan. Padilla, 423 F.3d at 391. Al-Marri urges us to ignore Padilla in light of its subsequent history. See Padilla v. Hanft, 432 F.3d 582, 583 (4th Cir.2005) (noting that the Government's transfer of Padilla to civilian custody for criminal trial after arguing before this court that he was an enemy combatant created "an appearance that the government may be attempting to avoid consideration of our decision by the Supreme Court"). That history is troubling but we see no need to avoid Padilla's narrow holding.

We do wish to respond to points concerning Padilla raised by our friend in dissent. First, we do not, as the dissent suggests, ignore Padilla's holding that an individual qualifying as an "enemy combatant" may be captured and detained in the United States. Padilla provides no precedent for al-Marri's military capture and detention in this country because al-Marri, for the reasons explained in text, is not an enemy combatant. We emphasize the place of al-Marri's capture and detention only to establish that, as an alien lawfully residing in this country, he is protected by the Due Process Clause and so cannot be seized and indefinitely detained by the military unless he qualifies as an enemy combatant. Second, we do not hold, in conflict with Padilla, that al-Marri cannot be detained in military custody because the Government could criminally prosecute him. If al-Marri, like Padilla, did qualify as an enemy combatant, then the Government could choose to either detain him or prosecute him (if it established that he was not entitled to immunity from criminal prosecution as a lawful combatant). That said, given

Supreme Court precedent offered substantial support for the narrow rulings in Hamdi and Padilla. In Quirin, which the Hamdi plurality characterized as the "most apposite precedent," 542 U.S. at 523, 124 S.Ct. 2633, the Supreme Court upheld the treatment, as enemy combatants, of men directed, outfitted, and paid by the German military to bring explosives into the United States to destroy American war industries during World War II. The Quirin Court concluded that even a petitioner claiming American citizenship had been properly classified as an enemy combatant because "[c]itizens who associate themselves with the military arm of the enemy government, and with its aid, guidance and direction enter this county bent on hostile acts, are enemy belligerents [combatants] within the meaning of ... the law of war." Quirin, 317 U.S. at 37-38, 63 S.Ct. 2. The Court cited the Hague Convention "which defines the persons to whom belligerent [i.e. combatant] rights and duties attach," id. at 30-31 n. 7, 63 S.Ct. 2, in support of its conclusion that the Quirin petitioners qualified as enemy combatants. Given the "declaration of war between the United States and the German Reich," id. at 21, 63 S.Ct. 2, and that all the Quirin petitioners, including one who claimed American citizenship, were directed and paid by the "military arm" of the German Reich, the Court held that the law of war classified them as enemy belligerents (or combatants) and so the Constitution permitted subjecting them to military jurisdiction. Id. at 48, 63 S.Ct. 2.

Hamdi and Padilla ground their holdings on this central teaching from Quirin, i.e., enemy combatant status rests on an individual's affiliation during wartime with the "military arm of the enemy government." Quirin, 317 U.S. at 37-38, 63 S.Ct. 2; Hamdi, 542 U.S. at 519, 124 S.Ct. 2633; see also Padilla, 423 F.3d at 391. In Quirin that enemy government was the German Reich; in Hamdi and Padilla, it was the Taliban government of Afghanistan.

---

the dissent's acknowledgment, that unlike Padilla, al-Marri has never been "in a combat zone," we do not see how his detention as an enemy combatant could achieve the asserted purpose of such detention, i.e. "the prevention of return to the field of battle." (quoting Padilla, 423 F.3d at 394-95).

Hamdi and Padilla also rely on this principle from Quirin to distinguish (but not disavow) Milligan. In Milligan, the Court rejected the Government's impassioned contention that a presidential order and the "laws and usages of war," 71 U.S. at 121-22, justified exercising military jurisdiction over Lamdin Milligan, an Indiana resident, during the Civil War. The Government alleged that Milligan had communicated with the enemy, had conspired to "seize munitions of war," and had "join[ed] and overthrowing the Government and duly constituted authorities of the United States." Id. at 6. The Court recognized that Milligan had committed "an enormous crime" during "a period of *182 war" and at a place "within ... the theatre of military operations, and which had been and was constantly threatened to be invaded by the enemy." Id. at 7, 130. But it found no support in the "laws and usages of war" for subjecting Milligan to military jurisdiction as a combatant, for although he was a "dangerous enem[y]" of the nation, he was a civilian, and had to be treated as such. Id. at 121-22, 130.

Quirin, Hamdi, and Padilla all emphasize that Milligan's teaching-that our Constitution does not permit the Government to subject civilians within the United States to military jurisdiction-remains good law. The Quirin Court explained that while the petitioners before it were affiliated with the armed forces of an enemy nation and so were enemy belligerents, Milligan was a "non-belligerent" and so "not subject to the law of war." 317 U.S. at 45, 63 S.Ct. 2. The Hamdi plurality similarly took care to note that Milligan "turned in large part on the fact that Milligan was not a prisoner of war" (i.e. combatant) and suggested that "[h]ad Milligan been captured while he was assisting Confederate soldiers by carrying a rifle against Union troops on a Confederate battlefield, the holding of the Court might well have been different." 542 U.S. at 522, 124 S.Ct. 2633. And in Padilla, we reaffirmed that " Milligan does not extend to enemy combatants" and so "is inapposite here because Padilla, unlike Milligan, associated with, and has taken up arms against the forces of the United States on behalf of, an enemy of the United States." 423 F.3d at 396-97. Thus, although Hamdi, Quirin, and Padilla distinguish Milligan, they recognize that its core holding remains the law of the land. That is, civilians within this country (even "dangerous enemies" like Milligan who perpetrate "enormous crime[s]" on behalf of "secret" enemy organizations bent on "overthrowing the Government" of this country) may not be subjected to military control and deprived of constitutional rights.

In sum, the holdings of Hamdi and Padilla share two characteristics: (1) they look to law-of-war principles to determine who fits within the "legal category" of enemy combatant; and (2) following the law of war, they rest enemy combatant status on affiliation with the military arm of an enemy nation.

In view of the holdings in Hamdi and Padilla, we find it remarkable that the Government contends that they "compel the conclusion" that the President may detain al-Marri as an enemy combatant. For unlike Hamdi and Padilla, al-Marri is not alleged to have been part of a Taliban unit, not alleged to have stood alongside the Taliban or the armed forces of any other enemy nation, not alleged to have been on the battlefield during the war in Afghanistan, not alleged to have even been in Afghanistan during the armed conflict there, and not alleged to have engaged in combat with United States forces anywhere in the world. See Rapp Declaration (alleging none of these facts, but instead that "Al-Marri engaged in conduct in preparation for acts of international terrorism intended to cause injury or adverse effects on the United States").

In place of the "classic wartime detention" that the Government argued justified Hamdi's detention as an enemy combatant, see Br. of Respondents at 20-21, 27, Hamdi, 542 U.S. 507, 124 S.Ct. 2633 (No. 03-6696), or the "classic battlefield" detention it maintained justified Padilla's, see Opening Br. for the Appellant at 16, 20, 29, 51, Padilla, 432 F.3d 386 (No. 05-6396), here the Government argues that al-Marri's seizure and indefinite military detention in this country are justified "because he engaged in, and continues to pose a very real threat of carrying out, ... acts of international terrorism." And instead of seeking judicial deference to decisions of "military officers who are engaged in the serious work of waging battle," Hamdi, 542 U.S. at 531-32, 124 S.Ct. 2633, the Government asks us to defer to the "multi-agency evaluation process" of government bureaucrats in Washington made eighteen months after al-Marri was taken into custody. Neither the holding in Hamdi nor that in Padilla supports the Government's contentions here.

...

...[T]he Hamdi plurality emphasized the narrowness of its holding, id. at 509, 516, 517, 124 S.Ct. 2633, and the "limited category" of individuals controlled by that holding, id. at 518, 124 S.Ct. 2633. In Padilla, we similarly saw no need to embrace a broader construction of the AUMF than that adopted by the Supreme Court in Hamdi. Indeed, the Government itself principally argued that Padilla was an enemy combatant because he, like Hamdi, "engaged in armed conflict" alongside the Taliban "against our forces in Afghanistan." [2]

Thus, the Government is mistaken in its representation that Hamdi and Padilla "recognized" "[t]he President's authority to detain 'enemy combatants' during the current conflict with al Qaeda." No precedent recognizes any such authority. Hamdi and Padilla evidence no sympathy for the view that the AUMF permits indefinite military detention beyond the "limited category" of people covered by the "narrow circumstances" of those cases. Therefore the Government's primary argument-that Hamdi and Padilla "compel the conclusion" that the AUMF authorizes the President "to detain al-Marri as an enemy combatant"-fails.

The Government offers no other legal precedent, rationale, or authority justifying its position that the AUMF empowers the President to detain al-Marri as an enemy combatant. The Hamdi plurality, however, noted that because it had not "elaborated" on "[t]he legal category of enemy combatant," "[t]he permissible bounds of the category will be defined by the lower courts as subsequent cases are presented to them." Hamdi, 542 U.S. at 522 n. 1, 124 S.Ct. 2633. As a "lower court"

---

[2] In doing so, the Government acknowledged, id. at 29-30, our distinguished colleague Judge Wilkinson's statement that "[t]o compare [Hamdi's] battlefield capture to the domestic arrest in Padilla v. Rumsfeld is to compare apples and oranges," Hamdi v. Rumsfeld, 337 F.3d 335, 344 (4th Cir.2003) (Wilkinson, J., concurring in the denial of rehearing en banc), but explained that Judge Wilkinson's observation came before the Government had proffered any evidence that Padilla had carried arms alongside the Taliban against United States armed forces during the conflict in Afghanistan. In other words, at the time Judge Wilkinson differentiated Hamdi from Padilla, the Government's allegations against Padilla mirrored its allegations against al-Marri here-that he had associated with al Qaeda and engaged in conduct in preparation for acts of terrorism. We agree with Judge Wilkinson's characterization: to compare Hamdi's battlefield capture to the domestic arrest of al-Marri is indeed "to compare apples and oranges." Id.

in this "subsequent case[ ]," we have searched extensively for authority that would support the Government's contention that al-Marri fits within the "permissible bounds" of "the legal category of enemy combatant." ... [W]e have found none.

...

The core assumption underlying the Government's position, notwithstanding Hamdi, Padilla, Quirin, Milligan, and Hamdan, seems to be that persons lawfully within this country, entitled to the protections of our Constitution, lose their civilian status and become "enemy combatants" if they have allegedly engaged in criminal conduct on behalf of an organization seeking to harm the United States. Of course, a person who commits a crime should be punished, but when a civilian protected by the Due Process Clause commits a crime he is subject to charge, trial, and punishment in a civilian court, not to seizure and confinement by military authorities.

We recognize the understandable instincts of those who wish to treat domestic terrorists as "combatants" in a "global war on terror." Allegations of criminal activity in association with a terrorist organization, however, do not permit the Government to transform a civilian into an enemy combatant subject to indefinite military detention, any more than allegations of murder in association with others while in military service permit the Government to transform a civilian into a soldier subject to trial by court martial. See United States ex rel. Toth v. Quarles, 350 U.S. 11, 23, 76 S.Ct. 1, 100 L.Ed. 8 (1955) (holding that ex-servicemen, "like other civilians, are entitled to have the benefit of safeguards afforded those tried in the regular courts authorized by Article III of the Constitution").

To be sure, enemy combatants may commit crimes just as civilians may. When an enemy combatant violates the law of war, that conduct will render the person an "unlawful" enemy combatant, subject not only to detention but also to military trial and punishment. Quirin, 317 U.S. at 31, 63 S.Ct. 2. But merely engaging in unlawful behavior does not make one an enemy combatant. Quirin well illustrates this point. The Quirin petitioners were first enemy combatants-associating themselves with the military arm of the German government with which the United States was at war. They became unlawful enemy combatants when they violated the laws of war by "without uniform com[ing] secretly through the lines for the purpose of waging war." Id. By doing so, in addition to being subject to military detention for the duration of the conflict as enemy combatants, they also became "subject to trial and punishment by military tribunals for acts which render their belligerency illegal." Id. Had the Quirin petitioners never "secretly and without uniform" passed our "military lines," id., they still would have been enemy combatants, subject to military detention, but would not have been unlawful enemy combatants subject to military trial and punishment.

Neither Quirin nor any other precedent even suggests, as the Government seems to believe, that individuals with constitutional rights, unaffiliated with the military arm of any enemy government, can be subjected to military jurisdiction and deprived of those rights solely on the basis of their conduct on behalf of an enemy organization. In fact, Milligan rejected the Government's attempt to do just this. There, the Court acknowledged that Milligan's conduct-not "mere association" with, cf. post at n.3, but also "joining and aiding" a "secret political organization, armed to oppose the laws, and seek[ing] by stealthy means to introduce the enemies of the country into peaceful communities, there to ... overthrow the power of the United States"-made him and his co-conspirators "dangerous enemies to their country." 71 U.S. at 6, 130. But the Government did not allege that Milligan took orders from any enemy government or took up arms against this country on the battlefield. And so the Court prohibited the Government from subjecting Milligan to military jurisdiction for his "enormous crime." Id.[3]

---

[3] The distinction between organizations and nations is not without rationale. The law of war refuses to classify persons affiliated with terrorist organizations as enemy combatants for fear that doing so would immunize them from prosecution and punishment by civilian authorities in the capturing country. See, e.g., Message from the President of the United States Transmitting the Protocol II Additional to the 1949 Geneva Conventions, and Relating to the Protection of Victims of Noninternational Armed Conflicts, S. Treaty Doc. No. 100-2, at IV (1987) (explaining President Reagan's recommendation against ratifying a treaty provision that "would grant combatant status to irregular forces" and so "give recognition and protection to terrorist groups"). Moreover, a rule permitting indefinite military detention as "enemy combatants" of members of an "armed" organization, even one "seek[ing] ... to ... overthrow" a government, in

Although Milligan was an "enem[y]" of the country and associated with an organization seeking to "overthrow[ ] the Government" of this country, he was still a civilian. Id. Milligan's conduct mirrors the Government's allegations against al-Marri. If the Government's allegations are true, like Milligan, al-Marri is deplorable, criminal, and potentially dangerous, but like Milligan he is a civilian nonetheless. those who met with Bin Laden and trained in terrorist camps in Afghanistan). ...

Moreover, the Government is now prosecuting Jose Padilla in civilian court for his crimes. This practice is hardly new. Even the civilian co-conspirators of the Quirin petitioners were tried for their crimes in civilian courts. See Cramer v. United States, 325 U.S. 1, 65 S.Ct. 918, 89 L.Ed. 1441 (1945); United States v. Haupt, 136 F.2d 661 (7th Cir.1943).

The Government's treatment of others renders its decision to halt al-Marri's criminal prosecution-on the eve of a pre-trial

---

addition to being contrary to controlling precedent, Milligan, 71 U.S. at 130, could well endanger citizens of this country or our allies. For example, another nation, purportedly following this rationale, could proclaim a radical environmental organization to be a terrorist group, and subject American members of the organization traveling in that nation to indefinite military detention.

The dissent properly recognizes the distinction between an organization and a nation's armed forces, acknowledging that an allegation of "mere association" with an organization, including al Qaeda, does not necessarily establish enemy combatant status permitting detention under the AUMF. Post at n.3. The dissent suggests, however, that if the Government alleges that a person affiliates with an organization and commits criminal acts with the " purpose of ... facilitating terrorist activities," id. (quoting Rapp Declaration (emphasis added)), that would qualify him for enemy combatant status, permitting military detention under the AUMF. But the Hamdi plurality outlined a procedure to verify an individual's status, not to determine whether he harbored a particular purpose or intent. In this country, the only appropriate way to determine whether a person can be imprisoned for harboring a particular purpose or intent is through the criminal process.

hearing on a suppression motion-puzzling at best. Al-Marri contends that the Government has subjected him to indefinite military detention, rather than see his criminal prosecution to the end, in order to interrogate him without the strictures of criminal process. We trust that this is not so, for such a stratagem would contravene Hamdi's injunction that "indefinite detention for the purpose of interrogation is not authorized." 542 U.S. at 521, 124 S.Ct. 2633. We note, however, that not only has the Government offered no other explanation for abandoning al-Marri's prosecution, it has even propounded an affidavit in support of al-Marri's continued military detention stating that he "possesses information of high intelligence value." See Rapp Declaration. Moreover, former Attorney General John Ashcroft has explained that the Government decided to declare al-Marri an "enemy combatant" only after he became a "hard case" by "reject[ing] numerous offers to improve his lot by ... providing information." John Ashcroft, Never Again: Securing America and Restoring Justice 168-69 (2006).

Finally, we note that the AUMF itself contains nothing that transforms a civilian into a combatant subject to indefinite military detention. ...

Moreover, assuming the Constitution permitted Congress to grant the President such an awesome and unprecedented power, if Congress intended to grant this authority it could and would have said so explicitly. The AUMF lacks the particularly clear statement from Congress that would, at a minimum, be necessary to authorize the classification and indefinite military detention of civilians as "enemy combatants."

...

Furthermore, shortly after Congress enacted the AUMF, it enacted another statute that did explicitly authorize the President to arrest and detain "terrorist aliens" living within the United States believed to have come here to perpetrate acts of terrorism. See Uniting and Strengthening America by Providing Appropriate Tools Required to Intercept and Obstruct Terrorism (USA PATRIOT ACT) Act of 2001 (hereinafter "Patriot Act"), Pub.L. No. 107-56, 115 Stat. 272. However, that statute only authorizes detention for a limited time pending deportation or trial, pursuant to civilian law enforcement processes, and accompanied by careful congressional oversight. See infra Section III.C.1. The explicit authorization for limited detention and criminal process in civilian courts in the Patriot

Act provides still another reason why we cannot assume that Congress silently empowered the President in the AUMF to order the indefinite military detention without any criminal process of civilian "terrorist aliens" as "enemy combatants."

...

In sum, the Government has not offered, and although we have exhaustively searched, we have not found, any authority that permits us to hold that the AUMF empowers the president to detain al-Marri as an enemy combatant. If the Government's allegations are true, and we assume they are for present purposes, al-Marri, like Milligan, is a dangerous enemy of this nation who has committed serious crimes and associated with a secret enemy organization that has engaged in hostilities against us. But, like Milligan, al-Marri is still a civilian: he does not fit within the "permissible bounds of" "[t]he legal category of enemy combatant." Hamdi, 542 U.S. at 522 n. 1, 124 S.Ct. 2633. Therefore, the AUMF provides the President no statutory authority to order the military to seize and indefinitely detain al-Marri.

Accordingly, we turn to the Government's final contention. The Government summarily argues that even if the AUMF does not authorize al-Marri's seizure and indefinite detention as an enemy combatant, the President has "inherent constitutional authority" to order the military to seize and detain al-Marri.

...

To sanction such presidential authority to order the military to seize and indefinitely detain civilians, even if the President calls them "enemy combatants," would have disastrous consequences for the Constitution-and the country. For a court to uphold a claim to such extraordinary power would do more than render lifeless the Suspension Clause, the Due Process Clause, and the rights to criminal process in the Fourth, Fifth, Sixth, and Eighth Amendments; it would effectively undermine all of the freedoms guaranteed by the Constitution. It is that power-were a court to recognize it-that could lead all our laws "to go unexecuted, and the government itself to go to pieces." We refuse to recognize a claim to power that would so alter the constitutional foundations of our Republic.

For the foregoing reasons, we reverse the judgment of the district court dismissing al-Marri's petition for a writ of habeas corpus. We remand the case to that court with instructions to issue a writ of habeas corpus directing the Secretary of Defense to release al-Marri from military custody within a reasonable period of time to be set by the district court. The Government can transfer al-Marri to civilian authorities to face criminal charges, initiate deportation proceedings against him, hold him as a material witness in connection with grand jury proceedings, or detain him for a limited time pursuant to the Patriot Act. But military detention of al-Marri must cease.

REVERSED AND REMANDED.

[Judge Hudson wrote a dissenting opinion.]

Page 609. Add before C.

Note

The court of appeals decision in Hamdan, reproduced in the main volume at p. 605, was reversed by the Supreme Court, Hamdan v. Rumsfeld, 548 U.S. 557 (2006). A majority of five justices ruled "that the military commission convened to try Hamdan lacks the power to proceed because its structure and procedures violate both the UCMJ and the Geneva Conventions." A four justice plurality also concluded that "the offense with which Hamdan…[was] charged [ed. conspiracy] is not an 'offens[e] that by … the law of war may be tried by military commissions.'" Sprinkled throughout the majority/plurality opinion, however, are phrases—"in the absence of specific congressional authorization," "[a]bsent a more specific congressional authorization" and the like—that suggest that a military commission process authorized by the Congress might pass muster.

Within three months after Supreme Court's decision in Hamdan, Congress responded, with the enactment of the Military Commissions Act of 2006. The MCA authorizes the establishment of military commissions by the President and generally prescribes the structure, procedures, and rules for the commissions. The Act lists and defines offenses triable before the commissions. The Act also withdraws habeas corpus jurisdiction, reenacting and expanding the scope of application of similar provisions in the Detainee Treatment Act of 2005. Also following similar provisions in the DTA, it provides for an exclusive route for appellate review of decisions of the military commissions. Selected provisions of the MCA are reproduced below.

The Military Commissions Act of 2006

SEC. 2. CONSTRUCTION OF PRESIDENTIAL AUTHORITY TO ESTABLISH MILITARY COMMISSIONS.

The authority to establish military commissions under chapter 47A of title 10, United States Code, as added by section 3(a), may not be construed to alter or limit the authority of the President under the Constitution of the United States and laws of the United States to establish military commissions for areas declared to be under martial law or in occupied territories should circumstances so require.

SEC. 3. MILITARY COMMISSIONS.

(a) MILITARY COMMISSIONS.—

(1) IN GENERAL.—Subtitle A of title 10, United States Code, is amended by inserting after chapter 47 the following new chapter:

"CHAPTER 47A—MILITARY COMMISSIONS

...

'§ 948a. Definitions

"In this chapter:

"(1) UNLAWFUL ENEMY COMBATANT.—

(A) The term 'unlawful enemy combatant' means—

"(i) a person who has engaged in hostilities or who has purposefully and materially supported hostilities against the United States or its co-belligerents who is not a lawful enemy combatant (including a person who is part of the Taliban, al Qaeda, or associated forces); or

"(ii) a person who, before, on, or after the date of the enactment of the Military Commissions Act of 2006, has been determined to be an unlawful enemy combatant by a Combatant Status Review Tribunal or another competent tribunal established under the authority of the President or the Secretary of Defense.

...

"(2) LAWFUL ENEMY COMBATANT.—The term 'lawful enemy combatant' means a person who is—

"(A) a member of the regular forces of a State party engaged in hostilities against the United States;

"(B) a member of a militia, volunteer corps, or organized resistance movement belonging to a State party engaged in such hostilities, which are under responsible command, wear a fixed distinctive sign recognizable at a distance, carry their arms openly, and abide by the law of war; or

"(C) a member of a regular armed force who professes allegiance to a government engaged in such hostilities, but not recognized by the United States.

...

"(5) GENEVA CONVENTIONS.—The term 'Geneva Conventions' means the international conventions signed at Geneva on August 12, 1949.

"§ 948b. Military commissions generally

"(a) PURPOSE.—This chapter establishes procedures governing the use of military commissions to try alien unlawful enemy combatants engaged in hostilities against the United States for violations of the law of war and other offenses triable by military commission.

"(b) AUTHORITY FOR MILITARY COMMISSIONS UNDER THIS CHAPTER.—The President is authorized to establish military commissions under this chapter for offenses triable by military commission as provided in this chapter.

"(c) CONSTRUCTION OF PROVISIONS.—The procedures for military commissions set forth in this chapter are based upon the procedures for trial by general courts-martial under chapter 47 of this title (the Uniform Code of Military Justice). Chapter 47 of this title does not, by its terms, apply to trial by military commission except as specifically provided in this chapter. The judicial construction and application of that chapter are not binding on military commissions established under this chapter.

"(d) INAPPLICABILITY OF CERTAIN PROVISIONS.—

(1) The following provisions of this title shall not apply to trial by military commission under this chapter:

"(A) Section 810 (article 10 of the Uniform Code of Military Justice), relating to speedy trial, including any rule of courtsmartial relating to speedy trial.

"(B) Sections 831(a), (b), and (d) (articles 31(a), (b), and (d) of the Uniform Code of Military Justice), relating to compulsory self-incrimination.

"(C) Section 832 (article 32 of the Uniform Code of Military Justice), relating to pretrial investigation.

"(2) Other provisions of chapter 47 of this title shall apply to trial by military commission under this chapter only to the extent provided by this chapter.

...

"(f) STATUS OF COMMISSIONS UNDER COMMON ARTICLE 3.—A military commission established under this chapter is a regularly constituted court, affording all the necessary 'judicial guarantees which are recognized as indispensable by civilized peoples' for purposes of common Article 3 of the Geneva Conventions.

"(g) GENEVA CONVENTIONS NOT ESTABLISHING SOURCE OF RIGHTS.—No alien unlawful enemy combatant subject to trial by military commission under this chapter may invoke the Geneva Conventions as a source of rights.

"§ 948c. Persons subject to military commissions

"Any alien unlawful enemy combatant is subject to trial by military commission under this chapter.

"§ 948d. Jurisdiction of military commissions

"(a) JURISDICTION.—A military commission under this chapter shall have jurisdiction to try any offense made punishable by this chapter or the law of war when committed by an alien unlawful enemy combatant before, on, or after September 11, 2001.

"(b) LAWFUL ENEMY COMBATANTS.—Military commissions under this chapter shall not have jurisdiction over lawful enemy combatants. Lawful enemy combatants who violate the law of war are subject to chapter 47 of this title. Courts-martial established under that chapter shall have jurisdiction to try a lawful enemy combatant for any offense made punishable under this chapter.

"(c) DETERMINATION OF UNLAWFUL ENEMY COMBATANT STATUS DISPOSITIVE.—A finding,

132

whether before, on, or after the date of the enactment of the Military Commissions Act of 2006, by a Combatant Status Review Tribunal or another competent tribunal established under the authority of the President or the Secretary of Defense that a person is an unlawful enemy combatant is dispositive for purposes of jurisdiction for trial by military commission under this chapter.

"(d) PUNISHMENTS.—A military commission under this chapter may, under such limitations as the Secretary of Defense may prescribe, adjudge any punishment not forbidden by this chapter, including the penalty of death when authorized under this chapter or the law of war.

...

"§ 948j. Military judge of a military commission

"(a) DETAIL OF MILITARY JUDGE.—A military judge shall be detailed to each military commission under this chapter. The Secretary of Defense shall prescribe regulations providing for the manner in which military judges are so detailed to military commissions. The military judge shall preside over each military commission to which he has been detailed.

"(b) QUALIFICATIONS.—A military judge shall be a commissioned officer of the armed forces who is a member of the bar of a Federal court, or a member of the bar of the highest court of a State, and who is certified to be qualified for duty under section 826 of this title (article 26 of the Uniform Code of Military Justice) as a military judge in general courts-martial by the Judge Advocate General of the armed force of which such military judge is a member.

...

"(f) PROHIBITION ON EVALUATION OF FITNESS BY CONVENING AUTHORITY.—The convening authority of a military commission under this chapter shall not prepare or review any report concerning the effectiveness, fitness, or efficiency of a military judge detailed to the military commission which relates to his performance of duty as a military judge on the military commission.

...

"§ 948m. Number of members; excuse of members; absent and additional members

"(a) NUMBER OF MEMBERS.

(1) A military commission under this chapter shall, except as provided in paragraph (2), have at least five members.

"(2) In a case in which the accused before a military commission under this chapter may be sentenced to a penalty of death, the military commission shall have the number of members prescribed by section 949m(c) of this title.

...

"§ 948r. Compulsory self-incrimination prohibited; treatment of statements obtained by torture and other statements

"(a) IN GENERAL.—No person shall be required to testify against himself at a proceeding of a military commission under this chapter.

"(b) EXCLUSION OF STATEMENTS OBTAINED BY TORTURE.—A statement obtained by use of torture shall not be admissible in a military commission under this chapter, except against a person accused of torture as evidence that the statement was made.

"(c) STATEMENTS OBTAINED BEFORE ENACTMENT OF DETAINEE TREATMENT ACT OF 2005.—A statement obtained before December 30, 2005 (the date of the enactment of the Defense Treatment Act of 2005) in which the degree of coercion is disputed may be admitted only if the military judge finds that—

"(1) the totality of the circumstances renders the statement reliable and possessing sufficient probative value; and

"(2) the interests of justice would best be served by admission of the statement into evidence.

"(d) STATEMENTS OBTAINED AFTER ENACTMENT OF DETAINEE TREATMENT ACT OF 2005.—A statement obtained on or after December 30, 2005 (the date of the enactment of the Defense Treatment Act of 2005) in which the degree of coercion is disputed may be admitted only if the military judge finds that—

"(1) the totality of the circumstances renders the statement reliable and possessing sufficient probative value;

"(2) the interests of justice would best be served by admission of the statement into evidence; and

"(3) the interrogation methods used to obtain the statement do not amount to cruel, inhuman, or degrading treatment prohibited by section 1003 of the Detainee Treatment Act of 2005.

...

"§ 949a. Rules

"(a) PROCEDURES AND RULES OF EVIDENCE.— Pretrial, trial, and post-trial procedures, including elements and modes of proof, for cases triable by military commission under this chapter may be prescribed by the Secretary of Defense, in consultation with the Attorney General. Such procedures shall, so far as the Secretary considers practicable or consistent with military or intelligence activities, apply the principles of law and the rules of evidence in trial by general courts-martial. Such procedures and rules of evidence may not be contrary to or inconsistent with this chapter.

"(b) RULES FOR MILITARY COMMISSION.—

(1) Notwithstanding any departures from the law and the rules of evidence in trial by general courts-martial authorized by subsection (a), the procedures and rules of evidence in trials by military commission under this chapter shall include the following:

"(A) The accused shall be permitted to present evidence in his defense, to cross-examine the witnesses who testify against him, and to examine and respond to evidence admitted against him on the issue of guilt or innocence and for sentencing, as provided for by this chapter.

"(B) The accused shall be present at all sessions of the military commission (other than those for deliberations or voting), except when excluded under section 949d of this title.

"(C) The accused shall receive the assistance of counsel as provided for by section 948k.

"(D) The accused shall be permitted to represent himself, as provided for by paragraph (3).

"(2) In establishing procedures and rules of evidence for military commission proceedings, the Secretary of Defense may prescribe the following provisions:

"(A) Evidence shall be admissible if the military judge determines that the evidence would have probative value to a reasonable person.

"(B) Evidence shall not be excluded from trial by military commission on the grounds that the evidence was not seized pursuant to a search warrant or other authorization.

"(C) A statement of the accused that is otherwise admissible shall not be excluded from trial by military commission on grounds of alleged coercion or compulsory self-incrimination so long as the evidence complies with the provisions of section 948r of this title.

...

"(E)(i) Except as provided in clause (ii), hearsay evidence not otherwise admissible under the rules of evidence applicable in trial by general courts-martial may be admitted in a trial by military commission if the proponent of the evidence makes known to the adverse party, sufficiently in advance to provide the adverse party with a fair opportunity to meet the evidence, the intention of the proponent to offer the evidence, and the particulars of the evidence (including information on the general circumstances under which the evidence was obtained). The disclosure of evidence under the preceding sentence is subject to the requirements and limitations applicable to the disclosure of classified information in section 949j(c) of this title.

"(ii) Hearsay evidence not otherwise admissible under the rules of evidence applicable in trial by general courts-martial shall not be admitted in a trial by military commission if the party opposing the admission of the evidence demonstrates that the evidence is unreliable or lacking in probative value.

"(F) The military judge shall exclude any evidence the probative value of which is substantially outweighed—

"(i) by the danger of unfair prejudice, confusion of the issues, or misleading the commission; or

"(ii) by considerations of undue delay, waste of time, or needless presentation of cumulative evidence.

...

"§ 949c. Duties of trial counsel and defense counsel

"(a) TRIAL COUNSEL.—The trial counsel of a military commission under this chapter shall prosecute in the name of the United States.

"(b) DEFENSE COUNSEL.

(1) The accused shall be represented in his defense before a military commission under this chapter as provided in this subsection.

"(2) The accused shall be represented by military counsel detailed under section 948k of this title.

"(3) The accused may be represented by civilian counsel if retained by the accused, but only if such civilian counsel—

"(A) is a United States citizen;

"(B) is admitted to the practice of law in a State, district, or possession of the United States or before a Federal court;

"(C) has not been the subject of any sanction of disciplinary action by any court, bar, or other competent governmental authority for relevant misconduct;

"(D) has been determined to be eligible for access to classified information that is classified at the level Secret or higher; and

"(E) has signed a written agreement to comply with all applicable regulations or instructions for counsel, including any rules of court for conduct during the proceedings.

"(4) Civilian defense counsel shall protect any classified information received during the course of representation of the accused in accordance with all applicable law governing the protection of classified information and may not divulge such information to any person not authorized to receive it.

"(5) If the accused is represented by civilian counsel, detailed military counsel shall act as associate counsel.

"(6) The accused is not entitled to be represented by more than one military counsel. However, the person authorized under regulations prescribed under section 948k of this title to detail counsel, in that person's sole discretion, may detail additional military counsel to represent the accused.

"(7) Defense counsel may cross-examine each witness for the prosecution who testifies before a military commission under this chapter.

...

"(f) PROTECTION OF CLASSIFIED INFORMATION.—

"(1) NATIONAL SECURITY PRIVILEGE.—

(A) Classified information shall be protected and is privileged from disclosure if disclosure would be detrimental to the national security. The rule in the preceding sentence applies to all stages of the proceedings of military commissions under this chapter.

"(B) The privilege referred to in subparagraph (A) may be claimed by the head of the executive or military department or government agency concerned based on a finding by the head of that department or agency that—

"(i) the information is properly classified; and

"(ii) disclosure of the information would be detrimental to the national security.

"(C) A person who may claim the privilege referred to in subparagraph (A) may authorize a representative, witness, or trial counsel to claim the privilege and make the finding described in subparagraph (B) on behalf of such person. The authority of the representative, witness, or trial counsel to do so is presumed in the absence of evidence to the contrary.

"(2) INTRODUCTION OF CLASSIFIED INFORMATION.—

"(A) ALTERNATIVES TO DISCLOSURE.—To protect classified information from disclosure, the military judge, upon motion of trial counsel, shall authorize, to the extent practicable—

"(i) the deletion of specified items of classified information from documents to be introduced as evidence before the military commission;

"(ii) the substitution of a portion or summary of the information for such classified documents; or "(iii) the substitution of a statement of relevant facts that the classified information would tend to prove.

...

"(C) ASSERTION OF NATIONAL SECURITY PRIVILEGE AT TRIAL.—During the examination of any witness, trial counsel may object to any question, line of inquiry, or motion to admit evidence that would require the disclosure of classified information. Following such an objection, the military judge shall take suitable action to safeguard such classified information. Such action may include the review of trial counsel's claim of privilege by the military judge in camera and on an ex parte basis, and the delay of proceedings to permit trial counsel to consult with the department or agency concerned as to whether the national security privilege should be asserted.

...

"§ 949m. Number of votes required

"(a) CONVICTION.—No person may be convicted by a military commission under this chapter of any offense, except as provided in section 949i(b) of this title or by concurrence of two-thirds of the members present at the time the vote is taken.

"(b) SENTENCES.

(1) No person may be sentenced by a military commission to suffer death, except insofar as—

"(A) the penalty of death is expressly authorized under this chapter or the law of war for an offense of which the accused has been found guilty;

"(B) trial counsel expressly sought the penalty of death by filing an appropriate notice in advance of trial;

"(C) the accused is convicted of the offense by the concurrence of all the members present at the time the vote is taken; and

"(D) all the members present at the time the vote is taken concur in the sentence of death.

"(2) No person may be sentenced to life imprisonment, or to confinement for more than 10 years, by a military commission under this chapter except by the concurrence of three-fourths of the members present at the time the vote is taken.

"(3) All other sentences shall be determined by a military commission by the concurrence of two-thirds of the members present at the time the vote is taken.

"(c) NUMBER OF MEMBERS REQUIRED FOR PENALTY OF DEATH.—

(1) Except as provided in paragraph (2), in a case in which the penalty of death is sought, the number of members of the military commission under this chapter shall be not less than 12.

"(2) In any case described in paragraph (1) in which 12 members are not reasonably available because of physical conditions or military exigencies, the convening authority shall specify a lesser number of members for the military commission (but not fewer than 9 members), and the military commission may be assembled, and the trial held, with not fewer than the number of members so specified. In such a case, the convening authority shall make a detailed written statement, to be appended to the record, stating why a greater number of members were not reasonably available

...

"§ 950f. Review by Court of Military Commission Review

"(a) ESTABLISHMENT.—The Secretary of Defense shall establish a Court of Military Commission Review which shall be composed of one or more panels, and each such panel shall be composed of not less than three appellate military judges. For the purpose of reviewing military commission decisions under this chapter, the court may sit in panels or as a whole in accordance with rules prescribed by the Secretary.

...

"(d) SCOPE OF REVIEW.—In a case reviewed by the Court of Military Commission Review under this section, the Court may act only with respect to matters of law.

"§ 950g. Review by the United States Court of Appeals for the District of Columbia Circuit and the Supreme Court

"(a) EXCLUSIVE APPELLATE JURISDICTION.—(1)(A) Except as provided in subparagraph (B), the United States Court of Appeals for the District of Columbia Circuit shall have exclusive jurisdiction to determine the validity of a final judgment rendered by a military commission (as approved by the convening authority) under this chapter....

...

"§ 950p. Statement of substantive offenses

"(a) PURPOSE.—The provisions of this subchapter codify offenses that have traditionally been triable by military commissions. This chapter does not establish new crimes that did not exist before its enactment, but rather codifies those crimes for trial by military commission.

"(b) EFFECT.—Because the provisions of this subchapter (including provisions that incorporate definitions in other provisions of law) are declarative of existing law, they do not preclude trial for crimes that occurred before the date of the enactment of this chapter

...

"§ 950v. Crimes triable by military commissions

"(a) DEFINITIONS AND CONSTRUCTION.—In this section:

"(1) MILITARY OBJECTIVE.—The term 'military objective' means—

"(A) combatants; and

"(B) those objects during an armed conflict—

"(i) which, by their nature, location, purpose, or use, effectively contribute to the opposing force's warfighting or war-sustaining capability; and

"(ii) the total or partial destruction, capture, or neutralization of which would constitute a definite military advantage to the attacker under the circumstances at the time of the attack.

"(2) PROTECTED PERSON.—The term 'protected person' means any person entitled to protection under one or more of the Geneva Conventions, including—

"(A) civilians not taking an active part in hostilities;

"(B) military personnel placed hors de combat by sickness, wounds, or detention; and

"(C) military medical or religious personnel.

"(3) PROTECTED PROPERTY.—The term 'protected property' means property specifically protected by the law of war (such as buildings dedicated to religion, education, art, science or charitable purposes, historic monuments, hospitals, or places where the sick and wounded are collected), if

141

such property is not being used for military purposes or is not otherwise a military objective. Such term includes objects properly identified by one of the distinctive emblems of the Geneva Conventions, but does not include civilian property that is a military objective.

"(4) CONSTRUCTION.—The intent specified for an offense under paragraph (1), (2), (3), (4), or (12) of subsection (b) precludes the applicability of such offense with regard to—

"(A) collateral damage; or

"(B) death, damage, or injury incident to a lawful attack.

"(b) OFFENSES.—The following offenses shall be triable by military commission under this chapter at any time without limitation:

"(1) MURDER OF PROTECTED PERSONS.—Any person subject to this chapter who intentionally kills one or more protected persons shall be punished by death or such other punishment as a military commission under this chapter may direct.

"(2) ATTACKING CIVILIANS.—Any person subject to this chapter who intentionally engages in an attack upon a civilian population as such, or individual civilians not taking active part in hostilities, shall be punished, if death results to one or more of the victims, by death or such other punishment as a military commission under this chapter may direct, and, if death does not result to any of the victims, by such punishment, other than death, as a military commission under this chapter may direct.

"(3) ATTACKING CIVILIAN OBJECTS.—Any person subject to this chapter who intentionally engages in an attack upon a civilian object that is not a military objective shall be punished as a military commission under this chapter may direct.

"(4) ATTACKING PROTECTED PROPERTY.—Any person subject to this chapter who intentionally engages in an attack upon protected property shall be punished as a military commission under this chapter may direct.

"(5) PILLAGING.—Any person subject to this chapter who intentionally and in the absence of military necessity appropriates or seizes property for private or personal use, without the consent of a person with authority to permit such appropriation or seizure, shall be punished as a military commission under this chapter may direct.

"(6) DENYING QUARTER.—Any person subject to this chapter who, with effective command or control over subordinate groups, declares, orders, or otherwise indicates to those groups that there shall be no survivors or surrender accepted, with the intent to threaten an adversary or to conduct hostilities such that there would be no survivors or surrender accepted, shall be punished as a military commission under this chapter may direct.

"(7) TAKING HOSTAGES.—Any person subject to this chapter who, having knowingly seized or detained one or more persons, threatens to kill, injure, or continue to detain such person or persons with the intent of compelling any nation, person other than the hostage, or group of persons to act or refrain from acting as an explicit or implicit condition for the safety or release of such person or persons, shall be punished, if death results to one or more of the victims, by death or such other punishment as a military commission under this chapter may direct, and, if death does not result to any of the victims, by such punishment, other than death, as a military commission under this chapter may direct.

...

"(11) TORTURE.—

"(A) OFFENSE.—Any person subject to this chapter who commits an act specifically intended to inflict severe physical or mental pain or suffering (other than pain or suffering incidental to lawful sanctions) upon another person within his custody or physical control for the purpose of obtaining information or a confession, punishment, intimidation, coercion, or any reason based on discrimination of any kind, shall be punished, if death results to one or more of the victims, by death or such other punishment as a military commission under this chapter may direct, and, if death does not result to any of the victims, by such punishment, other than death, as a military commission under this chapter may direct.

"(B) SEVERE MENTAL PAIN OR SUFFERING DEFINED.— In this section, the term 'severe mental pain or suffering' has the meaning given that term in section 2340(2) of title 18.

"(12) CRUEL OR INHUMAN TREATMENT.—

"(A) OFFENSE.—Any person subject to this chapter who commits an act intended to inflict severe or serious physical or mental pain or suffering (other than pain or suffering incidental to lawful sanctions), including serious physical abuse, upon another within his custody or control shall be punished, if death results to the victim, by death or such other punishment as a military commission under this chapter may direct, and, if death does not result to the victim, by such punishment, other than death, as a military commission under this chapter may direct.

"(B) DEFINITIONS.—In this paragraph:

"(i) The term 'serious physical pain or suffering' means bodily injury that involves—

"(I) a substantial risk of death;

"(II) extreme physical pain;

"(III) a burn or physical disfigurement of a serious nature (other than cuts, abrasions, or bruises); or

"(IV) significant loss or impairment of the function of a bodily member, organ, or mental faculty.

"(ii) The term 'severe mental pain or suffering' has the meaning given that term in section 2340(2) of title 18.

"(iii) The term 'serious mental pain or suffering' has the meaning given the term 'severe mental pain or suffering' in section 2340(2) of title 18, except that—

"(I) the term 'serious' shall replace the term 'severe' where it appears; and

"(II) as to conduct occurring after the date of the enactment of the Military Commissions Act of 2006, the term 'serious and non-transitory mental harm (which need not be prolonged)' shall replace the term 'prolonged mental harm' where it appears.

"(13) INTENTIONALLY CAUSING SERIOUS BODILY INJURY.—

"(A) OFFENSE.—Any person subject to this chapter who intentionally causes serious bodily injury to one or more persons, including lawful combatants, in violation of the law of war shall be punished, if death results to one or more of the victims, by death or such other punishment as a military commission under this chapter may direct, and, if death does not result to any of the victims, by such punishment, other than death, as a military commission under this chapter may direct.

"(B) SERIOUS BODILY INJURY DEFINED.—In this paragraph, the term 'serious bodily injury' means bodily injury which involves—

"(i) a substantial risk of death;

"(ii) extreme physical pain;

"(iii) protracted and obvious disfigurement; or

"(iv) protracted loss or impairment of the function of a bodily member, organ, or mental faculty.

. . . .

"(21) RAPE.—Any person subject to this chapter who forcibly or with coercion or threat of force wrongfully invades the body of a person by penetrating, however slightly, the anal or genital opening of the victim with any part of the body of the accused, or with any foreign object, shall be punished as a military commission under this chapter may direct.

"(22) SEXUAL ASSAULT OR ABUSE.—Any person subject to this chapter who forcibly or with coercion or threat of force engages in sexual contact with one or more persons, or causes one or more persons to engage in sexual contact, shall be punished as a military commission under this chapter may direct.

"(23) HIJACKING OR HAZARDING A VESSEL OR AIRCRAFT.— Any person subject to this chapter who intentionally seizes, exercises unauthorized control over, or endangers the safe navigation of a vessel or aircraft that is not a legitimate military objective shall be punished, if death results to one or more of the victims, by death or such other punishment as a military commission under this chapter may direct, and, if death does not result to any of the victims, by such punishment, other than death, as a military commission under this chapter may direct.

"(24) TERRORISM.—Any person subject to this chapter who intentionally kills or inflicts great bodily harm on one or more protected persons, or intentionally engages in an act that evinces a wanton disregard for human life, in a manner calculated to influence or affect the conduct of government or civilian population by intimidation or coercion, or to retaliate against government conduct, shall be punished, if death results to one or more of the victims, by death or such other punishment as a military commission under this chapter may direct, and, if death does not result to any of the victims, by such punishment, other than death, as a military commission under this chapter may direct.

"(25) PROVIDING MATERIAL SUPPORT FOR TERRORISM.—

"(A) OFFENSE.—Any person subject to this chapter who provides material support or resources, knowing or intending that they are to be used in preparation for, or in carrying out, an act of terrorism (as set forth in paragraph (24)), or who intentionally provides material support or resources to an international terrorist organization engaged in hostilities against the United States, knowing that such organization has engaged or engages in terrorism (as so set forth), shall be punished as a military commission under this chapter may direct.

"(B) MATERIAL SUPPORT OR RESOURCES DEFINED.—In this paragraph, the term 'material support or resources' has the meaning given that term in section 2339A(b) of title 18.

"(26) WRONGFULLY AIDING THE ENEMY.—Any person subject to this chapter who, in breach of an allegiance or duty to the United States, knowingly and intentionally aids an enemy of the United States, or one of the co-belligerents of the enemy, shall be punished as a military commission under this chapter may direct.

"(27) SPYING.—Any person subject to this chapter who with intent or reason to believe that it is to be used to the injury of the United States or to the advantage of a foreign power, collects or attempts to collect information by clandestine means or while acting under false pretenses, for the purpose of conveying such information to an enemy of the United States, or one of the co-belligerents of the enemy, shall be punished by death or such other punishment as a military commission under this chapter may direct.

"(28) CONSPIRACY.—Any person subject to this chapter who conspires to commit one or more substantive offenses triable by military commission under this chapter, and who knowingly does any overt act to effect the object of the conspiracy, shall be punished, if death results to one or more of the victims, by death or such other punishment as a military commission under this chapter may direct, and, if death does not result to any of the victims, by such punishment, other than death, as a military commission under this chapter may direct.

Notes

1.   In June, 2008, the Supreme Court handed down its latest pronouncement addressing the government's actions in the war against terrorism. Boumediene v. Bush, —S.Ct.—, 2008 WL 2369628. The issue before the Court was whether the congressional withdrawal in the MCA of federal court jurisdiction to consider habeas corpus petitions from enemy combatant detainees was lawful and effective. Justice Kennedy delivered the opinion of the court joined by Justices, Stevens, Souter, Ginsburg and Breyer.   He summarized the Court's ruling as follows:

> Petitioners are aliens designated as enemy combatants and detained at the United States Naval Station at Guantanamo Bay, Cuba. There are others detained there, also aliens, who are not parties to this suit.

> Petitioners present a question not resolved by our earlier cases relating to the detention of aliens at Guantanamo: whether they have the constitutional privilege of habeas corpus, a privilege not to be withdrawn except in conformance with the Suspension Clause, Art. I, § 9, cl. 2. We hold these petitioners do have the habeas corpus privilege. Congress has enacted a statute, the Detainee Treatment Act of 2005 (DTA), 119 Stat. 2739, that provides certain procedures for review of the detainees' status. We hold that those procedures are not an adequate and effective substitute for habeas corpus. Therefore § 7 of the Military Commissions Act of 2006 (MCA), 28 U. S. C. A. § 2241(e) (Supp. 2007), operates as an unconstitutional suspension of the writ. We do not address whether the President has authority to detain these petitioners nor do we hold that the writ must issue. These and other questions regarding the legality of the detention are to be resolved in the first instance by the District Court

2.   The implications of the Boumediene decision for the military commission trials at Guantanamo remain to be seen.   The ruling makes available to all of the detainees at Guantanamo the possibility

of seeking habeas corpus relief in a federal court, which, at a minimum, could delay the military commission trials even more. The Court in Boumediene also ruled that the habeas corpus provision of the Constitution applies to the detainees at Guantanamo. What additional constitutional rights will be afforded to them in connection with the military commission process and what form or content they will take remains to be clarified through future legal developments.

3. As of the present writing, no criminal cases have proceeded to trial before the military commissions although preliminary proceedings in a number of cases have been held, and one case has been completed through a negotiated plea of guilty (David Hicks).

Page 609. Add following the previous material also before C.

Note on the Choice between Civilian and Military Prosecution

In May, 2008, a report was issued titled "In Pursuit of Justice" authored by two former assistant United States Attorneys, Richard Zabel and James Benjamin. The report was prepared under the auspices of Human Rights First. The report examined 123 terrorist cases over the past 15 years and concluded that the civilian courts were able to produce just and reliable results while protecting national security. The report notes that prosecutors have used both specially tailored anti-terrorism statutes as well as general criminal laws; that the use of a federal statute, the Classified Information Procedures Act, has permitted an appropriate balancing of defendants' right to a fair trial with the need to protect confidential national security information; and that, where appropriate and necessary, severe sentences have been imposed in terrorism cases.

Consider in connection with the foregoing the following material which is taken from Norman Abrams, Anti-terrorism and Criminal Enforcement (3rd Edition, Thomson-West, 2008) pp. 833-835:

> The bases, too, on which the government is making the decision whether to treat some individuals as normal criminal arrestees and some as enemy combatants have not been publicly articulated. Examination of what is publicly known about the persons who have been treated in one category or the other does not entirely help to explicate the criteria that are being applied. One possible speculation is that the government is more likely to

use the enemy combatant approach when it believes that the individual being detained has important information and wishes to be able to interrogate at length, without being restricted by the procedural protections that attach in normal civilian criminal process. A second factor might be that the enemy combatant category is more likely to be used when the government considers the person to be guilty and too dangerous to release but does not have enough evidence to convict.

Some of the cases that have been prosecuted have made the choices being made seem puzzling. For example, John Walker Lindh was picked up on the battlefield, and prosecution was initiated in a United States district court in the Eastern District of Virginia. It is hard to see how his case differed from that of Hamdi, and on the face of things, the case for treating him as an enemy combatant seemed, if anything, stronger than the Padilla case. A possible explanation of the decision to prosecute Walker Lindh in a civilian forum is that it was the first one in this series, and at the time the government may not have yet sorted through how it was going to handle such cases.

Other cases, too, present similar conundrums as well. Zacarias Moussaoui, is a French citizen who was apprehended in the United States and was prosecuted in a U.S. District Court although at times, there were statements made by government officials that seemed to indicate there was a possibility that his case would be transferred to military jurisdiction. Richard Reid, a British citizen, the so-called "shoe bomber," was apprehended on an airplane bound for the United States, and he, too, was criminally charged in a civilian court in Massachusetts where the plane was diverted.

Under the present state of the law, unless the courts rule in his favor in the current litigation, Al–Marri is subject to being detained indefinitely in military custody, and any prospect of his being tried, whether before a military commission or a U.S. district court, will be decided, at the discretion of the government, as to whether and where.

Our criminal enforcement system, of course, is rife with choices that prosecutors make regarding the forum in which to prosecute. A frequent choice-of-forum issue is between a state or a federal prosecution, and many different kinds of considerations can affect that choice, including the legal advantages of prosecuting in one or the other forum. ... At an early stage and prior to the promulgation of any regulations establishing the procedures to be used before the military commissions, they appeared to have enormous legal and practical advantages for the government (and corresponding disadvantages for a defendant) in comparison with prosecution in a federal court. The gap between the two kinds of procedures has been narrowed at each successive stage of regulatory or legislative change. What comparative advantages and disadvantages remain between military and civilian prosecution under the procedures provided for in the MCA …?

…

1. Numerous pragmatic justifications have been offered by the government as to why military commissions are needed. Of course, ultimately, the use of a military commission is premised on the fact that we are at war and that cases against enemy combatants can be adjudicated under the laws of war before military commissions.

2. How many of the following justifications are likely to be applicable to some cases and not to others? How many of them, if applicable in a particular case, might be grounds for using a military commission instead of a federal district court?

   a. Military handling of a matter permits more effective interrogation of the defendant and a lengthier period in which to gather evidence;

   b. It is easier to maintain the confidentiality of classified information in a military commission (in this connection, compare the protection afforded to classified information in a civilian court under the Classified Information Procedures Act);

   c. Military trials can be conducted more quickly—it is possible to avoid prolonged delays and lengthy proceedings.

   d. It does not make sense to bring hundreds of persons captured in military encounters abroad to the United States to be tried in U.S. civil courts for being accessories to terrorism; there is even less justification for bringing such persons to the U.S. for trial when they are almost all foreign nationals.

   e. It is easier to close a military commission proceeding to the press and public than to close a civilian trial. Non-public proceedings may be desirable and even necessary in some of these cases.

   f. It is easier to keep the participants safe from retaliatory terrorist activity in a military setting.

g. Military commissions avoid the use of juries. Juries in these cases make for inefficiency, change the style of presentation of the evidence, and open up the possibility of the common man's passions and prejudices affecting the proceeding.

3. Can you think of other pragmatic factors that might be taken into account in deciding whether to prosecute in a military commission a person who is subject to the terms of the MCA?

CHAPTER 13

AN OVERVIEW OF RICO, CCE, AND THE OTHER FEDERAL STATUTES DEALING WITH ORGANIZATIONAL CRIME

Page 622. Add as a footnote to 21 U.S.C. § 848 cited in the first paragraph (Also see pp. 389-391 and 957-966 in the main volume).

Subsections (g)-(r)of 21 U.S.C. § 848, dealing with procedures for imposition of the death penalty were repealed in 2006 by Pub. L. 109-177, Title II, § 221 (2) (3) and (4) and 22(c), 120 Stat. 231.

CHAPTER 14

THE CRIMINAL CIVIL RIGHTS STATUTES

Page 652. Add to note 3c. before 3.

In United States v. Picklo, 190 Fed.Appx. 887 (11th Cir. 2006), the defendant was, in addition to other offenses, convicted of a violation of 18 U.S.C. § 242 in connection with a robbery he had perpetrated. The court stated:

> Picklo, a former investigator with the Florida Department of Insurance, asserts there was not sufficient evidence for the jury to find he acted under color of law in violation of 18 U.S.C. § 242 when he robbed and shot the victim because robbery was outside the scope of his duties as an investigator, he never identified himself as a law enforcement officer, and he was motivated purely by financial gain. To prove a defendant violated 18 U.S.C. § 242 by acting "under color of law" to deprive another of "any rights, privileges, or immunities secured or protected by the Constitution or laws of the United States," the government must establish beyond a reasonable doubt that (1) the defendant's conduct deprived the victim of rights secured or protected by the Constitution or federal law; (2) the defendant acted willfully; and (3) the defendant acted under color of law. ...

> ...

> "Misuse of power, possessed by virtue of state law and made possible only because the wrongdoer is clothed with the authority of state law, is action taken under color of state law." *Williams v. United States*, 341 U.S. 97, 71 S.Ct. 576, 578, 95 L.Ed. 774 (1951) (holding a private detective who took an oath as a special police officer was acting under color of law when he "flash[ed] his badge" while assaulting his victims). Further, it is not significant to the color of law analysis that the defendant's misuse of power "was motivated solely for personal reasons of pecuniary gain." *Brown v. Miller*, 631 F.2d 408, 411 (5th

Cir.1980) (color of law analysis under 42 U.S.C. § 1983). "[T]he lack of outward indicia suggestive of state authority-such as being on duty, wearing a uniform, or driving a patrol car-are not alone determinative of whether a police officer is acting under color of state law." *Revene v. Charles County Comm'rs,* 882 F.2d 870, 872 (4th Cir.1989).

Here, the evidence supported Picklo's conviction for deprivation of civil rights under 18 U.S.C. § 242. Frausto testified Picklo held up a "police badge" and said he was "with the North Florida Investigators," or "something like that." In addition, Frausto testified Picklo said, "By the way, Johnny is working with us," indicating there was an undercover operation. Moreover, Frausto believed Picklo was a law enforcement officer of some type, and he feared he would be arrested due to the check-cashing scheme. Frausto believed he had to follow Picklo's instructions because Picklo was a law enforcement officer. Frausto followed Picklo off the interstate into a nearby neighborhood, and Picklo got into the passenger's seat of Frausto's vehicle. Picklo used his official status to gain entry into Frausto's vehicle. Therefore, the evidence establishes Picklo acted under color of law because he identified himself as a state investigator, flashed a badge, and used his official status to get Frausto to follow his instructions.

...

Here, Picklo gained access to Frausto's vehicle using his status as a law enforcement officer, ... Picklo did not break into Frausto's vehicle. Frausto followed Picklo's instructions because Picklo told him that he was an investigator and flashed a badge. If Picklo had not indicated he was a law enforcement officer or investigator of some type, Frausto would have had no reason to follow him. Accordingly, we conclude there was sufficient evidence for a jury to find Picklo was acting under color of law and affirm Picklo's conviction under 18 U.S.C. § 242.

UNITED STATES V. GIORDANO
442 F.3d 30 (2d Cir.2006)

[The defendant was the sitting mayor of Waterbury, Connecticut at the time of the acts on which the prosecution was based. The victims were the 9 year old daughter and 11 year old niece of a prostitute who frequently came to his office.]

...

Giordano also challenges his conviction of two counts of violating 18 U.S.C. § 242. That statute "mak[es] it criminal to act (1) 'willfully' and (2) under color of law (3) to deprive a person of rights protected by the Constitution or laws of the United States." *United States v. Lanier,* 520 U.S. 259, 264, 117 S.Ct. 1219, 137 L.Ed.2d 432 (1997). The first count of the indictment charged that between November 2000 and July 2001, Giordano, "while acting under color of the laws of the State of Connecticut," deprived V1 of her Fourteenth Amendment right "to be free from aggravated sexual abuse and sexual abuse ... . Count two of the indictment contained the same charges as to V2.

Giordano argues that the evidence was insufficient as to the "under color of law" element of these counts. We disagree because the meaning of the statutory term "under color of ... law" is more expansive than Giordano maintains, and the evidence adduced at trial, viewed as it must be in the light most favorable to the government, was more than sufficient to allow a rational trier of fact to find the element satisfied beyond a reasonable doubt.

...."The fact that someone holds an office or otherwise exercises power under state law does not mean, of course, that any wrong that person commits is "under color of law." "It is clear that under 'color' of law means under 'pretense' of law. Thus acts of officers in the ambit of their personal pursuits are plainly excluded." *Screws v. United States,* 325 U.S. 91, 111, 65 S.Ct. 1031, 89 L.Ed. 1495 (1945). As we have observed, however, "there is no bright line test for distinguishing personal pursuits from actions taken under color of law." *Pitchell v. Callan,* 13 F.3d 545, 548 (2d Cir.1994)

Giordano argues that he cannot have acted under color of law because his actions, although they took place during his mayoralty, "were clearly a part of and derived from [a] personal relationship [he] had with [Jones][the prostitute]" that was unrelated to and predated his mayoralty. The color of law element may be satisfied by the fact that an official gains access to the victim in the course of official duty. ... But this is by no means a necessary condition: it is well-established that an official may act under color of law even when he or she encounters the victim outside the conduct of official business and acts for reasons unconnected to his or her office, so long as he or she employs the authority of the state in the commission of the crime. ... Thus we have found that officials acted under color of law even when, like Giordano, they came into contact with their victims in the course of their private affairs. ...

Nor do the facts that Giordano's crime had, as he asserts, "nothing whatever to do with [his] actual or pretended mayoral duties" or that he acted for "his own personal... gratification" end the "color of law" inquiry. The terms of 18 U.S.C. § 242 provide for enhanced penalties for a variety of acts, including aggravated sexual assault, none of which would be undertaken for official reasons, and some of which involve purely personal, albeit perverse, gratification. The language of the statute thus makes clear that the such acts cannot, by their nature alone, defeat an assertion that they were performed under "color of law."

Moreover, we have found that officials acted under color of law when their misuse of official power made the commission of a constitutional wrong possible, even though the official committed abusive acts for personal reasons far removed from the scope of official duties. In *Monsky v. Moraghan,* 127 F.3d 243 (2d Cir.1997), we concluded that a § 1983 complaint could not be dismissed for failure to plead action under color of law when it alleged that a state judge allowed his dog to approach and "aggressively nuzzle" a litigant who was researching records in the court clerk's office. *Id.* at 244. Although we noted that "[t]he complaint does not allege the typical actions of a state judicial officer that would plainly fall within the ambit of actions taken under color of law [such as] ... presiding at trial or rendering judgments," we concluded that the complaint adequately alleged action under color of law because it charged that the judge "was known to, and deferred to by, personnel of the office" and "was allowed to enter the office with his dog and remain there ... because he was a judge.". ...

Of particular relevance to the case before us, this Court found that a state official acted under color of state law even when acting outside the ambit of official duty because the official used his or her power to make the crime possible by causing the victim to submit. ...

In the same vein, the Eleventh Circuit held in *Griffin v. City of Opa-Locka,* 261 F.3d 1295 (11th Cir.2001), that the rape of a city employee by the city manager after hours in the employee's home was perpetrated "under color of law" because, *inter alia,* the manager "invoked his authority ... to create the opportunity to be alone with [the victim]" by coercing her into consenting to accept a ride home, "reminded her of his authority" immediately prior to the rape by saying " 'I can't believe you are telling me no after everything that I have done for you,' " and then "continued to invoke his authority over [her] to harass her and humiliate her even after the sexual assault" by summoning her to his office and referring obliquely to the rape in the presence of co-workers.

Considering the totality of the circumstances and drawing all inferences in the light most favorable to the government, the evidence was easily sufficient to show that Giordano, ..., threatened his victims by invoking a "special authority" to undertake retaliatory action, and that... he used his authority to cause the victims to submit to repeated abuse, in this case by causing the victims to fear that he would use his power to harm them if they reported the abuse. Both V1 and V2 testified that they did not like Giordano's repeated abuse, but that they were made to understand that he could jail or otherwise harm them and their families if they reported it. Jones, for her part, testified that on each occasion after Giordano was done abusing the girls and before they left he told her "to make sure the kids don't tell anyone [or] I'll get in trouble, I'll go to jail.... So I made sure they never said anything to anybody." [20]Jones also testified that Giordano told the girls the

---

[20] The dissent argues that any customers of a prostitute could make the same threat with equal credibility, and that Giordano's threats were the equivalent of any client's "demand[ ]" of confidentiality when engaging in an illegal act.. Similarly, the dissent asserts that such "threats" were more akin to warnings, that any friend would give to someone engaged in so many forms of illegal behavior. We respectfully disagree. The jury could very easily have concluded that the statements by Giordano that Jones would go to jail was more than a warning and that Giordano's threat carried far more weight than would a threat from a civilian customer. An ordinary citizen paying a prostitute for sex with children would be foolish in the extreme to arrange for the prostitute's prosecution, since his own conduct is a felony; any threat to do so would necessarily ring hollow. A mayor with manifest authority over the city's police has vastly more credibility in threatening prosecution. Nor did the fact that Jones acted at least in part from financial motives in making the girls available for abuse prevent the jury from rationally finding that Giordano acted under color of law in carrying out the repeated abuse. Jones

same thing directly: "They will get in trouble, and [she would] go to jail." She testified that she ensured they told no-one "because I was scared. I didn't want to go to jail." She further testified that Giordano repeatedly mentioned his presence at crime scenes, and understood from that and his request that she call him at home so he could tell his wife that he was needed on police business, that "he had a lot to do with the police .... He had control of what the police does ...." This evidence was sufficient to satisfy the government's burden of showing that Giordano invoked "the real or apparent power" of his office to make the continuing sexual abuse possible..

[I]t was ... entirely reasonable for the jury to infer that the aura of power that Giordano invoked as mayor then allowed him to convey to the two young victims that they would get in trouble, and that Jones would go to jail, if they told anyone of the abuse. The jury could reasonably have inferred as well that Giordano's apparent power, thereafter deprived the child victims of any opportunity to report what had happened or otherwise to resist their continuing victimization.

...

Giordano also challenges the sufficiency of the evidence as to the third element of a § 242 offense, arguing that V1 and V2 had no federally protected right to be free from aggravated sexual abuse

---

testified candidly and at some length about her crack habit and the fact that she prostituted the girls and her older niece because she needed the money for drugs. She also testified, however, that it was Giordano who first demanded that Jones bring children to perform oral sex, at a time when he was already the mayor, that she initially demurred, and that she "did anything [Giordano] asked her to" because she "figured [she]' d go to jail" if she refused. At some point after the abuse began in November of 2000, she wanted to stop bringing the girls because she "didn't like having to sit there and watching them do that. They didn't want to do it anymore." On occasion she failed to keep an appointment to bring the girls to see Giordano because she "didn't want to bring them up there" and because the girls did not want to go. Jones also testified that she told them not to tell anyone because she "was told to tell them that."

when such abuse did not satisfy the jurisdictional requirements of federal statutory sexual abuse crimes. This argument is baseless. Section 242 punishes those who, under color of law, subject a person to the "deprivation of any rights ... secured or protected by the Constitution," including rights secured by the Fourteenth Amendment, *Lanier,* 520 U.S. at 272 n. 7, 117 S.Ct. 1219. "It is incontrovertible that bodily integrity is necessarily violated when a state actor sexually abuses a schoolchild and that such misconduct deprives the child of rights vouchsafed by the Fourteenth Amendment." ...

We hold, in sum, that Giordano's crime was committed "under color of state law" within the meaning of § 242 because Giordano used the victim's fear of the power he wielded as mayor to keep them from reporting the ongoing abuse, and that the victims had a right under the Fourteenth Amendment to be free from sexual abuse by a state actor. We therefore reject Giordano's challenge to the sufficiency of the evidence as to the § 242 counts and affirm the district court's denial of his motions for acquittal.

Page 685. Add to note 3.

A recent application of 18 U.S.C. § 245 (B)(2)(C) involved alleged telephoned and emailed threats to an Arab American group and its individual members, United States v. Syring, 522 F.Supp.2d 125 (D.D.C. 2007). An example of one of the telephoned messages recorded on voice mail was the following: "This is Patrick Syring. I just read James Zogby's statements online on the MSNBC website, and I condemn him for his anti-Semitism and anti-American statements. The only good Lebanese is a dead Lebanese. The only good Arab is a dead Arab. Long live the IDF. Death to Lebanon and death to the Arabs." The court's opinion stated:

> On October 12, 2007 Defendant, Patrick Syring, filed a Motion to Dismiss the two-count Indictment in this case based upon the First, Fifth and Fourteenth Amendments to the Constitution of the United States, as well as Federal Rule of Criminal Procedure 12(b)(2). Defendant argues that the Indictment violates his rights under the First Amendment to the Constitution of the United States by attempting to criminalize protected speech, and also violates his due process rights under the Fifth and Fourteenth Amendments. For the same reasons, Defendant argues that the statutes under which he has been charged, 18 U.S.C. §§ 245(b)(2)(C) and 875(c), are unconstitutional as applied to his conduct.

...

161

Defendant Syring was indicted on August 15, 2007 on two charges, both related to alleged threats. The Indictment alleges that between July 17 and July 29, 2006, Defendant Syring sent three voice mail messages and four e-mail messages to employees of the Arab American Institute ("AAI"), a non-profit organization that represents the interests of Arab Americans in the United States. At all times relevant to the Indictment, AAI was located in Washington, D.C. and Defendant Syring lived in Arlington, Virginia

The Indictment contains two counts. Count One alleges that Defendant transmitted "e-mail and telephone communication to the offices of the [AAI] ... and, by threat of force ... attempt[ed] to and did willfully intimidate and interfere with [AAI] employees because of their race and national origin, that is because they were Arab and Lebanese Americans, and because they were and had been enjoying employment, and the perquisites thereof, by a private employer, [AAI]," in violation of 18 U.S.C. § 245(b)(2)(C). Count Two alleges that Defendant "willfully and knowingly did transmit in interstate commerce ... telephone and e-mail communication to [AAI] employees, in which [he] threatened to injure [AAI] employees," in violation of 18 U.S.C. § 875(c).

Significantly, Defendant has not moved to dismiss the Indictment based on an alleged defect. Instead, Defendant asserts that his communications constitute speech on social and political issues that is protected by the First Amendment, rather than "true threats" that may give rise to criminal charges. Defendant argues that whether his communications constitute "true threats" is a question of law, which must be decided by the Court, and is properly decided on a pretrial motion to dismiss. The Court notes that the D.C. Circuit has upheld district court pretrial dismissals of counts in indictments based on questions of law.

...

... [T]the First Amendment's protections are not absolute, and the Supreme Court has "long recognized that the government may regulate certain categories of expression consistent with the Constitution." The First Amendment permits "restrictions upon the content of speech in a few limited areas, which are 'of such slight social value as a step to truth that any benefit that may be derived from them is clearly outweighed by the social interest in order and morality.' The parties agree that the only such exception relevant to the instant case is that the First Amendment permits the imposition of criminal sanctions on the expression of "true threats."

The Indictment charges Defendant with violating two criminal laws by sending the communications described above. In particular, Count One charges Defendant with a violation of 18 U.S.C. § 245(b)(2)(C), which provides:

Whoever ... by force or threat of force willfully injures, intimidate or interferes with, or attempts to injure, intimidate or interfere with ... any person because of his race, color, religion or national origin and because he is or has been ... applying for or enjoying employment, or any perquisite thereof, by any private employer ... shall be fined under this title, or imprisoned for not more than one year, or both.

Count Two is brought pursuant to 18 U.S.C. § 875(c), which provides "Whoever transmits in interstate or foreign commerce any communication containing ... any threat to injure the person of another, shall be fined under this title or imprisoned not more than five years, or both." The Indictment thus charges Defendant with criminal action based on his speech.

The Supreme Court has cautioned that where a statute "makes criminal a form of pure speech, [it] must be interpreted with the commands of the First Amendment clearly in mind. What is a threat must be distinguished from what is constitutionally protected speech." As a result, courts have concluded that Section 875(c), as well as statutes worded similarly to Section 245(b)(2)(C), may only be constitutionally applied to speech insofar as it constitutes a true threat.

...[T]he Supreme Court defined true threats as "those statements where the speaker means to communicate a serious expression of an intent to commit an act of unlawful violence to a particular individual or group of individuals. The Supreme Court further emphasized that the "speaker need not actually intend to carry out the threat," because "the prohibition on true threats protects individuals from the fear of violence and from the disruption that fear engenders, in addition to protecting people from the possibility that the threatened violence will occur."

163

Courts determining whether communications constitute true threats have generally applied an objective standard.. Thus, courts in all jurisdictions consider whether a reasonable person would consider the statement a serious expression of an intent to inflict harm, although the circuits disagree on whether the proper perspective is that of a "reasonable listener" or a "reasonable speaker." ...

Moreover, in considering whether a communication is a true threat all circuits "consider context, including the effect of an allegedly threatening statement on the listener." This focus on context derives from *Watts,* wherein the Supreme Court explicitly considered the context of the defendant's speech in determining that his remarks constituted protected political hyperbole, rather than a true threat. *Watts,* 394 U.S. at 708, 89 S.Ct. 1399. Watts, an 18 year-old war protester, was convicted under 18 U.S.C. § 871, a statute that prohibits "knowingly and willfully ... [making] any threat to take the life of or to inflict bodily harm upon the President." Watts participated in a public rally at the Washington Monument, at which he told a discussion group of other young people "I have already received my draft classification as 1-A and I have got to report for my physical this Monday coming. I am not going. If they ever make me carry a rifle the first man I want to get in my sights is L.B.J." During Watts' trial, his counsel stressed that Watts' statement was conditional upon an event that he said would never occur and that both he and the crowd laughed after the statement was made. In ordering judgment entered for Watts, the Supreme Court concluded that "[t]aken in context, and regarding the expressly conditional nature of the statement and the reaction of the listeners, we do not see how it could be interpreted [as a true threat rather than political hyperbole]."

As a result, courts have determined that alleged threats must be analyzed "in light of [their] entire factual context," and have specified factors to be considered, including: the reaction of the recipient of the threat and of other listeners; whether the threat was conditional; whether the threat was communicated directly to its victim; whether the maker of the threat had made similar statements to the victim in the past; and whether the victim had reason to believe the maker of the threat had a propensity to engage in violence.

…

The parties disagree on whether the Court can determine pretrial if Defendant's communications constitute true threats. As noted above, Defendant (and *Amicus Curiae*) maintain that the question is one of law. In contrast, the Government asserts that "the determination of whether the conduct and communication at issue amounts to a true threat is a heavily fact-dependent, context driven one that is reserved for the jury as the finder of facts.". …

Courts in other jurisdictions have more directly addressed the question, and have concluded that "whether words used are a true threat is generally best left to the triers of fact. Surrounding factual circumstances may not easily be required to be recounted in all indictments. The initial burden is on the government to prove a 'true' threat. Only where the factual proof is insufficient as a matter of law should the indictment be dismissed.' " Thus, the Court should "dismiss the indictment only if the language [is] so facially insufficient that no reasonable jury could find that the language amounted to a true threat."

…

Defendant argues that the communications he sent to the AAI and its employees are not true threats, but are rather "deeply-held political views and [ ] opposition to the publicly expressed views of [AAI's President, Dr. James Zogby] and the AAIDefendant stresses that the communications "all concern events then unfolding between Israel and Hezbollah or, in the final instance, a shooting by a Muslim-American man at the Jewish Federation building in Seattle.". According to Defendant, his comments are "at worst, insulting political hyperbole," and therefore not true threats.

…

…Defendant's communications were made privately, via e-mails and voice mails directed to the AAI that specifically identified Dr. Zogby, as well as via more pointed communications addressed to individual employees at the AAI, one of which identified the recipient by her first name.

This distinction is one that courts have considered significant, noting that:

In targeting the recipient personally, the speaker leaves no doubt that he is sending the recipient a message of some sort. In contrast, political statements made at rallies or through the media are far more diffuse in their focus because they are generally intended, at least in part, to shore up political support for the speaker's position.

… [A]lthough Defendant argues that his communications were strictly political in nature, the same courts have concluded that "a threatening communication melded with some form of political expression … does not constitute protected speech simply because there is a political idea attached." … As such, the Court rejects Defendant's argument that his communications are inherently protected speech because they were prompted by comments made by Dr. Zogby that Defendant perceived as "anti-American, anti-Semitic, and pro-Hezbollah."

Defendant further argues that his communications are not true threats because, properly understood, his statement that "the only good Arab [or Lebanese] is a dead Arab [or Lebanese]" is a common phrase that is "dehumanizing but not a threat." Defendant bases this argument on statements purportedly made to the FBI by one of the AAI employees who received Defendant's communications. *Id.* Defendant likewise argues that his statement "Death to Lebanon[/Arabs]" is not a true threat because it is "simply a modified 'echo' of Hezbollah's mantra, 'Death to America,' " citing a speech by President Bush as support. Defendant thus invites the Court to determine the true meaning of his statements by moving beyond the face of the Indictment, and delving into the sufficiency of the evidence. The Court declines to do so on this Motion to Dismiss the Indictment. The Court notes that the D.C. Circuit has suggested that a district court may dismiss an indictment pretrial "on sufficiency-of-the-evidence grounds where the material facts are undisputed and only an issue of law is presented." It is obvious that material facts regarding the context of Defendant's communications are highly disputed. As such, the Court has focused its consideration on the allegations contained in the Indictment.

Nevertheless, Defendant is correct that the context of his communications may prove critical to properly understanding them. Indeed, the Government's opposition to Defendant's

Motion to Dismiss turns on just that assertion. The Government argues that, in addition to recounting the words of Defendant's communications, the allegations of the Indictment also demonstrate a number of factors that provide context necessary to understand the import of Defendant's words. In particular, the Government notes that Defendant's communications were repetitive and frequent within a period of days, and did not include conditional language. Again, many of the communications were directed specifically to the recipients, including one voice mail that addressed the recipient by her first name. Some of the communications alerted the recipients that Defendant was in Arlington, Virginia, i.e., in close physical proximity to the AAI offices in Washington. Finally, Defendant's last email made particular reference to a violent shooting, for which Defendant stated he held AAI responsible. In addition, that e-mail included the statement "The United States would be safer without you."

Defendant acknowledges these statements and the context provided in the Indictment, but nevertheless maintains that his statements cannot constitute a true threat because "[n]o one is targeted. There is no statement that Mr. Syring is going to do anything to anybody. There is no suggestion of anything imminent happening," Significantly, however, in *United States v. Khorrami,* 895 F.2d 1186 (7th Cir.1990) and *United States v. Gilbert,* 884 F.2d 454 (9th Cir.1989), *overruled on other grounds,* the courts upheld convictions under analogous threat statutes, notwithstanding the fact that, in each case, the defendants' mailings did not directly spell out the harm aimed at the recipient.

In *Khorrami,* the defendant sent communications to the headquarters of the Jewish National Fund ("JNF"), including (1) a "Wanted" poster with pictures of Israeli officials and JNF officers that stated "Must be Killed" and "Long live Palestine;" and (2) an altered copy of the JNF Mission's Calendar that included swastikas and typewritten statements with anti-Semitic content including "Death" to the "occupiers of beloved Palestine," ... *See* 894 F.2d at 1189. In upholding Khorrami's conviction, the Seventh Circuit rejected an argument that the poster was merely "political hyperbole," finding a reasonable jury could conclude that the poster constituted a true threat when viewed in context. Similarly, in *Gilbert,* the defendant mailed a letter and several posters to the founder of an adoption agency that placed minority children with white families. The letter " 'condemned' the [recipient's] actions and warned her to 'keep her human trash off of his property.' " The posters contained various messages threatening violence against minorities and those who associate with minorities. The Ninth Circuit likewise upheld Gilbert's conviction, finding that the mailings could be viewed as a threat in context. Specifically, the court stated that the recipient:

> received a letter from a man who was obviously an extremist and espoused the ideas of a traditionally violent group. The letter condemned [the recipient's] actions. The letter was accompanied by posters calling for a revolution-a term fraught with violence-and advocating lynch mobs, the shooting of black miscegenists, and the hanging of whites. While the mailings may not have said 'we're going to hurt you, Susan Smith,' they certainly said 'we don't like what you're doing, and we hurt people who do things we don't like.' The fact that a threat is subtle does not make it less of a threat.

Both *Khorrami* and *Gilbert* demonstrate the significance of context in determining whether speech constitutes a true threat. Defendant posits one interpretation of his communications, while the Government posits the diametric opposite. While both acknowledge that context is key to determining the true import of Defendant's words, much of the context to which they point does not appear on the face of the Indictment. The Court agrees with Defendant that on its face the Indictment does not present a compelling case. Nevertheless, even based on the meager context alleged in the Indictment, it possible that a reasonable jury could interpret Defendant's communications as "a serious expression of an intent to commit an act of unlawful violence to a particular individual or group of individuals." The Court therefore concludes that whether Defendant's communications constituted a true threat is an issue properly left to the jury as the trier of facts. As such, the Court shall deny Defendant's Motion to Dismiss the Indictment.

Page 692. Add to Note

The latest congressional consideration of hate crimes legislation occurred in 2007. A bill, H.R. 1592, which in many respects is similar to the bill reproduced in the main volume at p. 687, was passed by the House of Representatives in May, 2007. In the Senate, it was attached to a major defense bill that provided funding for the Iraq war. In conference in December, 2007, the hate crimes bill was stripped out of the defense bill and died in the Senate. H.R. 1592 is reproduced below. You may wish to examine what the differences are, if any, between H.R. 1592 and the proposed legislation reproduced in the main volume.

110th CONGRESS

1st Session

H. R. 1592

IN THE SENATE OF THE UNITED STATES

May 7, 2007

Received; read twice and referred to the Committee on the Judiciary

AN ACT

To provide Federal assistance to States, local jurisdictions, and Indian tribes to prosecute hate crimes, and for other purposes.

Be it enacted by the Senate and House of Representatives of the United States of America in Congress assembled,

SECTION 1. SHORT TITLE.

This Act may be cited as the 'Local Law Enforcement Hate Crimes Prevention Act of 2007'.

SEC. 2. DEFINITION OF HATE CRIME.

In this Act--

(1) the term 'crime of violence' has the meaning given that term in section 16, title 18, United States Code;

(2) the term 'hate crime' has the meaning given such term in section 280003(a) of the Violent Crime Control and Law Enforcement Act of 1994 (28 U.S.C. 994 note); and

(3) the term 'local' means a county, city, town, township, parish, village, or other general purpose political subdivision of a State.

SEC. 3. SUPPORT FOR CRIMINAL INVESTIGATIONS AND PROSECUTIONS BY STATE, LOCAL, AND TRIBAL LAW ENFORCEMENT OFFICIALS.

(a) Assistance Other Than Financial Assistance-

(1) IN GENERAL- At the request of State, local, or Tribal law enforcement agency, the Attorney General may provide technical, forensic, prosecutorial, or any other form of assistance in the criminal investigation or prosecution of any crime that--

(A) constitutes a crime of violence;

(B) constitutes a felony under the State, local, or Tribal laws; and

(C) is motivated by prejudice based on the actual or perceived race, color, religion, national origin, gender, sexual orientation, gender identity, or disability of the victim, or is a violation of the State, local, or Tribal hate crime laws.

(2) PRIORITY- In providing assistance under paragraph (1), the Attorney General shall give priority to crimes committed by offenders who have committed crimes in more than one State and to rural jurisdictions that have difficulty covering the extraordinary expenses relating to the investigation or prosecution of the crime.

(b) Grants-

(1) IN GENERAL- The Attorney General may award grants to State, local, and Indian law enforcement agencies for extraordinary expenses associated with the investigation and prosecution of hate crimes.

(2) OFFICE OF JUSTICE PROGRAMS- In implementing the grant program under this subsection, the Office of Justice Programs shall work closely with grantees to ensure that the concerns and needs of all affected parties, including community groups and schools, colleges, and universities, are addressed through the local infrastructure developed under the grants.

(3) APPLICATION-

(A) IN GENERAL- Each State, local, and Indian law enforcement agency that desires a grant under this subsection shall submit an application to the Attorney General at such time, in such manner, and accompanied by or containing such information as the Attorney General shall reasonably require.

(B) DATE FOR SUBMISSION- Applications submitted pursuant to subparagraph (A) shall be submitted during the 60-day period beginning on a date that the Attorney General shall prescribe.

(C) REQUIREMENTS- A State, local, and Indian law enforcement agency applying for a grant under this subsection shall--

(i) describe the extraordinary purposes for which the grant is needed;

(ii) certify that the State, local government, or Indian tribe lacks the resources necessary to investigate or prosecute the hate crime;

(iii) demonstrate that, in developing a plan to implement the grant, the State, local, and Indian law enforcement agency has consulted and coordinated with nonprofit, nongovernmental violence recovery service programs that have experience in providing services to victims of hate crimes; and

(iv) certify that any Federal funds received under this subsection will be used to supplement, not supplant, non-Federal funds that would otherwise be available for activities funded under this subsection.

(4) DEADLINE- An application for a grant under this subsection shall be approved or denied by the Attorney General not later than 30 business days after the date on which the Attorney General receives the application.

(5) GRANT AMOUNT- A grant under this subsection shall not exceed $100,000 for any single jurisdiction in any 1-year period.

(6) REPORT- Not later than December 31, 2008, the Attorney General shall submit to Congress a report describing the applications submitted for grants under this subsection, the award of such grants, and the purposes for which the grant amounts were expended.

(7) AUTHORIZATION OF APPROPRIATIONS- There is authorized to be appropriated to carry out this subsection $5,000,000 for each of fiscal years 2008 and 2009.

SEC. 4. GRANT PROGRAM.

(a) Authority To Award Grants- The Office of Justice Programs of the Department of Justice may award grants, in accordance with such regulations as the Attorney General may prescribe, to State, local, or Tribal programs designed to combat hate crimes committed by juveniles, including programs to train local law enforcement officers in identifying, investigating, prosecuting, and preventing hate crimes.

(b) Authorization of Appropriations- There are authorized to be appropriated such sums as may be necessary to carry out this section.

SEC. 5. AUTHORIZATION FOR ADDITIONAL PERSONNEL TO ASSIST STATE, LOCAL, AND TRIBAL LAW ENFORCEMENT.

There are authorized to be appropriated to the Department of Justice, including the Community Relations Service, for fiscal years 2008, 2009, and 2010 such sums as are necessary to increase the number of personnel to prevent and respond to alleged violations of section 249 of title 18, United States Code, as added by section 7 of this Act.

SEC. 6. PROHIBITION OF CERTAIN HATE CRIME ACTS.

(a) In General- Chapter 13 of title 18, United States Code, is amended by adding at the end the following:

'Sec. 249. Hate crime acts

'(a) In General-

'(1) OFFENSES INVOLVING ACTUAL OR PERCEIVED RACE, COLOR, RELIGION, OR NATIONAL ORIGIN- Whoever, whether or not acting under color of law, willfully causes bodily injury to any person or, through the use of fire, a firearm, or an explosive or incendiary device, attempts to cause bodily injury to any person, because of the actual or perceived race, color, religion, or national origin of any person--

'(A) shall be imprisoned not more than 10 years, fined in accordance with this title, or both; and

'(B) shall be imprisoned for any term of years or for life, fined in accordance with this title, or both, if--

'(i) death results from the offense; or

'(ii) the offense includes kidnaping or an attempt to kidnap, aggravated sexual abuse or an attempt to commit aggravated sexual abuse, or an attempt to kill.

172

'(2) OFFENSES INVOLVING ACTUAL OR PERCEIVED RELIGION, NATIONAL ORIGIN, GENDER, SEXUAL ORIENTATION, GENDER IDENTITY, OR DISABILITY-

'(A) IN GENERAL- Whoever, whether or not acting under color of law, in any circumstance described in subparagraph (B), willfully causes bodily injury to any person or, through the use of fire, a firearm, or an e.xplosive or incendiary device, attempts to cause bodily injury to any person, because of the actual or perceived religion, national origin, gender, sexual orientation, gender identity or disability of any person--

'(i) shall be imprisoned not more than 10 years, fined in accordance with this title, or both; and

'(ii) shall be imprisoned for any term of years or for life, fined in accordance with this title, or both, if--

'(I) death results from the offense; or

'(II) the offense includes kidnaping or an attempt to kidnap, aggravated sexual abuse or an attempt to commit aggravated sexual abuse, or an attempt to kill.

'(B) CIRCUMSTANCES DESCRIBED- For purposes of subparagraph (A), the circumstances described in this subparagraph are that--

'(i) the conduct described in subparagraph (A) occurs during the course of, or as the result of, the travel of the defendant or the victim--

'(I) across a State line or national border; or

'(II) using a channel, facility, or instrumentality of interstate or foreign commerce;

'(ii) the defendant uses a channel, facility, or instrumentality of interstate or foreign commerce in connection with the conduct described in subparagraph (A);

'(iii) in connection with the conduct described in subparagraph (A), the defendant employs a firearm, explosive or incendiary device, or other weapon that has traveled in interstate or foreign commerce; or

'(iv) the conduct described in subparagraph (A)--

'(I) interferes with commercial or other economic activity in which the victim is engaged at the time of the conduct; or

'(II) otherwise affects interstate or foreign commerce.

'(b) Certification Requirement- No prosecution of any offense described in this subsection may be undertaken by the United States, except under the certification in writing of the Attorney General, the Deputy Attorney General, the Associate Attorney General, or any Assistant Attorney General specially designated by the Attorney General that--

'(1) such certifying individual has reasonable cause to believe that the actual or perceived race, color, religion, national origin, gender, sexual orientation, gender identity, or disability of any person was a motivating factor underlying the alleged conduct of the defendant; and

'(2) such certifying individual has consulted with State or local law enforcement officials regarding the prosecution and determined that--

'(A) the State does not have jurisdiction or does not intend to exercise jurisdiction;

'(B) the State has requested that the Federal Government assume jurisdiction;

'(C) the State does not object to the Federal Government assuming jurisdiction; or

'(D) the verdict or sentence obtained pursuant to State charges left demonstratively unvindicated the Federal interest in eradicating bias-motivated violence.

'(c) Definitions- In this section--

'(1) the term 'explosive or incendiary device' has the meaning given such term in section 232 of this title;

'(2) the term 'firearm' has the meaning given such term in section 921(a) of this title; and

'(3) the term 'gender identity' for the purposes of this chapter means actual or perceived gender-related characteristics.

'(d) Rule of Evidence- In a prosecution for an offense under this section, evidence of expression or associations of the defendant may not be introduced as substantive evidence at trial, unless the evidence specifically relates to that offense. However, nothing in this section affects the rules of evidence governing impeachment of a witness.'.

(b) Technical and Conforming Amendment- The table of sections at the beginning of chapter 13 of title 18, United States Code, is amended by adding at the end the following new item:

§ 249. Hate crime acts

SEC. 7. SEVERABILITY.

If any provision of this Act, an amendment made by this Act, or the application of such provision or amendment to any person or circumstance is held to be unconstitutional, the remainder of this Act, the amendments made by this Act, and the application of the provisions of such to any person or circumstance shall not be affected thereby.

SEC. 8. RULE OF CONSTRUCTION.

Nothing in this Act, or the amendments made by this Act, shall be construed to prohibit any expressive conduct protected from legal prohibition by, or any activities protected by the free speech or free exercise clauses of, the First Amendment to the Constitution.

Passed the House of Representatives May 3, 2007

CHAPTER 15

PERJURY AND FALSE STATEMENTS-18 U.S.C. §§ 1621-1623; 1001

Page 704. Add to note 3.

For a recent prosecution under § 1623 based on the making of two irreconcilable contradictory statements under oath (defendant did not contend that the inconsistency could be reconciled), see United States v. Angulo-Hernandez, 175 Fed.Appx. 79 (7th Cir. 2006).

Pages 711-714.

For cases that invoke the "fundamental ambiguity"—"arguable ambiguity" distinction that is applied in Unted States v. Farmer in the main volume, see United States v. Richardson, 421 F.3d 17 (1st Cir. 2005) and United States v. Naegele, 341 B.R. 349 (D.D.C. 2006). In Naegele, a bankruptcy proceeding, the court ruled that one of the questions on a questionnaire that the defendant filled out under oath was fundamentally ambiguous. Defendant was an attorney who owned his own law firm as a sole proprietorship. The item in question asked defendant to state the gross amount of income that he had received from operation of his business. The indictment alleged that defendant, rather than stating his law firm's gross income, as purportedly required, reported his firm's net income. The court ruled that the questionnaire did not ask for gross income that the business received, or gross income "of" the business or "to" it, but rather suggested that defendant was supposed to report his "take-home" income from operation of his business which would be his law firm's gross income less business expenses. Nothing on the form suggested a contrary interpretation, and the accompanying instructions did not define "gross amount of income." Accordingly, defendant's allegedly false responses were insufficient to support criminal charges of making false statements in relation to his bankruptcy case.

Naegele involved other issues of fundamental ambiguity as well as literal truth claims under Bronston. The court described literal truth and fundamental ambiguity claims in connection with statements made under oath in a creditor proceeding as follows:

> Count 10 alleges that Naegele falsely testified at the creditors' meeting "that he had only rental vehicles when, in truth and in fact as he then well knew, he possessed a model year 2000 Chevrolet Malibu which he had acquired on or about April 17, 2000." According to the government, the Malibu had been purchased for Naegele by a client in exchange for a reduction in her legal fees, and Naegele owned it free and clear.

> Jeffrey Mervis, a representative of one of defendant's creditors, asked defendant whether he had a car in an exchange recorded in the government's version of the transcript as follows:

> MR. MERVIS: Do you have a car sir?

> DEFENDANT: No. Ah, I've, I've been renting a car from National Car (UI).

> MR. MERVIS: In Florida and LA and here or?

> DEFENDANT: In LA primarily. Ah, here, here, ah, ah, when I'm in Washington I often use the Metro.

> MR. MERVIS: Do you know what your, your automobile rental payments are?

> DEFENDANT: They've been running about a thousand a month.

Goverment's Draft Transcript at 7.

According to defendant's transcription of the meeting, defendant did not answer "no" when asked if he had a car; he responded only that he had "been renting a car from National Car." In that case, defendant argues, his response would have been misleading but literally true, because he *had* in fact been renting a car in addition to owning the one referred to in the indictment. *See* Defendant's Draft Transcript at 7.

The Court has reviewed the audio recording of the creditors' meeting and, on close listening, finds it at least arguable that defendant did answer "no" to Mervis's question before going on to state that he had been renting a car. Defendant's motion thus raises a factual question for the jury to decide after it hears the audio tape, not one appropriate for resolution now by the Court. Assuming, then, as the indictment alleges, that defendant denied having a car in the meeting, his response to Mervis's question was *not* literally true, because defendant did have a car when the question was asked.

Defendant argues, in the alternative, that even if he did answer "no" to Mervis's question, his response was literally true because the car was registered not in Naegele's name but in the name of a trust naming defendant's children as beneficiaries. *See* Defendant Timothy D. Naegele's Consolidated Reply to the Government's Opposition to Motions to Dismiss Counts Nine and Ten of the Indictment at 6-7 (citing *United States v. Strauch,* 59 F.3d 177 (Table), 1995 WL 377192, (9th Cir.1995) (unpublished), for the proposition that "an asset held in trust by a debtor for another is not property of the bankruptcy estate or the debtor"). This argument is unconvincing. Although defendant's response might be true under one (somewhat strained) interpretation of the term "have," it is assuredly not the case that defendant's statement is "literally true under the only possible interpretation," as is required for the *Bronston* defense. Defendant may put this argument to the jury in an attempt to show that his statement was not knowingly and fraudulently false..., but the Court will not dismiss Count 10 on this ground. In the context of perjury prosecutions, "it is up to the jury to determine how the defendant construed the question or answer and to decide, in that light, whether the defendant knowingly gave a false answer."

Defendant also argues that Count 10 should be dismissed because Mervis's question-"Do you have a car, sir?"-was fundamentally ambiguous. Defendant asserts that a reasonable person "could interpret that question equally well as meaning (1) 'do you have a car here today?' or (2) 'do you own a car?' or (3) 'do you have use of a car, e.g., a rental car?' " Even if defendant is correct that some ambiguity exists, because of the unlikely possibility that a reasonable person might assume scenarios (1) or (3), any ambiguity is not so "fundamental" as to render Count 10 fatally deficient. "Almost any question or answer can be interpreted in several ways when subjected to ingenious scrutiny after the fact," but "mere vagueness or ambiguity in the questions is not enough to establish a defense to perjury." When ambiguity is not fundamental, it is for the jury to resolve. ...Accordingly, the Court denies the defendant's motion to dismiss Count 10 on this ground, as well.

§ 1001 was amended on July 27, 2006. At the end of subsection (a), paragraph (3), insert: "If the matter relates to an offense under chapter 109A, 109B, 110, or 117, or section 1591, then the term of imprisonment imposed under this section shall be not more than 8 years."

Note: Chapter 109A, referred to in subsec. (a), above, is chapter 109A of this title, entitled Sexual Abuse, 18 U.S.C.A. § 2241 et seq.

Chapter 109B, referred to in subsec. (a), above, is chapter 109B of this title, entitled Sex Offender and Crimes Against Children Registry, 18 U.S.C.A. § 2250 et seq.

Chapter 110, referred to in subsec. (a), above, is chapter 110 of this title, entitled Sexual Exploitation and Other Abuse of Children, 18 U.S.C.A. § 2251 et seq.

Chapter 117, referred to in subsec. (a), above, is chapter 117 of this title, entitled Transportation for Illegal Sexual Activity and Related Crimes, 18 U.S.C.A. § 2421 et seq.

Section § 1591 referred to in subsec. (a), above, prohibits "Sex trafficking of children or by force, fraud, or coercion."

Consider the issue of materiality in United States v. Beltran, 136 Fed Appx. 59, 2005 WL 1394945 (9th Cir. 2005):

Finally, Beltran was convicted of violating 18 U.S.C. § 1001 for knowingly and willfully making a materially false statement in a matter within the jurisdiction of the executive branch of the U.S. government. A statement is material if it "has a natural tendency to influence, or was capable of influencing, the decision of the decisionmaking body to which it was addressed." Because the amount Beltran was actually carrying, $8,177, was below the $10,000 reporting requirement, the only way his statement that he was carrying $7,000 could have been material was if the misstatement had a tendency to influence, or was capable of influencing the Customs Agent. There is no record evidence that that was the case and the government has failed to explain how Beltran's misstatement was capable of influencing the Custom Agent's decisionmaking process. Notably, immediately upon being told Beltran was carrying $7,000, the Customs Agent referred Beltran to secondary inspection in order to verify the count. Therefore, the record evidence suggests that whether Beltran had told the Agent he had $7,000 or $8,177, he would have been sent to secondary inspection. Accordingly, Beltran's misstatement was immaterial as a matter of law. We reverse his conviction for violation of 18 U.S.C. § 1001.

Page 727. Add to note 11.

Also see United States v. Beaver, 515 F.3d 730 (7th Cir. 2008).

Page 728. Add as notes 13 and 14.

13. In United States v. Sattar, 395 F.Supp.2d 79 (S.D.N.Y.2005) (an earlier opinion in this case is reproduced at p. 583 of the main volume), the defendant argued that "broken promises of future intent cannot be the basis for a violation of 18 U.S.C. § 1001." The court rejected the argument holding that a knowingly false statement of present intent can be a false statement within the meaning of the statute. The government charged the defendant with having made knowingly false statements in affirmations that she signed and submitted to United States Attorney's Office, that she agreed to comply with Special Administrative Measures (SAMs) limiting prisoner's communications. The court stated:

> The jury was carefully instructed that, in order to find a violation of the statute, the Government was required to prove that the statements were untrue when made and that the defendant acted knowingly and willfully, and not simply that the defendant broke her promise recited in the affirmations.

Recall that the issue of whether false promises could a basis for a crime involving falsity was considered in the chapter on Mail Fraud. See United States v. Durland, main volume, p. 163.

14. Subsection (b) of § 1001 exempts from false statement liability under 1001 statements made to a judge by a party to a judicial proceeding. What is the policy basis for this exemption? What kinds of interpretative issues arise under this provision?

UNITED STATES V. HOLVATH
492 F.3d 1075 (9th Cir. 2007)

Before: HARRY PREGERSON, PAMELA ANN RYMER, and SUSAN P. GRABER, Circuit Judges.

GRABER, Circuit Judge:

... We must decide whether the exception in § 1001(b) for "statements ... submitted by [a] party ... to a judge" encompasses a false statement submitted to the judge in a presentence report ("PSR"), when the defendant in a criminal proceeding made the false statement to the probation officer during the defendant's presentence interview, rather than to the judge directly. We hold that when, but only when, the probation officer is required by law to include such a statement in the PSR and to submit the PSR to the judge, the statement falls within the exception in § 1001(b). We therefore reverse the district court's denial of Defendant's motion to dismiss the indictment.

On July 30, 2001, Defendant William Cody Horvath pleaded guilty to being a fugitive in possession of a firearm, in violation of 18 U.S.C. §§ 922(g)(2) and 924(a)(2). During the course of the judicial proceedings surrounding his plea, Defendant stated that he had served in the United States Marine Corps. Defendant now admits, and the record shows, that he never served in the Marine Corps.

Defendant first made his false statement at the change of plea hearing. After the court accepted his plea, a probation officer conducted a presentence interview with Defendant for the purpose of preparing a presentence report. Defendant told the probation officer that he had served in the Marine Corps. The probation officer followed up on Defendant's statement and reported in the PSR:

The defendant informed this officer that he was enlisted in the U.S. Marine Corps from May 1986 to May 1991 and received an honorable discharge. The defendant's highest rank was E5, and he received the Purple Heart for his service in Panama. The defendant advised that he was a field artillery spotter/scout and was based at Camp Lejeune, North Carolina. This officer requested documentation from the U.S. Marine Corps and the defendant to confirm the above information. At the time of this writing documentation or a DD214 was not available to this officer. At the time of the defendant's arrest in Spokane, Washington, he had in his possession a set of "dog tags" with the name William Horvath. The defendant's father informed that the defendant was in the U.S. Marine Corps.

The absence of documentary confirmation from the Marine Corps led the district court to question Defendant at the sentencing hearing about his alleged military service. Defendant was *not put under oath,* but his answers ultimately convinced the court of the truthfulness of his fabrications. In sentencing Defendant, the court relied on several mitigating factors, including Defendant's military service, to impose a lenient sentence: "I am going to go out on a limb in this case, Mr. Horvath, and what I'm going to do is put you on probation."

More than four years later, on January 4, 2006, the government determined that Defendant had lied about having served in the Marine Corps. The resulting indictment reads in its entirety:

On or about the 9th day of August, 2001, at Missoula, in the State and District of Montana, WILLIAM CODY HORVATH, in a matter within the jurisdiction of the judicial branch, knowingly and willfully made a materially false statement, to wit: when speaking to a probation officer preparing a presentence report which would aid the court in determining his sentence, WILLIAM CODY HORVATH claimed to have served in the United States Marine Corps, when in truth and in fact he never served in the United States Marine Corps, in violation of 18 U.S.C. § 1001(a)(2).

We review de novo questions of statutory interpretation. ...

... Defendant does not contest that he committed the proscribed conduct; that is, he knowingly and willfully made a materially false statement in a matter within the jurisdiction of the judicial branch of the Government of the United States. Instead, he argues that his conduct falls under the exception in § 1001(b), which provides:

...

Section 1001(b) contains three requirements: Defendant "must show that (1) he was a party to a judicial proceeding, (2) his statements were submitted to a judge or magistrate, and (3) his statements were made 'in that proceeding.' " *McNeil*, 362 F.3d at 572 (quoting 18 U.S.C. § 1001(b)). The parties-and we-agree that the first and third requirements are met: Defendant was a party to a judicial proceeding and made his statement in that proceeding. The only issue in dispute is the second requirement: whether Defendant's false statement to the probation officer, which was submitted to the judge in the PSR, qualifies as having been "submitted by [a] party ... to a judge." 18 U.S.C. § 1001(b).

Defendant's false statements at the change of plea hearing and at the sentencing hearing clearly fall under the protection of § 1001(b), because Defendant made the statements directly to a judge in a judicial proceeding.[1] The question in this case is whether Defendant's identical false statement, made to the probation officer during the presentence interview, likewise is protected by the exception that Congress created in § 1001(b). Because the probation officer was required by law to submit this particular false statement to the judge, we conclude that it is protected by § 1001(b).

The record does not fully explain why the government did not charge Defendant with perjury for his false statement made under oath during the change of plea hearing. *See* 18 U.S.C. § 1621 (criminalizing perjury). The government suggested that its decision not to charge may have related to the materiality of the false statement. Although the false statement plainly was material at the sentencing hearing, it may have been difficult to prove the materiality of the false statement at the change of plea hearing, which concerned only Defendant's guilt.

"A United States probation officer shall make a presentence investigation of a defendant that is required pursuant to the provisions of Rule 32(c) of the Federal Rules of Criminal Procedure, and shall, before the imposition of sentence, report the results of the investigation to the court." 18 U.S.C. § 3552(a). Rule 32(d)(2) of the Federal Rules of Criminal Procedure further specifies that "[t]he presentence report must ... contain ... the defendant's history and characteristics." A probation officer therefore is required to report all material aspects of a defendant's "history and characteristics" to the court in the PSR.

As the government concedes, Defendant's alleged prior military service was material biographical information to be considered by the judge at sentencing. Indeed, § 1001(a) criminalizes only *material* lies, and the indictment accordingly charged Defendant with having "knowingly and willingly made a *materially* false

---

[1] The indictment does not charge Defendant with any crime for his lies at those hearings. The indictment charges Defendant with a violation of § 1001(a) only for his false statement to the probation officer.

statement." (Emphasis added.) The materiality of Defendant's false statement is further demonstrated by the district judge's explicit reliance on Defendant's alleged military service in sentencing Defendant to a lenient sentence of probation. In summary, when Defendant told the probation officer that he had served in the Marine Corps, the probation officer was required by law to include the substance of that statement in the PSR. Dutifully performing his job, the probation officer did so....

The probation officer here did not include, and the law did not require him to include, a verbatim transcript of Defendant's statement. The probation officer was free to choose the text that described Defendant's statement, so long as he conveyed the information accurately. But the absence of Defendant's own words does not detract from our conclusion that the probation officer was a mere conduit for this information. ...

Nor does it matter that Defendant did not submit the statement *directly* to the judge. The text of § 1001(b) does not require direct submission, and many typical submissions reach the judge indirectly. For example, parties commonly submit papers and filings to a judge by handing them to the clerk of the court or to a judicial assistant. As the government concedes, § 1001(b) protects those submissions. Similarly, a defendant would not lose the protection of § 1001(b) simply because he or she hired a courier to take a written statement to the judge.

Because Rule 32 required the probation officer to submit Defendant's false statement of personal history to the judge, and because the probation officer exercised no discretion in doing so, he was acting as a conduit between Defendant and the judge. We therefore conclude that § 1001(b) protects Defendant's false statement.

...

We pause to make explicit the limited reach of our holding. A defendant's statement to a probation officer is protected under § 1001(b) only if the law requires the probation officer to include the statement in the PSR and submit the PSR to the court. In these circumstances, the statement is submitted (albeit indirectly) by the defendant to a judge in a judicial proceeding. Because § 1001(b) extends the exemption only to parties and their counsel, statements by others (such as Defendant's father, who "informed [the probation officer] that the defendant was in the U.S. Marine Corps") are not protected by § 1001(b). Additionally, our holding in no way affects the ability of the government to prosecute defendants for perjury for lies told under oath.[8]

We need not, and do not, address the policy issues that inhere in the government's arguments. Our only task is to understand what Congress meant when it chose to exempt from criminal liability certain kinds of lies to the federal government. Under 18 U.S.C. § 1001(b), criminal liability does not attach to materially false statements submitted by a party to a judge in a judicial proceeding, even if the party makes the statements knowingly and willfully.

...

REVERSED and REMANDED.

RYMER, Circuit Judge, dissenting:

This is a tough issue. Given that the majority sees the statute differently from the way I do, I take comfort in its effort to craft a narrow rule. Nevertheless, the choice boils down to: are all statements, representations, writings or documents given by a defendant to a probation officer in connection with the probation officer's preparation of a PSR "submitted ... to a judge" for purposes of § 1001(b)-or, are they "submitted ... to a [probation officer]." In my view, the conundrum is resolved by the statute itself.

---

[8] To the extent that the government suggests that liability under 18 U.S.C. § 1001 does, or should, reach all materially false statements not covered by the criminal statute for perjury, 18 U.S.C. § 1621, we are not persuaded. Although § 1001 liability extends to statements not made under oath, there is no suggestion in the history of § 1001 or our precedents that every lie told to the judiciary entails either criminal liability for perjury under § 1621 or criminal liability for making a false statement under § 1001. The facts of this case provide one clear example: Defendant's false statement to the judge at the sentencing hearing, when he was not under oath, is plainly shielded from liability under both § 1621 and § 1001.

Section 1001(b) says that it immunizes submissions by a party or that party's counsel "to a judge or magistrate." If this means what it says, then plainly and literally "to a judge" means *to a judge.*

I do not disagree that statements, representations, writings, or documents filed with or handed to a file clerk, or the judge's courtroom deputy clerk, or the judge's secretary, are "submitted ... to the judge" because the judge would receive these things personally if only he or she had enough time and arms. In that role clerical staff are conduits in the purest sense of the word. They don't add (or subtract) value; they simply transmit.

But a probation officer is quite different. In the capacity relevant here, preparation of a presentence report (PSR), a probation officer is an investigator and advisor who must gather, sort, and distill information that Federal Rule of Criminal Procedure 32 requires. That universe of information may include (but is by no means limited to) whatever the defendant, if he chooses to be interviewed, may impart. For sure, the *report* is submitted to a judge. Yet if the defendant submits to an interview, and makes a statement, he makes the statement to a probation officer; if he lies, he lies *to* the *probation officer,* not "to the judge."

. . .

Beyond this, while a defendant's statements to a probation officer may indirectly be for the judge's consumption, they are directly "to" the probation officer and directly influence the *probation officer's* sentencing recommendations. By contrast, the defendant's direct shot at a submission *to the judge* is allocution. Fed.R.Crim.P. 32(i)(4)(A)(ii). *That* is plainly protected by § 1001(b).

Absent anything more concrete than the majority has pointed to, it is hard to believe that Congress intended the exception for submissions "to a judge" to encourage those convicted of federal crimes to fabricate tales to a probation officer for the purpose of influencing a more favorable sentence. While Congress obviously did intend to allow some false statements, representations, writings, and documents to be made to a judge in the course of adversarial litigation to avoid chilling advocacy on the margin between pushing the envelope and being misleading and lying, it did not immunize falsehoods altogether even in the judge's arena as it drew a line at knowingly making a false material statement under oath. 18 U.S.C. § 1623. Additionally, the adversary system, counsels' ethical obligations, and other means available to judicial officers kick in to further truth-seeking in the courtroom. Similar balances do not apply in the probation officer's arena. Statements to probation officers are not made under penalty of perjury and the process is not adversarial. Absent § 1001, there are scant incentives for truth-speaking.

In sum, the words "to a judge" seem clear to me. "To a judge" is not "to a probation officer." Thus, § 1001(b) in its plain, literal sense excepts submissions *to a judge,* which a probation officer isn't. However, even if there is ambiguity, given a choice between immunizing all false statements made by a defendant to a probation officer in connection with sentencing and immunizing none of them, I would chose none. The same concerns that animate the exception for lies or misrepresentations to a judge and magistrate, who are adjudicative officers with other powers to deal with flagrant abuses of the process and with perjury, don't apply with the same force when lies are to probation officers, who perform functions that are vitally important to the administration of criminal justice but who are neither adjudicative officers nor armed with their authority.

Consequently, I dissent.

Page 750-751. Add to note 1.

Does the "exculpatory no" doctrine apply in a prosecution for perjury? For a case indicating that the Brogan rejection of the exculpatory no doctrine applies in a perjury prosecution based upon testimony before a grand jury, see United States v. Burke, 425 F.3d 400 (7th Cir. 2005).

Page 752. Add following note 3.

UNITED STATES V. SAFAVIAN
451 F.Supp. 2d 232 (D.D.C. 2006)

PAUL L. FRIEDMAN, District Judge.

This matter is before the Court on defendant David Safavian's motion for judgment of acquittal pursuant to Rule 29 of the Federal Rules of Criminal Procedure and his motion for a new trial pursuant to Rule 33 of the Federal Rules of Criminal Procedure. The Court heard oral argument on these motions on August 24, 2006. Upon consideration of the motions, oppositions, replies, and arguments of the parties, the Court concludes that both motions must be denied.

I. BACKGROUND

From May 16, 2002 until January 2004, David Safavian was the Chief of Staff for the Administrator of the General Services Administration ("GSA"). On August 3, 2002, the defendant, lobbyist Jack Abramoff, and seven other individuals, including a member of the United States House of Representatives, members of the Representative's staff, and other lobbyists employed at the same law firm as Jack Abramoff, flew by private jet to Scotland to play golf at St. Andrew's golf course. Mr. Safavian, Mr. Abramoff, and the others continued on to London, England. Mr. Safavian and Mr. Abramoff eventually returned to the United States by private jet on August 11, 2002.

Prior to going on the golfing trip, in July 2002, Mr. Safavian sought and received an ethics opinion from a GSA ethics officer regarding whether he could participate in the trip. Both the GSA Office of the Inspector General ("GSA-OIG") and the Senate Committee on Indian Affairs subsequently conducted investigations into the Scotland trip. The GSA-OIG's investigation was opened in March 2003 after the receipt of an anonymous tip. On February 22, 2004, the Washington Post published the first of a series of articles about Mr. Abramoff's dealings with several Indian tribes, triggering the Senate Committee's investigation. In the course of each of these investigations, Mr. Safavian was questioned about his involvement in the trip. He responded to each of the inquiries both orally and by providing documents. Mr. Safavian also wrote a letter accompanying the documents he provided to the Senate.

A grand jury thereafter returned a five count indictment against Mr. Safavian, charging him with three counts of making false statements or acts of concealment under 18 U.S.C. § 1001(a)(1) and two counts of obstruction under 18 U.S.C. § 1505. Specifically, Count One of the indictment alleged that the defendant obstructed the GSA-OIG investigation, in violation of 18 U.S.C. § 1505; Count Two alleged that he made a false statement and committed acts of concealment in connection with seeking the GSA ethics opinion prior to the trip, in violation of 18 U.S.C. § 1001(a)(1); Count Three alleged that he made a false statement and committed acts of concealment in the course of the GSA-OIG investigation, in violation of 18 U.S.C. § 1001(a)(1); Count Four alleged that he obstructed the Senate Committee investigation, in violation of 18 U.S.C. § 1505; and Count Five alleged that he made a false statement, committed acts of concealment, and provided false documentation in the course of the Senate Committee investigation, in violation of 18 U.S.C. § 1001(a)(1).

189

Mr. Safavian's trial before this Court began on May 22, 2006. On June 20, 2006, the jury returned a verdict finding him guilty on Count One, which alleged that he had obstructed "the official investigation being conducted by the GSA-OIG into [Mr.] Safavian's participation in an 'international golfing trip provided by lobbyists.' " The jury acquitted Mr. Safavian on Count Four, which alleged that he had obstructed "the inquiry by Senator John McCain as Chairman of the Senate Committee on Indian Affairs, into allegations of misconduct by lobbyists for Native American tribes." Mr. Safavian was found guilty on all three counts of false statements under 18 U.S.C. § 1001(a)(1).

Because each of the false statement/concealment counts under 18 U.S.C. § 1001(a)(1) alleged multiple false statements or acts of concealment, the Court used a special verdict form over the objection of the defendant. With respect to Count Two, the jury found that Mr. Safavian had both "concealed his assistance to Mr. Abramoff in GSA-related activities" and that he had "falsely stated to the GSA ethics officer that Mr. Abramoff did all his work on Capitol Hill, when in truth and fact, Mr. Safavian well knew, prior to the August 2002 Scotland trip that Mr. Abramoff was seeking to lease or purchase GSA-controlled property." With respect to Count Three, the jury found that Mr. Safavian had "concealed his assistance to Mr. Abramoff in GSA-related activities." With respect to Count Five, the jury found that Mr. Safavian had "falsely stated in a letter to the Committee that Mr. Abramoff did not have any business with GSA at the time Mr. Safavian was invited on the trip to Scotland, when in truth and fact, Mr. Safavian well knew, prior to the August 2002 Scotland trip that Mr. Abramoff was seeking to lease or purchase GSA-controlled property."

II. MOTION FOR JUDGMENT OF ACQUITTAL

The defendant moved for judgment of acquittal on all counts pursuant to Rule 29 of the Federal Rules of Criminal Procedure at the close of the government's case. At that time, the Court reserved ruling on the motion. At the close of the defendant's case, the Court ruled in part on the defendant's Rule 29 motion, finding that there was not sufficient evidence to support the allegation in Count Two of the indictment that the defendant had falsely stated to the GSA that Jack Abramoff "did not have any business with and was not seeking to do business with GSA." That portion of Count Two was stricken from the indictment after the close of the defendant's case and prior to jury instructions and closing arguments. The jury was given an amended indictment to reflect that change. Defendant now renews his Rule 29 motion with respect to the four counts on which the jury found him guilty.

...

A. Fifth Amendment Due Process

Defendant argues that the Court must set aside the jury's verdict on all four counts because he did not receive adequate notice of his right not to speak and the potential criminal implications of making false statements if he did choose to speak, thereby violating his Fifth Amendment due process rights. The government responds that this argument should have been made before trial in a motion to suppress the defendant's statements pursuant to Rule 12(b)(3) of the Federal Rules of Criminal Procedure, and it therefore is waived under Rule 12(e). The government further argues that even if the Court were to consider this new argument, it fails on the merits. The Court agrees with the government.

The proper remedy for a due process violation under the Fifth Amendment would have been for the defendant to move to suppress his various statements to the government officials with whom he spoke. Mr. Safavian was well aware of what statements he was alleged to have made to GSA ethics officers, a GSA-OIG agent, and a Senate Committee investigator, as they were charged in the indictment itself. He did not at any time prior to trial move to suppress these statements on the ground that his constitutional rights had been violated... He therefore waived any ability to raise this argument post-trial under Rule 29.

Even if Mr. Safavian had raised this argument prior to trial, he would not have succeeded in view of the Supreme Court's decision in Brogan v. United States, 522 U.S. 398, 118 S.Ct. 805, 139 L.Ed.2d 830 (1998). ...The Court held that although the false statements that the individual was convicted of making consisted of merely denying that he had committed certain illegal acts, such a denial nevertheless could result in criminal liability under the statute. In concluding that the plain language of 18 U.S.C. § 1001 admits of no exception for an "exculpatory no," the majority opinion stated that while the dissenters appeared to object to the harshness of the result, they could have equally sought to mitigate the asserted harshness of the statute as applied under the rationale that " § 1001 has no application unless the defendant has been warned of the consequences of lying, or indeed unless the defendant has been put under oath." Id. at 407, Clearly, the majority considered and dismissed such an argument in upholding the conviction of the defendant in that case, who received no

191

warning prior to making his false statement. Justice Ginsburg, in a concurring opinion, further noted the breadth of the statute (albeit somewhat disapprovingly):

> Because the questioning occurs in a noncustodial setting, the suspect is not informed of the right to remain silent. Unlike proceedings in which a false statement can be prosecuted as perjury, there may be no oath, no pause to concentrate the speaker's mind on the importance of his or her answers.

Id. at 411. Justice Ginsburg, nevertheless, concurred in the outcome, which upheld the defendant's conviction. Clearly, no prior warning is required under 18 U.S.C. § 1001.

Defendant also argues that his statements could not be the predicate for a prosecution because he should have received an administrative warning under Garrity v. New Jersey, 385 U.S. 493, 87 S.Ct. 616, 17 L.Ed.2d 562 (1967), because he was threatened with the prospect of discipline. But there is absolutely no evidence that such a threat existed. ...

Mr. Safavian initiated contact with the GSA ethics officers. He himself testified that he voluntarily went to the GSA-OIG agent's office after receiving a phone call, describing the meeting as "not tense" and "informal." As for his communications with Deputy Chief Investigative Counsel for the Senate Committee on Indian Affairs Bryan Parker, Mr. Safavian and Mr. Parker both testified that after responding to the Senate request for documents, Mr. Safavian was the one to initiate a phone call to Mr. Parker following up on his response, and eventually sending to the Committee a letter and documentation. Mr. Safavian may have cooperated with the GSA-OIG and Senate Committee investigations out of a well-founded belief that for him to do otherwise might be a poor reflection on him as a public official. Nevertheless, his own testimony shows that he was not coerced or threatened and that there was not any immediate or direct threat of harm to his job when he chose to speak with either GSA-OIG Agent Gregory Rowe or Senate Investigator Bryan Parker. The fact that certain government investigators give warnings as a matter of policy in no way affects the analysis of whether such a warning is constitutionally required. The Court finds that under the circumstances presented here it was not.

B. Legal Duty to Disclose

Defendant argues that the conviction on Count Three, which was predicated on the jury's finding that Mr. Safavian had committed an act of concealment, and the jury's verdict with respect to the concealment portion of Count Two must be set aside because he had no legal duty to disclose the information concealed. He argues first, that the Court should have determined as a matter of law whether he was under a duty to disclose the facts in question, and, second, that no such duty existed. The Court already has concluded that the issue of a legal duty to disclose was a matter for the jury, and therefore included the legal duty as an element of 18 U.S.C. § 1001(a)(1) in the jury instructions. See Jury Instructions for Count Two, Count Three, Count Five. The Court sees no reason to revisit the question now. The Court further finds that there was more than sufficient evidence for the jury to find that such a duty existed. Finally, even had it decided this question itself as a matter of law, the Court would have reached the same conclusion as the jury apparently did: that under the circumstances presented in all three of the counts brought under 18 U.S.C. § 1001(a)(1), Mr. Safavian was under a legal duty to disclose material facts to the GSA ethics officers, to the GSAOIG agent, and to the Senate Committee investigator.

The evidence presented at trial supported the jury's finding that such a duty existed. In United States v. Cisneros, 26 F.Supp.2d 24 (D.D.C.1998), the court found that Mr. Cisneros, at the time under consideration for a position in the cabinet of the President of the United States, was under a legal duty to disclose based on an Executive Order requiring that applicants for government employment "possess such traits as reliability, trustworthiness, and loyalty." In this case, the government presented to the jury evidence that Mr. Safavian owed a duty as a public servant based on the fourteen principles from the "Standards of Ethical Conduct" that were issued in a January 20, 2001 Executive Order, and were later codified in the Code of Federal Regulations as the "General Principles" that make up the "Basic obligation of public service." 5 C.F.R. § 2635.101(b); Mr. Safavian was trained on these principles of public service when he became the GSA Chief of Staff. 5/31/06 (p.m.) Tr. 18:9-17. ...

C. Literal Truth Defense

Defendant claims that his convictions under 18 U.S.C. § 1001(a)(1) must be set aside because the government has not borne its "burden to negate any reasonable interpretations that would make a defendant's statement factually correct." The government responds that the literal truth defense is only proper under the "false statement" prong of 18 U.S.C. § 1001 and not under the "concealment prong" under which Mr. Safavian was indicted and convicted. The Court rejects the defendant's argument as a basis for judgment of acquittal.

While 18 U.S.C. § 1001 is frequently referred to as the "false statements" statute, it actually contains three different prongs under which the government bring charges. 18 U.S.C. § 1001(a)(2), or the "false statement prong" of the false statements statute, creates criminal liability for one who "makes any materially false, fictitious, or fraudulent statement or representation." 18 U.S.C. § 1001(a)(3) relates to the use of false writings or documents. The defendant was indicted and convicted under 18 U.S.C. § 1001(a)(1), or the "concealment prong" of the false statements statute, which creates criminal liability for one who "falsifies, conceals, or covers up by any trick, scheme, or device a material fact." Within each count of the indictment, however, the grand jury alleged both acts of concealment and false statements under this concealment prong. Regardless of the government's argument that the literal truth defense is not appropriate to charges brought under the concealment prong, the Court permitted the jury to be instructed that the literal truth constituted a defense to the false statements alleged under the concealment prong, but not to the acts of concealment themselves. The jury nevertheless found Mr. Safavian guilty under 18 U.S.C. § 1001(a)(1) on Counts Two and Five for making false statements.

The Court agrees with the government that the literal truth defense is inherently illogical with respect to the acts of concealment defendant was convicted of committing under Counts Two and Three. The Court therefore will consider the defendant's argument with respect only to the false statements that Mr. Safavian was convicted of making under Counts Two and Five. Mr. Safavian argues that these statements were literally true-that is, that Mr. Abramoff in fact "did all his work on Capitol Hill" and that Mr. Abramoff in fact "did not have any business with GSA at the time [Mr.] Safavian was invited on the trip to Scotland." The problem with Mr. Safavian's arguments for why these statements are the "literal truth" is that they rely on a recitation of the evidence in a light that is clearly most favorable to him. Under Rule 29, the Court must view the evidence in the light most favorable to the government.

Mr. Safavian asserts, as he did before trial in his motion to dismiss, that the term "doing business" should be understood to mean only what is stated in the federal regulations or GSA ethics manual as they relate to GSA contracting practices, and not as the term is understood by the average person. The Court rejected this view at trial and rejects it now. The meaning of the words he used such as "business" or "work"-as in "all Mr. Abramoff's work was on Capitol Hill"-were susceptible to multiple reasonable definitions, and therefore could only be understood by "considering the term[s] in context, taking into account the setting in which [they] appeared and the purpose for which [they were] used." Mr. Safavian's understanding of these terms was presented to the jury in the form of both the expert witness Anthony Anikeeff, who testified as to GSA contracting procedures, and Mr. Safavian's own testimony as to his understanding of these terms when he used them. The jury was free to consider, and reject this evidence, which it apparently did. The Court does not find that Mr. Safavian has met the burden of showing that no reasonable juror could have found that he did not speak the literal truth when making the false statements for which he was convicted.

...

Page 756. Add as notes 4, 5, 6, 7 and 8.

4. Whereas the Martha Stewart case involved prosecution of the false statement offense along with an obstruction of justice count, United States v. Brown, 459 F.3d 509, 530-531 (5th Cir. 2006) involved perjury charges combined with obstruction :

> Brown essentially argues that perjury and obstruction are separable and distinct offenses; consequently, the mere fact that one perjures himself does not mean that he has obstructed justice. Thus, the obstruction conviction must be reversed because '[t]he government introduced no evidence ... [to] establish that Brown's testimony had any effect (actual, natural, or probable) on the Grand Jury proceeding.' [U]nder the precedent of this circuit, ... false testimony as to one's knowledge relating to the subject of a grand jury inquiry does in fact establish obstruction; not because the perjury ipso facto establishes obstruction, but because the perjurious testimony has the effect of 'closing off entirely the avenue[ ] of inquiry being pursued.' . . . .

5. Suppose the government combines all three offenses, perjury, false statements and obstruction in one indictment. Indeed, this is not an uncommon pattern of charging related offenses. A prominent recent case involving this combination of charges is United States v. Libby, a prosecution of the former chief of staff of the Vice President of the United States. The basic facts in the Libby

case are recounted in the following excerpt from United States v. Libby, 432 F. Supp. 2d 81 (D.D.C. 2006):

On October 28, 2005, the defendant was charged in a five-count indictment with obstruction of justice in violation of 18 U.S.C. § 1503 (2000), two counts of false statements in violation of 18 U.S.C. § 1001(a)(2) (2000), and two counts of perjury in violation of 18 U.S.C. § 1623 (2000). All of these charges arise from a criminal investigation into the possible unauthorized disclosure of classified information about Valerie Plame Wilson's affiliation with the Central Intelligence Agency ("CIA") to several journalists.. And specifically, the charges against the defendant are predicated upon statements that he allegedly made to Special Agents of the Federal Bureau of Investigation ("FBI") in October and November, 2003, and testimony he provided to a grand jury in March 2004. The allegedly false statements related to conversations the defendant had with news reporters Tim Russert, Judith Miller, and Matthew Cooper in June and July 2003.

While these purportedly false statements were made against the backdrop of Ambassador Joseph Wilson's comments about the validity of President George W. Bush's proclamation in his January 28, 2003 State of the Union address that "[t]he British government has learned that Saddam Hussein recently sought significant quantities of uranium from Africa," Ambassador Wilson's comments have only peripheral pertinence to this case. Moreover, although the Special Counsel's criminal investigation initially focused on whether government officials illegally disclosed Ms. Wilson's employment with the CIA, the defendant has not been charged with any such violation. Rather, the only question the jury will be asked to resolve in this matter will be whether the defendant intentionally lied when he testified before the grand jury and spoke with FBI agents about statements he purportedly made to the three news reporters concerning Ms. Wilson's employment. The prosecution of this action, therefore, involves a discrete cast of characters and events, and this Court will not permit it to become a forum for debating the accuracy of Ambassador Wilson's statements, the propriety of the Iraq war or related matters leading up to the war, as those events are not the basis for the charged offenses. At best, these events have merely an abstract relationship to the charged offense. [1]

Nonetheless, this Court recognizes that the charged offenses occurred against this backdrop and appreciates that some reference to Ambassador Wilson, his trip to Niger, and his wife during the trial is probably inevitable. Any testimony or other evidence relating to these subjects, however, will be admitted for limited purposes-to establish what the principal players (the defendant, the three news reporters, and any other key witnesses) knew about Ambassador Wilson's wife's affiliation with the CIA and when they knew it, and as evidence of the defendant's purported motive to reveal Ms. Wilson's affiliation with the CIA to reporters. In fact, as to this first basis of admissibility, as the indictment makes clear, one aspect of the government's case will be an attempt to establish the defendant's knowledge of Ms. Wilson's affiliation with the CIA before his conversations with Miller, Russert, and Cooper. However, whether the information possessed by any of the principal players was true or not is immaterial to this case; rather, what will be relevant in regards to either the prosecution or defense is what, if anything, they knew about the subject and when they acquired that information. And documents reflecting what these principal players may have known (or did not know) could be used to attack the credibility and recollection of these potential witnesses.

---

[1] This reality is not altered simply because the government intends to introduce into evidence at trial various news articles that discuss Ambassador Wilson's trip to Niger. *See* Government's Response to Court's Inquiry Regarding News Articles the Government Intends to Offer as Evidence at Trial. The government does not intend to introduce these articles for the truth of the matters asserted, *id.* at 1, but rather, only for the limited purpose of demonstrating that the defendant had a motive to make the statements to the media representatives that form the basis for the charged offenses.

In response to the charges filed against him, the defendant relates that one aspect of his defense will be that he was not engaged in a sinister effort to punish Ambassador Wilson or Valerie Plame Wilson; rather, any discussions he had with the reporters concerning Ambassador Wilson, his trip to Niger, or Valerie Plame Wilson were conducted solely for the purpose of refuting the accuracy of Ambassador Wilson's pronouncements. According to the defendant, his requests for documents relating to discussions he had with other government officials or news reporters that show that he was simply engaged in legitimate efforts to rebut the merits of Ambassador Wilson's findings are material to the preparation of his defense, as their content would arguably support his claim that the government's position that he intended to make false statements, commit perjury, and obstruct justice is incorrect. In limited respect, the Court agrees. ... Therefore, if the government is in possession of documents that show the defendant's intent to participate or his actual participation in such legitimate efforts, those documents must be produced ....

6. The indictment in the Libby case included the following specific allegations:

... [D]efendant herein, did knowingly and corruptly endeavor to influence, obstruct and impede the due administration of justice, namely proceedings before Grand Jury, by misleading and deceiving the grand jury as to when, and the manner and means by which, LIBBY acquired and subsequently disclosed to the media information concerning the employment of Valerie Wilson by the CIA.

32. It was part of the corrupt endeavor that during his grand jury testimony, defendant LIBBY made the following materially false and intentionally misleading statements and representations, in substance, under oath:

a. When LIBBY spoke with Tim Russert of NBC News, on or about July 10, 2003:

i. Russert asked LIBBY if LIBBY knew that Wilson's wife worked for the CIA, and told LIBBY that all the reporters knew it; and

ii. At the time of this conversation, LIBBY was surprised to hear that Wilson's wife worked for the CIA;

b. LIBBY advised Matthew Cooper of Time magazine on or about July 12, 2003, that he had heard that other reporters were saying that Wilson's wife worked for the CIA, and further advised him that LIBBY did not know whether this assertion was true; and

c. LIBBY advised Judith Miller of the New York Times on or about July 12, 2003 that he had heard that other reporters were saying that Wilson's wife worked for the CIA but LIBBY did not know whether that assertion was true.

33. It was further part of the corrupt endeavor that at the time defendant LIBBY made each of the above-described materially false and intentionally misleading statements and representations to the grand jury, LIBBY was aware that they were false, in that:

a. When LIBBY spoke with Tim Russert of NBC News on or about July 10, 2003:

i. Russert did not ask LIBBY if LIBBY knew that Wilson's wife worked for the CIA, nor did he tell LIBBY that all the reporters knew it; and

ii. At the time of this conversation, LIBBY was well aware that Wilson's wife worked at the CIA; in fact, LIBBY had participated in multiple prior conversations concerning this topic, including on the following occasions:

- In or about early June 2003, LIBBY learned from the Vice President that Wilson's wife worked for the CIA in the Counterproliferation Division;

- On or about June 11, 2003, LIBBY was informed by a senior CIA officer that Wilson's wife was employed by the CIA and that the idea of sending him to Niger originated with her;

- On or about June 12, 2003, LIBBY was informed by the Under Secretary of State that Wilson's wife worked for the CIA;

- On or about June 14, 2003, LIBBY discussed. "Joe Wilson" and "Valerie Wilson" with his CIA briefer, in the context of Wilson's trip to Niger;

- On or about June 23, 2003, LIBBY informed reporter Judith Miller that Wilson's wife might work at a bureau of the CIA;

199

- On or about July 7, 2003, LIBBY advised the White House Press Secretary that Wilson's wife worked for the CIA;

- In or about June or July 2003, and in no case later than on or about July 8, 2003, LIBBY was advised by the Assistant to the Vice President for Public Affairs that Wilson's wife worked for the CIA;

- On or about July 8, 2003, LIBBY advised reporter Judith Miller of his belief that Wilson's wife worked at the CIA; and

- On or about July 8, 2003, LIBBY had a discussion with the Counsel to the Office of the Vice President concerning the paperwork that would exist if a person who was sent on an overseas trip by the CIA had a spouse who worked at the CIA;

b. LIBBY did not advise Matthew Cooper, on or about July 12, 2003, that LIBBY had heard other reporters were saying that Wilson's wife worked for the CIA, nor did LIBBY advise him that LIBBY did not know whether this assertion was true; rather, LIBBY confirmed to Cooper, without qualification, that LIBBY had heard that Wilson's wife worked at the CIA; and

c. LIBBY did not advise Judith Miller, on or about July 12,2003, that LIBBY had heard other reporters were saying that Wilson's wife worked for the CIA, nor did LIBBY advise her that LIBBY did not know whether this assertion was true;

In violation of Title 18, United States Code, Section 1503.

COUNT TWO

(False Statement)

THE GRAND JURY FURTHER CHARGES:

1. The Grand Jury realleges Paragraphs 1-26 of Count One as though fully set forth herein.

2. During the course of the criminal investigation conducted by the Federal Bureau of Investigation and the Department of Justice, the following matters, among others, were material to that investigation:

a. When, and the manner and means by which, defendant LIBBY learned that Wilson's wife was employed by the CIA;

b. Whether and when LIBBY disclosed to members of the media that Wilson's wife was employed by the CIA;

c. The language used by LIBBY in disclosing any such information to the media, including whether LIBBY expressed uncertainty about the accuracy of any information he may have disclosed, or described where he obtained the information; and

d. LIBBY's knowledge as to whether any information he disclosed was classified at the time he disclosed it.

3. On or about October 14 and November 26, 2003, in the District of Columbia,

I. LEWIS LIBBY,

also known as "SCOOTER LIBBY,"

defendant herein, did knowingly and willfully make a materially false, fictitious, and fraudulent statement and representation in a matter within the jurisdiction of the Federal Bureau of Investigation, an agency within the executive branch of the United States. in that the defendant, in response to questions posed to him by agents of the Federal Bureau of Investigation, stated that:

During a conversation with Tim Russert of NBC News on July 10 or 11, 2003, Russert asked LIBBY if LIBBY was aware that Wilson's wife worked for the CIA. LIBBY responded to Russert that he did not know that, and Russert replied that all the reporters knew it. LIBBY was surprised by this statement because, while speaking with Russert, LIBBY did not recall that he previously had learned about Wilson's wife's employment from the Vice President.

4. As defendant LIBBY well knew when he made it, this statement was false in that when LIBBY spoke with Russert on or about July 10 or 11, 2003:

a. Russert did not ask LIBBY if LIBBY knew that Wilson's wife worked for the CIA, nor did he tell LIBBY that all the reporters knew it; and

b. At the time of this conversation, LIBBY was well aware that Wilson's wife worked at the CIA;

In violation of Title 18, United States Code, Section 1001(a)(2).

...

201

COUNT FOUR

(Perjury)

THE GRAND JURY FURTHER CHARGES:

1. The Grand Jury realleges Paragraphs 1-30 of Count One as though fully set forth herein.

2. On or about March 5, 2004, in the District of Columbia,

I. LEWIS LIBBY,

also known as "SCOOTER LIBBY,"

defendant herein, having taken an oath to testify truthfully in a proceeding before a grand jury of the United States, knowingly made a false material declaration, in that he gave the following testimony regarding a conversation that he represented he had with Tim Russert of NBC News, on or about July 10, 2003 (underlined portions alleged as false):

....And then he said, you know did you know that this - excuse me, did you know that Ambassador Wilson's wife works at the CIA? And I was a little taken aback by that. I remember being taken aback by it. And I said - he may have said a little more but that was- he said that. And I said, no, I don't know that. And I said no, I don't know that intentionally because I didn't want him to take anything I was saying as in any way confirming what he said, because at that point in time I did not recall that I had ever known, and I thought this is something that he was telling me that I was first learning. And so I said, no, I don't know that because I want to be very careful not to confirm it for him, so that he didn't take my statement as confirmation for him.

Now, I had said earlier in the conversation, which I omitted to tell you, that this - you know, as always, Tim, our discussion is off-the-record if that's okay with you, and he said, that's fine.

So then he said - I said - he said. sorry - he, Mr. Russert said to me, did you know that Ambassador Wilson's wife, or his wife, works at the CIA? And I said, no. I don't know that. And then he said, yeah-yes, all the reporters know it. And I said again, I don't know that. I just wanted to be clear that I wasn't confirming anything for him on this. And you know, I was struck by what he was saying in that he thought it was an important fact, but I didn't ask him anymore about it because I didn't want to be digging in on him, and he then moved on and finished the conversation, something like that.

3. In truth and fact, as LIBBY well knew when he gave this testimony, it was false in that:

a. Russert did not ask LIBBY if LIBBY knew that Wilson's wife worked for the CIA, nor did he tell LIBBY that all the reporters knew it; and

b. At the time of this conversation, LIBBY was well aware that Wilson's wife worked at the CIA;

In violation or Title 18, United States Code, Section 1623.

COUNT FIVE

(Perjury)

THE GRAND JURY FURTHER CHARGES:

1. The Grand Jury realleges Paragraphs 1-30 of Count One as though fully set forth herein.

2. On or about March 5, 2004 and March 24, 2004, in the District of Columbia,

I. LEWIS LIBBY,

also known as "SCOOTER LIBBY,"

defendant herein, having taken an oath to testify truthfully in a proceeding before a grand jury of the United States, knowingly made a false material-declaration, in that he gave the following testimony regarding his conversations with reporters concerning the employment of Joseph Wilson's wife by the CIA (underlined portions alleged as false):

a. Testimony Given on or about March 5, 2004 Regarding a Conversation With Matthew Cooper on or About July 12, 2003:

Q. And it's your specific recollection that when you told Cooper about Wilson's wife working at the CIA, you attributed that fact to what reporters -

A. Yes.

Q. - plural, were saying. Correct?

A. *I was very clear to say reporters are telling us that because in my mind I still didn't know it as a fact. I thought I was - all I had was this information that was coming in from the reporters.*

....

203

Q. And at the same time you have a specific recollection of telling him, you don't know whether it's true or not, you're just telling him what reporters are saying?

A. *Yes, that's correct, sir. And I said, reporters are telling us that, I don't know if it's true. I was careful about that because among other things, I wanted to be clear I didn't know Mr. Wilson. I don't know - I think I said. I don't know if he has a wife but this is what we're hearing.*

b. Testimony Given on or about March 24, 2004 Regarding Conversations With Reporters:

Q. And let me ask you this directly. Did the fact that you knew that the law could turn, the law as to whether a crime was committed, could turn on where you learned the information from, affect your account for the FBI when you told them that you were telling reporters Wilson's wife worked at the CIA but your source was a reporter rather than the Vice-President?

A. *No, it's a fact. It was a fact, that's what I told the reporters.*

Q. And you're, you're certain as you sit here today that every reporter you told that Wilson's wife worked at the CIA, you sourced it back to other reporters?

A. *Yes, sir,* because it was important for what I was saying and because it was - that's what - *that's how I did it.*

....

Q. The next set of questions from the Grand Jury are-concern this fact. If you did not understand the information about Wilson's wife to have been classified and didn't understand it when you heard it from Mr. Russert, why was it that you were so deliberate to make sure that you told other reporters that reporters were saying it and not assert it as something you knew?

A. I want - I didn't want to - I didn't know if it was true and I didn't want people - I didn't want the reporters to think it was true because I said it. I - *all I had was that reporters are telling us that, and by that I wanted them to understand it wasn't coming from me and that it might not be true.* Reporters write things that aren't true sometimes, or get things that aren't true. *So I allied to be clear they didn't, they didn't think it was me saying it. I didn't know it was true and I wanted them to understand that.* Also, it was important to me to let them know that because what I was telling them was that I don't know Mr. Wilson. We didn't ask for his mission. That I didn't see his report. *Basically we didn't know anything about him until this stuff came out in June. And among the other things, I didn't know he had a wife. That was one of the things I said to Mr. Cooper. I don't know if he's married. And so I wanted to be very clear about all this stuff that I didn't, I didn't know about him. And the only thing I had, I thought at the time, was what reporters are telling us.*

....

Well, talking to the other reporters about it, I don't see as a crime. What I said to the other reporters is what, you know - *I told a couple reporters what other reporters had told us,* and I don't see that as a crime.

3. In truth and fact, as LIBBY well knew when he gave this testimony, it was false in that LIBBY did not advise Matthew Cooper or other reporters that LIBBY had heard other reporters were saying that Wilson's wife worked for the CIA, nor did LIBBY advise Cooper or other reporters that LIBBY did not know whether this assertion was true;

7. Libby was alleged to have lied to the FBI and the grand jury not about who had first disclosed the fact that Valerie Plame worked as a CIA agent but rather what he said to the individual reporters and what they had said to him. Was these lies material to the grand jury's investigation?

The reporters contradicted Libby's testimony about their respective conversations with Libby. Ordinarily, a swearing contest between individuals, by itself, is not an adequate basis for proving perjury or false statement or obstruction. What more was required here? What else did the government need to prove in order to make out a strong case for the prosecution?

Why would Libby lie about something where reputable witnesses would be likely to contradict him?

Is there a difference between the allegations regarding perjury and the allegations regarding the false statement charge even though they relate to the same conversations? What accounts for the difference?

"Scooter" Libby was convicted by a jury verdict and sentenced to 30 months in prison. On July 2, 2007, President Bush commuted his sentence but did not pardon him so the felony conviction remains intact.

8. For an example of a case where a prosecution for a substantive offense failed and the government then pursued a perjury prosecution, see United States v. Benkhala, 437 F. Supp. 2d 541, 541-551 (E.D. Va. 2006). Defendant was first prosecuted for supplying services to the Taliban in Afghanistan by attending a jihad training camp there. Four witnesses testified at his trial about his participation in a jihad training camp, but only one of them stated that these activities occurred in Taliban-controlled territory. He was acquitted of the charge because of the absence of sufficient evidence linking these activities to the Taliban .

Subsequently, he was called twice to testify before a grand jury and in each instance testified that he did not participate in any training relevant to combat, fired any weapons, etc. Based on that testimony he was indicted for perjury. The court denied the defendant's motion to dismiss on collateral estoppal grounds since the prior acquittal had turned on the location of the training camp activities while in the perjury prosecution the location of his jihad training camp activities was irrelevant. The only question was whether he had testified falsely about not having participated in combat training.

Defendant also alleged that the grand jury investigation was a mere pretext to establish the foundation for a perjury prosecution-- that the government knew what his testimony would be before he was called to testify. The court ruled that as alleged in the indictment, the grand jury was conducting an investigation into the participation in and facilitation of jihad training camps in Afghanistan and Pakistan and the defendant was called to testify to identify individuals with a violent ideology against the United States who undertook combat training in furtherance of this end. The subject matter of the questions asked of the defendant in the grand jury was material to this investigation.

Further, the court stated,

Arguably, Petitioner's prior false statements provided the government with notice that he might testify falsely.... However this falls far short of proving that the government asked him to testify for the purpose of eliciting perjury....

CHAPTER 16

OBSTRUCTION OF JUSTICE: INTERFERENCE WITH WITNESSES

Page 763. Add to note 1.

In United States v. Quattrone, 441 F.3d 153 (2d Cir. 2006), the court overturned the conviction because of a failure to properly instruct on the nexus requirement. The trial court had charged the jury, "... if you find that either, A, the defendant directed he destruction of documents that were called for by a grand jury subpoena, or that B, defendant directed the destruction of documents that he had reason to believe were within the scope of the grand jury's investigation, then this nexus requirement will be satisfied." The appellate court concluded that "More is required; a defendant must know that his corrupt actions 'are likely to affect the ... proceeding." And, "Under our analysis, it would be sufficient to show that Quattrone knew that his actions were likely to affect the proceeding."

Also see United States v. Macari, 453 F.3d 926 (7th Cir. 2006), cert. denied, 127 S.Ct. 688 (2006): A grand jury investigating union activities had been ongoing for at least four years; the FBI was sporadically gathering and presenting evidence to this grand jury. Defendant was aware of this grand jury investigation when he advised a union member to lie about the union's criminal activities. There was some ambiguity in the facts regarding what the defendant had said to the union member. The union member testified that the defendant had told him that "if 'law enforcement' ever asked him... he was to deny it." A tape of the conversation included the union member's statement to the defendant, "Covelli was involved in the grand jury and Covelli got, you know, he's the second person this month," and the defendant then stating, "I think you should say you don't know nothing." The court construed the conversation as the defendant having instructed the witness to lie to the grand jury.

See United States v. Matthews, 505 F.3d 698 (7th Cir. 2007) where the charges were attempted obstruction and conspiracy to obstruct. The defendant contended that acts before he became aware of grand jury proceedings could not have furthered a conspiracy to impair the availability of the firearm for use in an official proceeding. However, under the statute the defendant could obstruct justice even before the judicial proceeding was ongoing, and the evidence permitted the conclusion that defendant thought judicial proceedings likely if he did not dispose of the firearm.

Page 771. Consider in connection with the paragraph preceding the Arthur Andersen case.

As noted, subsection (c) was added to § 1512 by the Sarbanes-Oxley Act. What specific changes in the crime of obstruction through document destruction were introduced by subsection (c)? In 2008, the penalty provisions applicable to § 1512 were amended. The penalties were generally increased. The specific changes were as follows:

Subsec. (a)(3)(A). Pub.L. 110-177, § 205(1)(A), rewrote subpar. (A), which formerly read: "**(A)** in the case of murder (as defined in section 1111), the death penalty or imprisonment for life, and in the case of any other killing, the punishment provided in section 1112." It now says: "in the case of a killing, the punishment provided in sections 1111 and 1112."

Subsec. (a)(3)(B). Pub.L. 110-177, § 205(1)(B), struck out "20 years" and inserted "30 years" in the matter following clause (ii).

Subsec. (a)(3)(C). Pub.L. 110-177, § 205(1)(C), struck out "10 years" and inserted "20 years".

Subsec. (b). Pub.L. 110-177, § 205(2), struck out "ten years" and inserted "20 years" in the undesignated matter at the end.

Subsec. (d). Pub.L. 110-177, § 205(3), struck out "one year" and inserted "3 years" in the undesignated matter at the end.

In addition, Sarbanes-Oxley added § 1519 which provides as follows:

§ 1519. Destruction, alteration, or falsification of records in Federal investigations and bankruptcy

Whoever knowingly alters, destroys, mutilates, conceals, covers up, falsifies, or makes a false entry in any record, document, or tangible object with the intent to impede, obstruct, or influence the investigation or proper administration of any matter within the jurisdiction of any department or agency of the United States or any case filed under title 11, or in relation to or contemplation of any such matter or case, shall be fined under this title, imprisoned not more than 20 years, or both.

If the Arthur Andersen LLP had been prosecuted under § 1519, what would have been the likely outcome? What is the relationship between §§ 1519 and 1512?

Page 776-777. Add to note 1

In United States v. Gotti, 459 F.3d 296 (2d Cir. 2006), the court ruled that the evidence was sufficient to permit the jury to conclude that the defendant had an improper purpose in "suggesting" to a witness (via a command to his stepfather over whom he had authority under the hierarchical structure of the Gambino Family) to plead the Fifth Amendment to ensure that witness did not implicate him.

Page 777. In connection with note 3.

For a case rejecting a challenge to jury instructions on the "nexus" issue in connection with a witness tampering charge under § 1512 (b)(1) see United States v. Darif, 446 F.3d 701 (7th Cir. 2006) (the district court's instruction was adequate because they made "clear to the jury that the witness tampering charge was related to 'a particular proceeding.'" See also United States v. Vampire Nation, 451 F.3d 189 (3d Cir. 2006) which involved a prosecution under § 1512 (b)(2). The Third Circuit held that the jury instructions were adequate under Arthur Andersen because the jury had been instructed that "that Banks could be found guilty of witness tampering only if he acted with the specific intent to induce [another person] to withhold evidence from an official proceeding."

Page 778. In connection with note 4.

In United States v. Ronda, 455 F.3d 1273 (11th Cir. 2006), on facts very similar to those in United States v. Veal, the Eleventh Circuit distinguished Arthur Andersen (which involved a prosecution under § 1512(b)(2)) and declined to apply it to convictions under § 1512(b)(3), reasoning that although Arthur Andersen required that "the acts of obstruction relate to 'an official proceeding,'" § 1512(b)(3) makes no mention of "an official proceeding." See also United States v. Byrne, 435 F.3d 16 (1st Cir. 2006), where the First Circuit declined to "resolve the exact contours of any nexus requirement in subsection (b)(3)," and rather deferred consideration "for a future case that requires resolution of that issue."

Page 778. Add as note 5 before C.

5. United States v. Reich, 479 F.3d 179 (2d Cir. 2007), involved, inter alia, a prosecution for obstruction under 18 U.S.C.§ 1512(c)(2). Defendant, a lawyer had commenced an arbitration proceeding against a brokerage firm that he alleged had mishandled his account. The brokerage firm filed a lawsuit seeking to enjoin Reich and other investors who had filed arbitration claims from arbitrating against it. The magistrate in the matter issued an order denying the brokerage firm's motion for a preliminary injunction staying arbitration. While the brokerage firm's mandamus application to the U.S. circuit court seeking to compel the magistrate to issue a ruling on its summary judgment motion was pending, the lawyer representing the brokerage firm received a faxed judicial order purporting to have been issued by the magistrate in the case. In response to this order, the attorney for the brokerage firm wrote a letter to the Second Circuit withdrawing his application for a writ of mandamus, since he understood the order to have been rendered moot. He also contacted the Chief Judge to inquire how he should proceed regarding other issues, and he circulated the order to various arbitration panels and attorneys representing the brokerage firm in other jurisdictions. This faxed order turned out to have been forged, and the evidence pointed toward it having emanated from defendant Reich's home. Regarding the obstruction count, the court stated:

> Reich challenges as insufficient the evidence supporting his conviction for obstruction of justice under 18 U.S.C. § 1512(c)(2), which subjects to criminal liability one who "corruptly ... obstructs, influences, or impedes any official proceeding, or attempts to do so." In *United States v. Aguilar,* 515 U.S. 593, 115 S.Ct. 2357, 132 L.Ed.2d 520 (1995), the Supreme Court construed the intent element of 18 U.S.C. § 1503, whose relevant language is substantially similar to the relevant language in 18 U.S.C. § 1512(c)(2), to include a "nexus requirement." ... To satisfy this requirement, the defendant's

conduct must "have a relationship in time, causation, or logic with the judicial proceedings"; in other words, "the endeavor must have the natural and probable effect of interfering with the due administration of justice." Reich concedes that the necessary nexus can exist when the discretionary actions of a third person are required to obstruct the judicial proceeding, but he alleges that the evidence adduced at trial failed to establish such a nexus because it was not foreseeable to Reich that the third party, [the lawyer for the brokerage firm] would act on the forged Order in such a way as to obstruct the judicial proceeding.

This Circuit has not previously applied *Aguilar's* nexus requirement to § 1512(c)(2). We have, however, applied it not only to § 1503, but also to 18 U.S.C. § 1505, which subjects to criminal liability one who "corruptly ... influences, obstructs, or impedes ... the due and proper administration of the law under which any pending proceeding is being had before any department or agency of the United States," *see United States v. Quattrone,* 441 F.3d 153, 174 (2d Cir.2006). The language of § 1505 is even more similar to § 1512(c)(2) than is § 1503, and given that the parties have not disputed *Aguilar's* application to § 1512(c)(2), there is no reason not to apply it.... Accordingly, we hold that § 1512(c)(2) incorporates a "nexus requirement" as articulated in *Aguilar.*

Reich has failed to show that the evidence was insufficient to establish a nexus between his actions and obstruction of the proceeding. ...Because the forged Order appeared to render moot ... [the brokerage firm's] application to the Second Circuit for a writ of mandamus, it was foreseeable that upon receiving the forged Order, ... [its lawyer] would withdraw the application, as he in fact did. In addition, because the forged Order expressly invited the parties to contact Chief Judge Korman regarding further proceedings, it was foreseeable that ...[he] would contact Chief Judge Korman, as he in fact did. This evidence is clearly sufficient to establish a "relationship in time, causation, or logic" between Reich's transmission of the forged Order and effects on the judicial proceeding, as *Aguilar* requires. Moreover, that relationship is much closer than those found insufficient in *Aguilar* ... where the defendant... merely made false statements to [an] agent... who might or might not later testify before a grand jury. It is also closer in time, causation, and logic than the relationship found sufficient in

Quattrone, where the defendant sent an email to his staff endorsing a suggestion to destroy documents that might eventually be subpoenaed by a grand jury. Here, by contrast, Reich directly injected a false order into ongoing litigation to which he was a party. The forged Order purported to enjoin a party from acting in an arbitration, directed the parties to contact Chief Judge Korman, and mooted a party's application before the Second Circuit, thereby inducing that party to withdraw it. ...

.Reich also claims that no "obstruction" occurred within the meaning of § 1512(c)(2) because there was no evidence that "the fairness or outcome of the ...lawsuit was affected in any way." He observes that unlike the language of § 1503, which contemplates action affecting the "due administration of justice," § 1512(c)(2) contemplates only actions affecting "any official proceeding." This difference, Reich contends, indicates Congress's intent not to criminalize under § 1512(c)(2) actions that impact the administration of justice but that do not "actually" affect the outcome of the official proceedings. This interpretation, however, is inconsistent with the plain language of the statute, which encompasses all actions that "corruptly ... influence[ ]" a proceeding-or even attempt to do so-not merely those that affect its ultimate outcome. Moreover, the injection of the forged Order into the ... lawsuit at the very least "influence[d]" the proceedings, in that it caused a litigant to withdraw a filing and contact a judge, and caused Magistrate Judge Mann to issue an order explaining the falsity of the forged Order and to convene a status conference to discuss it.

Page 780. Add to note 8.

A somewhat unusual set of facts prosecuted under the obstruction statute is United States v. Rand, 2007 WL 1029431 (7th Cir. 2007):

In the fall of 2001, Kalady was arrested for executing an identity fraud scheme in which he counterfeited U.S. birth certificates to obtain passports for illegal aliens. He was released on bond but confined to his home and monitored by an electronic bracelet around his ankle. Under the terms of his release, he had to remain within 500 feet of his residence unless he had permission from a Pretrial Services officer to go beyond that distance. Kalady's arraignment was delayed due to problems with his health, but it was ultimately scheduled for December 6, 2001.

Kalady was a huge man, weighing in at 450 pounds, and he suffered serious health problems as a result of his weight. Like most all defendants facing federal criminal charges, he did not want to go to prison. So in November 2001, as the date for his arraignment drew close, he told his brother, Michael, that he wanted to fake his own death so he could get out of his predicament. Kalady's plan, ultimately, was to kill another person and use the corpse as a double for himself.

Kalady discussed his plan with Rand, who had previously lived with him. During the discussion, Kalady told Rand to "get a homeless guy, kill him, and pretend that he's me." Kalady also asked Rand to find a homeless man who looked like Kalady, someone who visited "soup kitchens or missions" so Kalady could use the body to "replace" his own. Kalady suggested that Rand go to places where "bums go" since they didn't have families looking after them. Rand agreed to find someone Kalady could use to pull off his scheme.

...

Rand was charged and went to trial on two counts. Count 1 charged him with aiding and abetting Kalady in the murder of White, under § 1512(a)(1)(C). The statute provides:

> Whoever kills ... another person, with intent to ... prevent the communication by any person to a law enforcement officer or judge of the United States of information relating to the commission or possible commission of a Federal offense or a violation of conditions of ... release pending judicial proceedings; shall be punished [according to law].

A jury found Rand guilty..... He was sentenced to a life term on the first count .... His appeal is limited to challenging his conviction on the first count.

The government's theory of the case was that Kalady, aided and abetted by Rand, killed White intending to prevent a Pretrial Services officer from communicating to the court that he violated his conditions of release by leaving his house. Rand argues that § 1512 does not apply to these facts-it is plainly addressed, he says, to what is commonly understood to be witness tampering. He argues that because White was not "a

213

witness, victim or informant," his killing by Kalady is not a violation of the statute.

...

Kalady clearly murdered White and, viewing the evidence in the light most favorable to the government, Rand clearly aided and abetted that nefarious act. But did Rand violate § 1512? We think the answer is "yes."

Rand argues that the statute, on these facts, only prohibits the killing of victims, witnesses, and informants, and because White does not fall into any of these categories, his killing does not fit under the statute. This argument, we think, ignores the plain language of the statute.

...

Count 1 of the indictment against Rand tracked the language of § 1512(a)(1)(C). It charges that Rand (with Michael Kalady and others) aided and abetted the violation:

> with the intent to prevent the communication by a United States Pretrial Services Officer to a law enforcement officer and judge of the United States of information relating to the commission and possible commission of a Federal offense and a violation of defendant Joseph Kalady's conditions of release pending judicial proceedings, which killing was a murder in the first degree, as defined in Title 18, United States Code, Section 1111.

We believe that a plain reading of § 1512(a)(1)(C) demonstrates that the murder victim does not have to be a witness or an informant. The statute makes it a federal crime to kill or attempt to kill " *another person* "-regardless of who that person is-in order to prevent the communication of information by *"any person"* to the court. The statute does not only provide that it is a federal crime to kill another person in order to prevent *that* person from communicating information to the court.

Page 781. Add as note 10.

Numerous cases involve attempts to get a witness to lie or withhold information but without the use of threats or intimidation. See, e.g., U.S. v. LaShay, 417 F.3d 715 (7th Cir. 2005) (defendant repeated urged witness to "remember" certain facts);

U.S. v. Lucas, 499 F.3d 769 (8th Cir. 2007) (defendant asked two people to claim ownership of firearm found in his apartment); U.S. v. Tampas, 2007 WL 2126807 (11th Cir. 2007) (defendant asked accountant to create spread sheet attributing two years' worth of contractor's receipts to jobs performed by contractor for company).

There are also numerous cases where threats or intimidation were utilized to get the witness to lie or withhold information. See, e.g., U.S. v. Matthews, 431 F.3d 1296 (11th Cir. 2005)(defendant reminded witness that one can never predict exact time of one's death and advised another witness that defendant had a lot of friends in prison in which the witness was incarcerated); United States v. Hoskins, 164 Fed. Appx. 602 (9th Cir. 2006) (cover letter defendant sent to witness contained a contextually ominous statement that defendant was sending it "in case anything happens to you in the future. Let's hope that's not the case").

Page 786. Add to note 1.

For a recent case holding that witness tampering can still be pursued under 18 U.S.C. § 1503 even after the enactment of § 1512, see United States v. LeMoure, 474 F.3d 37 (1st Cir. 2007). LeMoure also ruled that the defendant could be convicted of both the § 1503 and § 1512 offenses under the doctrine of Blockburger v. United States, 284 U.S. 299 (1932).

CHAPTER 17

The Choice Between Federal or State Prosecution, or Duplicative Prosecutions

Pages 795-99.

The recent federal prosecution of Michael Vick, then a star NFL quarterback for the Atlanta Falcons, makes an interesting case to test the factors that determine whether there will be a federal or state prosecution, and then whether there will be a second prosecution in the other jurisdiction.

Vick was charged in 2007 with conspiracy to violate the Travel Act and animal fighting laws, 7 U.S.C. § 2156(a)(1) and § 2156(b). He and his co-conspirators purchased pit bulls in interstate commerce, then trained them to fight against other pit bulls, both at Vick's Virginia property and in other states. Stakes in these fights ran as high as thousands of dollars, and weaker dogs were apparently brutally executed by hanging and drowning. Vick pled guilty to these charges and was sentenced to 23 months imprisonment.

Considering the factors described in the main text, what was the federal interest in prosecuting Vick? Given Vick's celebrity status, is this just an example of the big case factor, with federal prosecutors seeking the limelight? Or are there reasons for a federal prosecution? Note that elements of the case clearly involved more than one jurisdiction, so that the federal courts' national service of process could have been important. Many of the dogs traveled in interstate commerce. Moreover, fights at Vick's Virginia property presumably drew the owners of out-of-state dogs, who bet significant sums of money against the pit bulls fighting for Vick's "Bad Newz Kennels."

A month after Vick's federal sentencing, state prosecutors in Virginia indicted Vick on cruelty to animals and dogfighting charges. A trial date is set for June 2008, and Vick's attorneys are likely to raise double jeopardy concerns. Although Virginia and the United States are clearly separate sovereigns under the dual

217

sovereignty doctrine, a Virginia statute provides that "if the same act be a violation of both a state and a federal statute, a prosecution under the federal statute shall be a bar to a prosecution under the state statute." Va. Code Ann. § 19.2-294. The materials later in this chapter consider the constitutional and statutory limitations on duplicative prosecutions.

Page 807. *Insert as a new note at the end of note 2.*

Sometimes cases that should be in state court end up on the federal docket. Other cases that seem, on their face, to call for federal prosecution end up in state court. For example, in May 2008, 125 suspects, including 95 students, were arrested in connection with a major drug investigation at San Diego State University. In breaking up a large drug ring, police seized $60,000 cash, fifty pounds of marijuana, handguns, and other drugs.

There was substantial federal involvement in the case, and the facts seem to favor federal charges. Campus police began the investigation when a student died after using cocaine and alcohol, but they soon sought federal support. The DEA launched a five-month sting operation called Operation Sudden Fall, in which federal agents posed as students to purchase drugs from numerous dealers. The DEA's lengthy investigation made the case. There were guns involved, and the drug ring operated near a college – in fact, the dealers catered to students. Moreover, one of the non-student suspects allegedly had ties to the Mexican Mafia gang.

Despite all of the federal involvement, the defendants were prosecuted on state charges, and we wondered why. A cynic might posit the authorities perceived college drug dealers differently than young, inner city gang members, and were less inclined to subject them to the more serious penalties available in federal court. But it seems likely that the caseload pressures in the Southern District of California played a significant role. In 2007, the Southern District of California was the fourth busiest district in the country, behind the Western District of Texas, the Southern District of Texas, and the District of Arizona. All are border districts, where prosecutions involving fast-tracked deportation proceedings may limit prosecutors' ability to bring drug cases that would typically merit federal attention.

Treating college students differently than inner city gang members seems unfair, and at first blush caseload pressures seem like a much more satisfactory rational for bringing the cases to state court. Moreover, caseload pressures are a constant factor in the exercise of prosecutorial discretion. But is it really desirable to treat drug traffickers in San Diego differently than those in Iowa, based only on each district's caseload? Should an Iowan get a harsher federal sentence than someone who did precisely the same thing in Southern California?

Pages 818-20. Add to Note 2.

The excerpt from Professor Guerra suggests that multijurisdictional drug task forces warrant reconsideration of the dual sovereignty doctrine, because it is no longer accurate to say that the federal and state sovereigns are operating independently. Two recent drug cases illustrate both the interdependence of the federal and state charges and the unwillingness of the federal courts to question the dual sovereignty doctrine or to apply the sham exception to that doctrine.

United States v. Barrett, 496 F.3d 1079 (10th Cir. 2007), arose out of a bloody confrontation that ensued when state officers attempted to serve an arrest warrant and a search warrant for a methamphetamine lab. The federal charges included intentionally killing a state law enforcement officer during the commission of a violent drug felony, 21 U.S.C. § 848(e)(1)(B). Because Barrett owned several guns and had previously threatened "to kill the first cop through the door" in the event of a raid, the drug task force sought the aid of the Oklahoma Highway Patrol's Tactical Team to handle the raid. Barrett, tipped off that a suspected police vehicle was approaching, vowed to go out in a blaze of glory. Before the police reached Barrett's door, he opened fire with a Colt Sporter .223 rifle, spewing bullets from three magazines taped together. One officer was killed when a bullet pierced his aorta as he scrambled for safety behind his vehicle. After Barrett wounded another officer in the shoulder, he was shot and taken into custody.

Both federal and state officials investigated the crime scene. Oklahoma State Bureau of Investigation agents investigated with a new warrant issued after the shooting, while federal Drug Enforcement Administration task force agents searched pursuant to the original warrant.

The state took the lead in prosecuting Barrett, charging him with first degree murder, shooting with intent to kill, and two counts of discharging a firearm with intent to kill. His first trial resulted in a hung jury, and the second jury found him guilty only of lesser charges: first-degree manslaughter (rather than murder) and assault and battery with a dangerous weapon (rather than shooting with intent to kill). Barrett was acquitted of discharging a firearm with intent to kill. He was sentenced to twenty years and ten years, to be served consecutively. In both state trials, Barrett argued that he acted in self-defense, claiming that he did not know he was firing on law enforcement officers.

The federal indictment was filed a few months after the end of the second state trial. A federal jury convicted Barrett on three counts, and he received life sentences on two counts and a death sentence on the § 848(e)(1)(B) count. The court of appeals rejected Barrett's double jeopardy arguments, reasoning that regardless of their collaboration, the federal government and the State of Oklahoma are separate sovereigns, and concluding that the federal prosecution was not a "sham." Indeed, the court observed, there was less collaboration between federal and state authorities in this case than in *Bartkus*.

As you think about the application of the dual sovereignty doctrine, you should also ask why federal charges were brought against Barrett and what *federal* interest the prosecutors thought they were vindicating. There's nothing in the public record explaining this, so we can only speculate. Does the federal government have a general interest in punishing someone who kills a *state* law enforcement officer? If not, does it have an interest when the state officials are enforcing *state* drug laws, given the overlap between state and federal law? Or is there a federal interest only when the operation in question is carried out jointly, so that federal as well as state officials are endangered? If there were no federal officials involved in the melee at Barrett's home, does the federal government have a separate sovereign interest in the murder prosecution?

Page 820-21. Insert at the end of note 3.

In *United States v. Vanhoesen*, 529 F. Supp. 2d 358, (N.D.N.Y. 2008), federal drug charges against two brothers were brought only when state charges hit procedural hurdles. Both brothers claimed – unsuccessfully – that their cases fell within the sham exception to dual sovereignty. The first federal charges against Raymond Vanhoesen were filed after state charges for possession and sale of crack cocaine were dismissed based on the right to a speedy trial. When a state appellate court reversed the trial court's speedy trial decision, federal prosecutors dropped the initial federal charges. When the state charges were dismissed on a different ground, federal charges were refiled, and the court rejected Raymond's double jeopardy objection. Although the timing of the prosecutions might show that they were interrelated, it did not establish the federal prosecution as a sham. Federal prosecutors have a legitimate interest in the result of a state trial; "'a federal prosecutor may, in deciding whether to pursue a subsequent prosecution, take into consideration what he deems an inadequate result obtained in the state trial.'"

Federal charges against Raymond's brother Jermaine Vanhoesen were filed after the state appellate court reversed his conviction and remanded for a new trial. At the time the federal charges were filed, Jermaine was considering the state's offer of a plea agreement requiring a term of 5 to 10 years of imprisonment. Federal prosecutors offered to drop the federal charges if Jermaine pled guilty to the state charges and received a sentence of at least seven and a half years imprisonment. The state prosecutors then changed the terms of their offer to match the federal deal, and when Jermaine declined to plead guilty, the state charges were dropped. Jermaine moved to dismiss the federal indictment, arguing that the federal prosecution fell within the sham exception to the dual sovereignty doctrine. The court rejected his argument, holding that the federal prosecutors did not sufficiently control the state prosecution to make the federal prosecution a sham.

Page 822. *Insert at the end of Note 4.*

What if someone prosecuted in a foreign country is later charged by federal prosecutors for the same conduct? A foreign country would clearly seem to be a separate sovereign for double jeopardy purposes. But states with their own limitations on successive prosecutions may treat foreign countries differently than other domestic jurisdictions.

For example, a California statute prohibits prosecution when the defendant was already acquitted or convicted of a charge "under the laws of the United States, or of another state or territory of the United States based upon the act or omission in respect to which he or she is on trial." Cal. Penal Code § 656. Before this section was amended in 2004, however, it extended to prosecutions in foreign countries.

This amendment may play a major role in the legal battle over a 27-year-old murder mystery. In 1981, Kazumi Miura was walking with her husband, Kazuyoshi, in a Los Angeles parking lot when someone opened fire from a passing car, hitting Kazumi in the head and Kazuyoshi in the leg. After Jimmy Sakoda, known as the "samurai detective" in the LAPD, convinced the district attorney that Mr. Miura planned the shooting, the DA's office aided Japanese authorities in an investigation. In 1994, a Japanese court convicted Mr. Miura for his involvement, but in 1998 the Tokyo High Court reversed the conviction on evidentiary grounds.

Then, in 2008, authorities used a 1988 warrant to arrest Mr. Miura in the Northern Mariana Islands, a U.S. commonwealth territory. Los Angeles prosecutors hope to try him under California law, but Mark Geragos, Miura's attorney, has argued that the state's double jeopardy statute was amended after Miura was cleared in Japan. Therefore, Geragos claims, the California prosecution should be dismissed. Note that if the state charges are dismissed, there may be pressure to come up with a federal charge that would reach Miura.

CHAPTER 18

THE SENTENCING GUIDELINES

Delete pages 869-891 and substitute the following:

Notes

1. *Booker* transformed the Guidelines from mandatory to advisory standards that must be "considered" by the sentencing courts, subject to appellate review for reasonableness. In his dissenting opinion Justice Scalia noted the irony of a remedial choice that "in order to rescue from nullification a statutory scheme designed to eliminate discretionary sentencing, discards the provisions that eliminate discretionary sentencing." In Justice Breyer's view, making the Guidelines only advisory was the cost of preserving "real offense" sentencing. The system can no longer *require* a judge to increase a defendant's sentence on the basis of facts not proven to a jury beyond a reasonable doubt. However, consideration of relevant facts beyond just the elements of the offense or the issues presented to the jury helps to ensure that similarly situated defendants receive similar sentences. The remedial majority opinion preserves "real offense" sentencing by concluding that the Guidelines just *recommend* an increase on the basis of those facts, which does not violate the Fifth or Sixth Amendments.

Look again at the analysis of the remedial opinion. A great deal of Justice Breyer's argument turns on the importance of preserving "real offense" sentencing. It's important to understand what he meant, and why he thought it was so important to preserve real offense sentencing, even though the cost was making the Guidelines only advisory.

The Guidelines definition of "relevant conduct" incorporates more than just the elements of the offense, looking at many characteristics of the "real offense" that are not part of the statutory definition of the offense. Sometimes this means facts that were never presented to a jury–or even included in the indictment–but note that this can and does go even further. Indeed, *United States v. Watts*, 519 U.S. 148 (1997) (per curiam), held that it was proper to increase the defendants' Guidelines offense levels on the basis of the judges' finding, by a preponderance of the evidence, that the defendants had committed drug and weapons offenses of which their juries had just *acquitted* them, because the actions in question were part of the "real offenses" of which the juries did convict them. Many people find that shocking. But in Justice Breyer's view, if a defendant did use a gun or traffic in large quantities of a drug, it's vital to consider those facts at sentencing to insure that truly similar cases receive similar sentences–even if that issue was never presented to a jury, or the proof that was presented fell short of the reasonable doubt standard, but is enough to meet the preponderance standard. The central insight of the merits opinion, however, is that a defendant is entitled to have a jury determine, beyond a reasonable doubt, whether he did use a gun or traffic in larger quantities of a drug (and so forth) before these facts can provide a basis for an increase in his sentence. The system can't require a judge to increase a defendant's sentence on the basis of such facts without the usual procedural safeguards of trial by jury or proof beyond a reasonable doubt.

The remedial majority preserves real offense sentencing but avoids trial by jury and proof beyond a reasonable doubt by concluding that the Guidelines no longer *require* an increase in the defendant's sentence based on the judge's finding that he possessed a gun or was involved in a larger transaction. They just recommend an increase on the basis of those facts. The remedial majority argues that's what judges were doing before the passage of the Guidelines, and nothing in the Fifth or Sixth Amendments is offended by this traditional practice.

Does *Booker*'s reading of the Sixth Amendment undermine *Watts*? That depends on how far the courts are willing to extend the distinction drawn in the remedial portion of *Booker*. Can a decision predicated on the right to have a jury determine critical sentencing facts be squared with increasing the defendant's sentence on facts the jury plainly rejected? The Sixth Circuit, sitting en banc, has heard argument in a case challenging the constitutionality of using acquitted conduct to determine a sentence under the advisory guideline regime. *United States v. White*, 503 F.3d 487 (6th Cir. 2007).

2. After *Booker*, the lower courts took very different approaches to the key question of what it means to "consider" the Guidelines. At the one end of the spectrum, some courts concluded that the Guidelines should be given heavy weight, because following the traditional departure methodology was necessary to minimize

unwarranted sentencing disparity arising from judicial discretion. At the other end of the spectrum, some courts concluded that *Booker* gave primacy not to the Guidelines, but to § 3553(a) (reprinted text at 863-64), which requires the court to "impose a sentence sufficient, but not greater than necessary, to comply with" a list of statutory purposes.

The Supreme Court has now resolved some of the issues raised by *Booker*. In *Rita v. United States*, 127 S.Ct. 2456 (2007), the Court held that courts of appeals may--but need not--apply a presumption of reasonableness to sentences within the Guidelines range. However, *Rita* made it clear that under *Booker* courts may *not* adopt a presumption of *un*reasonableness for all sentences outside of the Guidelines range. That would come too close to making the Guidelines mandatory.

Next, in the case that follows, the Court turned to the question of whether the justification required for a non-Guideline *Booker* sentence must be proportional to the size of the variance, with a very large variance requiring an exceptional justification.

GALL V. UNITED STATES, 128 S.CT. 586 (2007)
Justice STEVENS delivered the opinion of the Court.

* * * *

We now hold that, while the extent of the difference between a particular sentence and the recommended Guidelines range is surely relevant, courts of appeals must review all sentences-whether inside, just outside, or significantly outside the Guidelines range-under a deferential abuse-of-discretion standard. We also hold that the sentence imposed by the experienced District Judge in this case was reasonable.

* * * *

[Brian Gall joined a drug trafficking operation while in his second year at the University of Iowa. He netted about $30,000 for delivering drugs. Just a few months after joining the conspiracy Gall stopped using drugs, and soon thereafter he withdrew from the conspiracy as well. He graduated from college, moved out of state, and became a master carpenter. He used no illegal drugs after leaving college. Three and a half years after he left the conspiracy, he was indicted in federal court for conspiracy to distribute ecstasy, cocaine and marijuana. Gall, who admitted his participation, surrendered to authorities and while awaiting the outcome of his case started a prosperous window installation business. He entered into a plea agreement that reflected these facts. Gall's presentencing report recommended 30 to 37 months imprisonment.

Noting his reliance on § 3553(a), the district judge sentenced Gall to only 36 months probation. The court found that this sentence was "sufficient, but not greater than necessary to serve the purposes of sentencing." The key factors upon which the judge based his decision were Gall's age at the time of the offense and his post offense conduct, particularly his withdrawal from the conspiracy, his graduation from college, and his employment and work history. The court also emphasized that Gall would face a substantial restriction in his liberty, strict reporting requirements, and regular alcohol and drug testing.

The Court of Appeals reversed Gall's sentence, holding that a departure from the Guideline sentence range must be accompanied by a proportionately strong justification. Here, the downward variance was 100 %: Gall got zero prison time, although the Guidelines recommended at least 30 months. The Eighth Circuit held that the district judge's explanation did not justify such a drastic departure.]

III

In *Booker* we invalidated both the statutory provision, 18 U.S.C. § 3553(b)(1) (2000 ed., Supp. IV), which made the Sentencing Guidelines mandatory, and § 3742(e) (2000 ed. and Supp. IV), which directed appellate courts to apply a *de novo* standard of review to departures from the Guidelines. As a result of our decision, the Guidelines are now advisory, and appellate review of sentencing decisions is limited to determining whether they are "reasonable." Our explanation of "reasonableness" review in the *Booker* opinion made it pellucidly clear that the familiar abuse-of-discretion standard of review now applies to appellate review of sentencing decisions.

It is also clear that a district judge must give serious consideration to the extent of any departure from the Guidelines and must explain his conclusion that an unusually lenient or an unusually harsh sentence is appropriate in a particular case with sufficient justifications. For even though the Guidelines are advisory rather than mandatory, they are, as we pointed out in *Rita*, the product of careful study based on extensive empirical evidence derived from the review of thousands of individual sentencing decisions.

In reviewing the reasonableness of a sentence outside the Guidelines range, appellate courts may therefore take the degree of variance into account and consider the extent of a deviation from the Guidelines. We reject, however, an appellate rule that requires "extraordinary" circumstances to justify a sentence outside the Guidelines range. We also reject the use of a rigid mathematical formula that uses the percentage of a departure as the standard for determining the strength of the justifications required for a specific sentence.

As an initial matter, the approaches we reject come too close to creating an impermissible presumption of unreasonableness for sentences outside the Guidelines range. Even the Government has acknowledged that such a presumption would not be consistent with *Booker*.

The mathematical approach also suffers from infirmities of application. On one side of the equation, deviations from the Guidelines range will always appear more extreme-in percentage terms-when the range itself is low, and a sentence of probation will always be a 100% departure regardless of whether the Guidelines range is 1 month or 100 years. Moreover, quantifying the variance as a certain percentage of the maximum, minimum, or median prison sentence recommended by the Guidelines gives no weight to the "substantial restriction of freedom" involved in a term of supervised release or probation.

We recognize that custodial sentences are qualitatively more severe than probationary sentences of equivalent terms. Offenders on probation are nonetheless subject to several standard conditions that substantially restrict their liberty. Probationers may not leave the judicial district, move, or change jobs without notifying, and in some cases receiving permission from, their probation officer or the court. They must report regularly to their probation officer, permit unannounced visits to their homes, refrain from associating with any person convicted of a felony, and refrain from excessive drinking. USSG § 5B1.3. Most probationers are also subject to individual "special conditions" imposed by the court. Gall, for instance, may not patronize any establishment that derives more than 50% of its revenue from the sale of alcohol, and must submit to random drug tests as directed by his probation officer.

Most importantly, both the exceptional circumstances requirement and the rigid mathematical formulation reflect a practice-common among courts that have adopted "proportional review"-of applying a heightened standard of review to sentences outside the Guidelines range. This is inconsistent with the rule that the abuse-of-discretion standard of review applies to appellate review of all sentencing decisions-whether inside or outside the Guidelines range.

As we explained in *Rita,* a district court should begin all sentencing proceedings by correctly calculating the applicable Guidelines range. As a matter of administration and to secure nationwide consistency, the Guidelines should be the starting point and the initial benchmark. The Guidelines are not the only consideration, however. Accordingly, after giving both parties an opportunity to argue for whatever sentence they deem appropriate, the district judge should then consider all of the § 3553(a) factors to determine whether they support the sentence requested by a party. In so doing, he may not presume that the Guidelines range is reasonable. He must make an individualized assessment based on the facts presented. If he decides that an outside-Guidelines sentence is warranted, he must consider the extent of the deviation and ensure that the justification is sufficiently compelling to support the degree of the variance. We find it uncontroversial that a major departure should be supported by a more significant justification than a minor one. After settling on the appropriate sentence, he must adequately explain the chosen sentence to allow for meaningful appellate review and to promote the perception of fair sentencing.

Regardless of whether the sentence imposed is inside or outside the Guidelines range, the appellate court must review the sentence under an abuse-of-discretion standard. It must first ensure that the district court committed no significant procedural error, such as failing to calculate (or improperly calculating) the Guidelines range, treating the Guidelines as mandatory, failing to consider the § 3553(a) factors, selecting a sentence based on clearly erroneous facts, or failing to adequately explain the chosen sentence-including an explanation for any deviation from the Guidelines range. Assuming that the district court's sentencing decision is procedurally sound, the appellate court should then consider the substantive reasonableness of the sentence imposed under an abuse-of-discretion standard. When conducting this review, the court will, of course, take into account the totality of the circumstances, including the extent of any variance from the Guidelines range. If the sentence is within the Guidelines range, the appellate court may, but is not required to, apply a presumption of reasonableness. But if the sentence is outside the Guidelines range, the court may not apply a presumption of unreasonableness. It may consider the extent of the deviation, but must give due deference to the district court's decision that the § 3553(a) factors, on a whole, justify the extent of the variance. The fact that the appellate court might reasonably have concluded that a different sentence was appropriate is insufficient to justify reversal of the district court.

Practical considerations also underlie this legal principle. "The sentencing judge is in a superior position to find facts and judge their import under § 3553(a) in the individual case. The judge sees and hears the evidence, makes credibility determinations, has full knowledge of the facts and gains insights not conveyed by the record." "The sentencing judge has access to, and greater familiarity with, the individual case and the individual defendant before him than the Commission or the appeals court." *Rita,* 127 S.Ct., at 2469. Moreover, "[d]istrict courts have an institutional advantage over appellate courts in making these sorts of determinations, especially as they see so many more Guidelines sentences than appellate courts do."[2]

"It has been uniform and constant in the federal judicial tradition for the sentencing judge to consider every convicted person as an individual and every case as a unique study in the human failings that sometimes mitigate, sometimes magnify, the crime and the punishment to ensue." The uniqueness of the individual case, however, does not change the deferential abuse-of-discretion standard of review that applies to all sentencing decisions. As we shall now explain, the opinion of the Court of Appeals in this case does not reflect the requisite deference and

---

[2]District judges sentence, on average, 117 defendants every year. Administrative Office of United States Courts, 2006 Federal Court Management Statistics 167. The District Judge in this case, Judge Pratt, has sentenced over 990 offenders over the course of his career. Only a relatively small fraction of these defendants appeal their sentence on reasonableness grounds. See *Koon,* 518 U.S., at 98, 116 S.Ct. 2035 ("In 1994, for example, 93.9% of Guidelines cases were not appealed"); *Likens,* 464 F.3d, at 827, n. 1 (Bright, J., dissenting) (noting that the District Judge had sentenced hundreds of defendants and that "[w]e have reviewed only a miniscule number of those cases"); cf. United States Sentencing Commission, 2006 Sourcebook of Federal Sentencing Statistics 135-152.

does not support the conclusion that the District Court abused its discretion.

IV

As an initial matter, we note that the District Judge committed no significant procedural error. He correctly calculated the applicable Guidelines range, allowed both parties to present arguments as to what they believed the appropriate sentence should be, considered all of the § 3553(a) factors, and thoroughly documented his reasoning. The Court of Appeals found that the District Judge erred in failing to give proper weight to the seriousness of the offense, as required by § 3553(a)(2)(A), and failing to consider whether a sentence of probation would create unwarranted disparities, as required by 3553(a)(6). We disagree.

Section 3553(a)(2)(A) requires judges to consider "the need for the sentence imposed ... to reflect the seriousness of the offense, to promote respect for the law, and to provide just punishment for the offense." The Court of Appeals concluded that "the district court did not properly weigh the seriousness of Gall's offense" because it "ignored the serious health risks ecstasy poses." Contrary to the Court of Appeals' conclusion, the District Judge plainly did consider the seriousness of the offense. ("The Court, however, is bound to impose a sentence that reflects the seriousness of joining a conspiracy to distribute MDMA or ecstasy"). It is true that the District Judge did not make specific reference to the (unquestionably significant) health risks posed by ecstasy, but the prosecutor did not raise ecstasy's effects at the sentencing hearing. Had the prosecutor raised the issue, specific discussion of the point might have been in order, but it was not incumbent on the District Judge to raise every conceivably relevant issue on his own initiative.

The Government's legitimate concern that a lenient sentence for a serious offense threatens to promote disrespect for the law is at least to some extent offset by the fact that seven of the eight defendants in this case have been sentenced to significant prison terms. Moreover, the unique facts of Gall's situation provide support for the District Judge's conclusion that, in Gall's case, "a sentence of imprisonment may work to promote not respect, but derision, of the law if the law is viewed as merely a means to dispense harsh punishment without taking into account the real conduct and circumstances involved in sentencing."

Section 3553(a)(6) requires judges to consider "the need to avoid unwarranted sentence disparities among defendants with similar records who have been found guilty of similar conduct." The Court of Appeals stated that "the record does not show that the district court considered whether a sentence of probation would result in unwarranted disparities." As with the seriousness of the offense conduct, avoidance of unwarranted disparities was clearly considered by the Sentencing Commission when setting the Guidelines ranges. Since the District Judge correctly calculated and carefully reviewed the Guidelines range, he necessarily gave significant weight and consideration to the need to avoid unwarranted disparities.

Moreover, as we understand the colloquy between the District Judge and the AUSA, it seems that the judge gave specific attention to the issue of disparity when he inquired about the sentences already imposed by a different judge on two of Gall's codefendants. * * * *

From these facts, it is perfectly clear that the District Judge considered the need to avoid unwarranted disparities, but also considered the need to avoid unwarranted *similarities* among other co-conspirators who were not similarly situated. The District Judge regarded Gall's voluntary withdrawal as a reasonable basis for giving him a less severe sentence than the three codefendants discussed with the AUSA, who neither withdrew from the conspiracy nor rehabilitated themselves as Gall had done. We also note that neither the Court of Appeals nor the Government has called our attention to a comparable defendant who received a more severe sentence.

Since the District Court committed no procedural error, the only question for the Court of Appeals was whether the sentence was reasonable- *i.e.,* whether the District Judge abused his discretion in determining that the 3553(a) factors supported a sentence of probation and justified a substantial deviation from the Guidelines range. As we shall now explain, the sentence was reasonable. The Court of Appeals' decision to the contrary was incorrect and failed to demonstrate the requisite deference to the District Judge's decision.

V

The Court of Appeals gave virtually no deference to the District Court's decision that the § 3553(a) factors justified a significant variance in this case. Although the Court of Appeals correctly stated that the appropriate standard of review was abuse of discretion, it engaged in an analysis that more closely resembled *de novo* review of the facts presented and determined that, in its view, the degree of variance was not warranted.

The Court of Appeals thought that the District Court "gave too much weight to Gall's withdrawal from the conspiracy because the court failed to acknowledge the significant benefit Gall received from being subject to the 1999 Guidelines." This criticism is flawed in that it ignores the critical relevance of Gall's voluntary withdrawal, a circumstance that distinguished his conduct not only from that of all his codefendants, but from the vast majority of defendants convicted of conspiracy in federal court.

The Court of Appeals thought the District Judge "gave significant weight to an improper factor" when he compared Gall's sale of ecstasy when he was a 21-year-old adult to the "impetuous and ill-considered" actions of persons under the age of 18. The appellate court correctly observed that the studies cited by the District Judge do not explain how Gall's "specific behavior in the instant case was impetuous or ill-considered."

In that portion of his sentencing memorandum, however, the judge was discussing the "character of the defendant," not the nature of his offense. He noted that Gall's criminal history included a ticket for underage drinking when he was 18 years old and possession of marijuana that was contemporaneous with his offense in this case. In summary, the District Judge observed that all of Gall's criminal history "including the present offense, occurred when he was twenty-one-years old or younger" and appeared "to stem from his addictions to drugs and alcohol." The District Judge appended a long footnote to his discussion of Gall's immaturity. The footnote includes an excerpt from our opinion in *Roper v. Simmons,* 543 U.S. 551, 569 (2005), which quotes a study stating that a lack of maturity and an undeveloped sense of responsibility are qualities that " 'often result in impetuous and ill-considered actions.' " * * * Given the dramatic contrast between Gall's behavior before he joined the conspiracy and his conduct after withdrawing, it was not unreasonable for the District Judge to view Gall's immaturity at the time of the offense as a mitigating factor, and his later behavior as a sign that he had matured and would not engage in such impetuous and ill-considered conduct in the future. Indeed, his consideration of that factor finds support in our cases.

Finally, the Court of Appeals thought that, even if Gall's rehabilitation was dramatic and permanent, a sentence of probation for participation as a middleman in a conspiracy distributing 10,000 pills of ecstasy "lies outside the range of choice dictated by the facts of the case." If the Guidelines were still mandatory, and assuming the facts did not justify a Guidelines-based downward departure, this would provide a sufficient basis for setting aside Gall's sentence because the Guidelines state that probation alone is not an appropriate sentence for comparable offenses. But the Guidelines are not mandatory, and thus the "range of choice dictated by the facts of the case" is significantly broadened. Moreover, the Guidelines are only one of the factors to consider when imposing sentence, and § 3553(a)(3) directs the judge to consider sentences other than imprisonment.

The District Court quite reasonably attached great weight to Gall's self-motivated rehabilitation, which was undertaken not at the direction of, or under supervision by, any court, but on his own initiative. This also lends strong support to the conclusion that imprisonment was not necessary to deter Gall from engaging in future criminal conduct or to protect the public from his future criminal acts. See 18 U.S.C. §§ 3553(a)(2)(B), (C).

The Court of Appeals clearly disagreed with the District Judge's conclusion that consideration of the § 3553(a) factors justified a sentence of probation; it believed that the circumstances presented here were insufficient to sustain such a marked deviation from the Guidelines range. But it is not for the Court of Appeals to decide *de novo* whether the justification for a variance is sufficient or the sentence reasonable. On abuse-of-discretion review, the Court of Appeals should have given due deference to the District Court's reasoned and reasonable decision that the § 3553(a) factors, on the whole, justified the sentence. Accordingly, the judgment of the Court of Appeals is reversed.

It is so ordered.

The concurring opinions of Justices Scalia and Souter and the dissenting opinions of Justices Thomas and Alito have been omitted.

What is the combined effect of *Booker, Rita, and Gall*? Here are some of the key questions, which are discussed in the notes that follow:

- How much discretion do district courts now have in sentencing individual offenders? And what are they doing with this discretion?

- Can a judge vary from the Guidelines range because she disagrees with the Commission on some policy judgment, such as the relative seriousness of crack cocaine?

- Can a judge vary from the Guidelines range to offset the effects of other institutional features of the Guidelines, such as the availability of downward departures for defendants who provide "substantial assistance" to the government by testifying against others?

- Has disparity—one of the core concerns driving sentencing reform—increased?

Discretion

Under *Gall* the sentencing court may be reversed only for a procedure error or abuse of discretion. Moreover, the abuse of discretion standard applies not only to cases that are within or close to the Guideline range, but also to sentences that fall far outside the Guideline range. But what does that mean in practice? What counts as an abuse of discretion?

A second case decided the same day applied the principles announced in *Gall* to sentencing for crack cocaine. In *Kimbrough v. United States*, 128 S. Ct. 558 (2007), the Court considered whether the potentially harsh disparity between sentences for crack and powder cocaine can be an appropriate factor in a judge's decision to deviate from the Guidelines sentencing range. *See supra* at 67. The Court answered in the affirmative, noting that the Sentencing Commission itself had repeatedly criticized the 100-to-1 powder-to-crack ratio used by the Guidelines. After *Booker*, the Guidelines are advisory, and although they provide the starting point for any sentencing decision, in the crack context the Sentencing Commission merely adopted the ratio prescribed by the statutory mandatory minimum sentences. Therefore, the Court concluded "it would not be an abuse of discretion for a district court to conclude when sentencing a particular defendant that the crack/powder disparity yields a sentence 'greater than necessary' to achieve § 3553(a)'s purposes, even in mine run cases."

Taken together, *Kimbrough* and *Gall* indicate that the district courts do have substantial sentencing discretion. This had the effect of reversing precedents from many circuits, and the lower courts are now working out exactly what it means in practice. It's clear that sentences that would have been reversed before *Gall* are now being upheld. One example is the case of Richard Rowan, who pled guilty to the illegal possession of child pornography and would have faced 46 to 57 months in prison if sentenced within the applicable Guidelines range. After the District Court sentenced him to only a lengthy term of probation and sex-offender therapy,

234

the government appealed and the Fifth Circuit vacated the sentence as unreasonable. But the Supreme Court remanded the case for reconsideration in light of *Gall*, and on remand the Fifth Circuit affirmed the probationary sentence in a brief opinion, finding no procedural error and noting the District Court's careful consideration of the § 3553(a) factors. *See United States v. Rowan*, No. 05-30536, 2008 WL 2332527, at *1 (5th Cir. Jun. 9, 2008).

On the other hand, appellate courts continue to reverse some sentences. Those decisions frequently focus on a "procedural" error (which means the abuse of discretion standard does not apply) even though it seems clear in some cases that the reviewing court also views the resulting sentence as unreasonable. For example, in *United States v. Livesay*, 525 F.3d 1081 (11th Cir. 2008), the district court sentenced a major player in a $1.4 billion criminal fraud scheme to probation even though his Guidelines range was 78 to 97 months imprisonment. The government filed a § 5K1.1 motion recommending a downward departure of 3 levels, but the district court departed downward by 18 levels. The Court of Appeals for the Eleventh Circuit reversed (as it had already done twice in the same case), concluding that the district judge had failed to address the relevant § 5K1.1 factors, and had failed to adequately explain the reasons for its variance and how co-defendants whose sentences he compared were similarly situated.

The court of appeals also reversed the sentences in *United States v. Williams*, 524 F.3d 209 (2nd Cir. 2008), on ostensibly procedural grounds. Two defendants were arrested together by local authorities for selling crack cocaine in the City of Yonkers, New York. Federal charges of conspiracy to possess with intent to distribute 50 grams or more of crack cocaine were filed, and both pled guilty. In sentencing one defendant the judge emphasized that the case should be in state, not federal court, and that for such a defendant landing in federal court was "a random event." Noting that "the nature and circumstances of the offense are not particularly federal," and finding the applicable Guideline "excessive," she stated a personal policy that she would impose a sentence within the range the defendant would have received if he had pled guilty in state court. Although the Guideline range was 70 to 87 months, she imposed a sentence of only 36 months. The court of appeals vacated the sentence on procedural grounds, finding that instead of using the Guidelines as the starting point and benchmark, the district judge had erroneously used the plea and sentencing policies of the local district attorney as her benchmark. The appellate court expressed concern that this approach would create disparity even within a single state, and would base federal sentences on policies that might reflect nothing more than local resource constraints.

Discretion to Disagree With the Commission

Does *Kimbrough* mean that district courts are free to vary from the Guideline range whenever they disagree with the policy basis of a particular Guideline? Maybe not. Indeed, some portions of the *Kimbrough* opinion suggest a narrower reading. The Court compared the institutional strengths of the sentencing court and the Commission. The sentencing judge is in the best position to find and gauge the importance of facts concerning individual cases. The Commission's strength lies in its ability to study and collect empirical data, and then formulate sentencing ranges tailored to § 3553(a)'s objectives. But in formulating the crack Guidelines, the Commission was not acting in its characteristic institutional role; it did not base the Guidelines on empirical data and its own institutional expertise. Rather, it based the crack Guidelines on the mandatory minimum sentences set by Congress. Moreover, the Commission subsequently issued multiple reports finding the crack Guidelines did *not* implement the purposes of § 3553(a), and proposing amendments that were blocked by Congress. In this portion of its opinion, the Court suggested–but did not hold–that the district court's decision to vary may be given greatest respect when it is based on a finding that a particular case falls outside the heartland. Conversely, the Court suggested—but did not hold—that a district court's decision to vary may receive closer review when based solely on the judge's view that an empirically based Guideline fails to properly reflect § 3553(a) factors in general.

Kimbrough didn't settle all of the questions about the district court's authority in crack cases, and the next wave of cases raises some interesting questions. Sitting en banc, a closely divided Eighth Circuit reversed a sentence because the district court had employed a 20-to-1 ratio, rather than 100-to-1. The majority concluded that *Kimbrough* allows a judge to deviate from the 100-to-1 ratio based on the individual circumstances of a case, but "the district court may not categorically reject the ratio set forth by the Guidelines." *United States v. Spears*, 2008 WL 2485329 at 1 (8th Cir. 2008) (en banc). The dissent argued that a judge who finds the 100-to-1 ratio inherently unjust does not abuse his discretion in adopting a 20-to-1 ratio at the outset. Moreover, a study of nationwide district court rulings expressing a preference for a particular crack/powder differential could assist the Sentencing Commission in revising the Guidelines. This case raises several questions. The first is which approach is more consistent with *Kimbrough*. The second is whether it makes sense for each district judge to adopt his or her own preferred ratio, instead of following the Guidelines. On the other hand, if the judge has no ratio in mind, would it really be possible to determine whether an individual sentence is too harsh?

Discretion and Institutional Features

Some of the most difficult issues facing the courts arise in cases where structural or institutional features of the Guidelines create what an individual sentencing judge may see as "unwarranted sentencing disparities." § 5K1.1 authorizes downward departures, upon the government's motion, for a defendant who provides "substantial assistance" in the investigation and prosecution of other persons who have committed offenses. The Guidelines make no provision for departure to avoid disparities between the sentences of co-defendants, and substantial assistance departures under § 5K1.1 make such disparities inevitable. The government does not need the cooperation of all defendants. Instead, it rewards some for assisting in the prosecution of the others. What if the government gets substantial assistance from one of the most culpable defendants, who knows the most and can implicate everyone else? In such a case, how should a district court evaluate a claim that a sentence should be reduced to avoid disparity among co-defendants caused by § 5K1.1 departures? Issa Jaber, who pled guilty to charges related to his participation in a meth ring, faced 70-87 months under the Guidelines based on drug type and quantity. But Jaber's boss, who recruited him, was sentenced to only 51 months based on the substantial assistance he provided authorities in the prosecution of other defendants, including Jaber. The district court judge concluded that giving Jaber a longer sentence than his more culpable co-felon would have been an unjustified sentencing disparity, so she departed (or varied) downward. *United States v. Jaber*, 362 F. Supp. 2d 365 (D. Mass. 2005).

A similar issue can arise if the court concludes that the government failed to move for a downward departure for substantial assistance though the defendant did as much to assist the government as others for whom such motions have been made. In *United States v. McCormick*, No. 8:04CR218, 2008 WL 268441 (D.Neb. Jan. 29, 2008), the district court found that it would be "unfair and inequitable" not to reduce the sentence of a defendant who attempted to cooperate. McCormick furnished information about his accomplice and pled guilty, expecting that he would be rewarded with a reduced sentence. But the government declined to move for a substantial assistance departure, finding that it no longer needed McCormick's testimony because his accomplice pled guilty in state court and would not be prosecuted in the federal system. Despite the absence of a § 5K1.1 motion the court reduced the defendant's sentence by 50 percent, which he noted was the typical departure for substantial assistance.

At first blush, both the *Jaber* and *McCormick* decisions seem appropriate. In each case, the district court adjusted the sentence to meet the statutory directive under § 3553(a)(6) to avoid unwarranted disparity. But the Sentencing Reform Act itself also recognizes that defendants who actually provide the government substantial assistance should receive reduced sentences. 28 U.S.C. § 994(n) states:

> The Commission shall assure that the guidelines reflect the general appropriateness of imposing a lower sentence than would otherwise be imposed, including a sentence that is lower than that established by statute as a minimum sentence, to take into account a defendant's substantial assistance in the investigation or prosecution of another person who has committed an offense.

And 18 U.S.C. § 3553(e) authorizes sentences below mandatory minimums set by statute, but only upon motion of the government. So, within the statutory scheme, is the disparity produced by substantial assistance "unwarranted"? Should the sentencing court be able to use its *Booker/Gall* discretion to second guess the government on the cases in which substantial assistance has been provided, or to nullify the incentives for cooperation by granting similar benefits to co-defendants who did not cooperate? Is this consistent with §§ 994(n) and 3553(e)?

Similar questions have arisen in connection with other structural features of the Guidelines, including downward departures under § 5K3.1. Is it appropriate for a judge to consider the disparity between sentences in early disposition ("fast track") districts and those in districts without early disposition programs? Circuits are currently split on whether this disparity can be considered "unwarranted" under § 3553(a). Congress gave the Attorney General power to create these programs to help alleviate caseloads in districts in the southwestern United States that are swamped with immigration proceedings. One view is that, by allowing the creation of early disposition programs at the district level, Congress approved any disparities that would be created among the districts. However, the First Circuit emphasizes that, like the crack Guidelines in *Kimbrough*, early disposition departures were not promulgated by the Commission in its typical institutional capacity. *See United States v. Rodriguez*, 527 F.3d 221 (1st Cir. Jun. 4, 2008). Do you see a difference between the disparities created by the crack Guidelines and fast track departures? When it authorized fast track programs did Congress effectively take the issue of disparity off the table for district courts balancing under § 3553(a)? Or should courts be able to take a holistic approach to individual cases, weighing the potential disparity created by fast track programs and then deciding whether, in a district without a fast track program, a shorter sentence would be sufficient to meet the goals of sentencing?

Disparity

In *Booker*, Justice Scalia wrote separately to express his concern that the reasonableness standard of appellate review would do nothing to fix the disparities that would, he predicted, be the inevitable result of instructing the district courts to consider a variety of unranked priorities under the SRA and the Guidelines. What do we mean by disparity in this context? And is it indeed increasing?

The Sentencing Reform Act instructs sentencing judges to avoid "unwarranted sentence disparities among defendants with similar records who have been found guilty of similar conduct." § 3553(a)(6). Data comparing the sentencing patterns from circuit to circuit and district to district provide a useful way to measure disparity by giving us some sense of whether similarly situated defendants get the same sentences in different courts. The Sentencing Commission data presented below allow a comparison of the percentage of defendants who were sentenced within the Guidelines range in each court. And, for defendants sentenced above or below the Guidelines range, we can also see the percentage of cases in which the government sought (or "sponsored") the change and the cases in which the government opposed it.

Although most of our discussion will focus on the period after *Booker*, it's important to recognize that there was already a great deal of statistical disparity from district to district and circuit to circuit before *Booker*. For example, before *Booker* the rate of substantial assistance departures varied enormously from district to district. In FY 2003, nationally 15.9 % of defendants received downward departures for substantial assistance. But more than 30 % received such departures in five districts, and fewer than 10 %

received such departures in sixteen other districts. Although some of this variation might have reflected differences in the types of cases found in each court, a Sentencing Commission study concluded that there were major differences in how the districts defined substantial assistance.

The concern, of course, is that by making the Guidelines merely advisory *Booker* could increase disparity.   After *Booker*, the percentage of within-Guideline sentences did drop, but not as much as many critics of *Booker* had feared.   Now that we have the clarifications provided by *Rita, Gall,* and *Kimbrough*, the picture that emerges is one of significant variation from district to district and circuit to circuit, with some districts and circuits showing much lower rates of within-Guideline sentences. But it's critical to distinguish those departures that were sponsored by the government (because, for example, the defendant provided substantial assistance in the prosecution of another case, and was rewarded by the government with a motion under § 5K1.1).

Here is a look at the Commission's first post-*Gall* and *Kimbrough* data. At the national level, during the first four months following *Gall* and *Kimbrough* there seems to have been very little change.

Guideline Sentences
FY 2007 and Post Gall/Kimbrough
(Dec. 10 - May 1, 2008)

		Within Range	§ 5K1.1 Subst. Assistance	§ 5K3.1 early disposition	Other gov't sponsored departures	Down departures & Booker below range
National	**FY 07**	60.8 %	14.4	7.5%	3.7 %	12.0 %
	Dec10-May1	59.80%	13.30%	8.10%	3.80%	13.40%

One percent fewer defendants were sentenced within range after *Gall* and *Kimbrough*, and downward departures and variances not sponsored by the government increased by less than one and a half percent. Substantial assistance departures were down, but other government sponsored departures rose slightly.

However, when we break the data down by circuits and districts within the same circuit, we see a very different picture.

240

The next chart shows the pre and post *Gall/Kimbrough* data from four circuits. If you focus first on the last fiscal year's data, in bold, you will see that even before *Kimbrough* and *Gall* there was a remarkably wide variation in both the percentage of defendants who were sentenced within the Guidelines and the percentages who received downward departures for various reasons. The percentage of defendants sentenced within range was only 42% in one circuit and nearly 72% in another. Substantial assistance ranged from more than a third of defendants in one circuit to less than 9 percent in another. And downward departures and variances ranged from a high of 14.3% to a low of 6.3%.

Guideline Sentences
FY 2007 and Post *Gall/Kimbrough* (Dec. 10 - May 1, 2008)

		Within Range	§ 5K1.1 Subst. Assistance	§ 5K3.1 early disposition	Other gov't sponsored departures	Down departures & *Booker* below range
D.C. Circ.	**FY 07**	**41.7 %**	**33.9 %**	**0.0 %**	**8.9 %**	**14.3 %**
	Dec10-May1	44.0 %	34.5 %	0.0 %	6.9 %	14.7 %
Fourth Circ.	**FY 07**	**72.3 %**	**16.8 %**	**0.0 %**	**1.0 %**	**8.6 %**
	Dec10-May1	67.4 %	16.0 %	0.0 %	1.1 %	13.1 %
Fifth Circ.	**FY 07**	**71.8 %**	**8.4 %**	**6.5 %**	**4.8 %**	**6.3 %**
	Dec10-May1	70.6 %	7.4 %	7.9 %	5.4 %	6.9 %
Ninth Circ.	**FY 07**	**44.2 %**	**10.0 %**	**27.7 %**	**5.2 %**	**11.3 %**
	Dec10-May 1	44.0 %	9.7 %	29 %	4.7 %	11.6 %

Now compare FY 07 with the early post *Gall* and *Kimbrough* data. Although this reflects only a short period and the effects of those decisions have not been fully felt, the data show relatively little change in the percentage of downward departures and variances not sponsored by the government. Indeed, to the degree there is change, the circuits seem to be coming closer together, because the Fourth Circuit's rate has come closer to that of its sister circuits.

This early data from the circuit level does not confirm fears that disparity will substantially increase as a result of the decisions in *Gall* and *Kimbrough*. (Of course, this still may occur as district judges get used to having this discretion). But the early data does reveal big differences among the circuits, and most of the differences are attributable to government sponsored departures, not to downward departures and variances by the courts. Note that some of this variation reflects real differences between the cases in these circuits. The variation in "§ 5K3.1 early disposition" departures reflects the variation in the immigration caseload. In the Ninth Circuit more than a quarter of defendants received government-sponsored downward departures in early disposition ("fast track") programs that are used when illegal immigrants agree to plead guilty and to be deported when they finish serving their sentences. The Fourth Circuit doesn't have the flood of immigration related cases that come out of Arizona and Southern California.

The final chart compares pre and post *Gall/Kimbrough* sentences for the Third and Fourth Circuits, and for two districts within each of the circuits.

Guideline Sentences
FY 2007 and Post *Gall/Kimbrough*
(Dec. 10 - May 1, 2008)

		Within Range	§ 5K1.1 Subst. Assistance	§ 5K3.1 early disposition	Other gov't sponsored departures	Down departures & Booker below range
Third Circ.	FY 07	52.6 %	27.1 %	0.0 %	1.7 %	17.5 %
	Dec10-May1	53.2 %	26.6 %	0.0 %	1.2 %	17.1 %
E.D. PA	FY 07	41.3 %	33.6 %	0.0 %	1.3 %	21.8 %
	Dec10-May1	41.3 %	36.0 %	0.0 %	0.5 %	20.2 %
W.D. PA	FY 07	70.6 %	11.7 %	0.0 %	1.0 %	15.4 %
	Dec10-May1	70.1 %	13.9 %	0.0 %	0.7 %	13.9 %
Fourth Circ.	FY 07	72.3 %	16.8 %	0.0 %	1.0 %	8.6 %
	Dec10-May1	67.4 %	16.0 %	0.0 %	1.1 %	13.1 %
D. MD	FY 07	51.5 %	26.8 %	0.0 %	2.6 %	18.2 %
	Dec 10-May 1	49.4 %	19.2 %	0.0 %	3.8 %	26.2 %
E.D. VA	FY 07	79.8 %	5.9 %	0.0%	0.5 %	12.3 %
	Dec 10-May1	75.0 %	4.6 %	0.0 %	1.0 %	17.6 %

These two circuits present quite different profiles, but the real surprise is the variation within each circuit. There are certainly differences between the cases in each district, but it's hard to avoid the conclusion that there are also differences in how similar cases are treated. But note that much of this variation was present before the decisions in *Gall* and *Kimbrough* (and some predated *Booker*). The next question is, who's responsible for the variation? Look at the variation from court to court in government-sponsored departures, as well as downward departures and below range sentences based on *Booker*. For example, within the Third Circuit, within-range sentences are less than 42% in the Eastern District of Pennsylvania, but more than 70% in the Western District of the same state. The districts vary, however, by about 20% on substantial assistance rates, but only about 6% in non-government sponsored downward departures and variances. Similarly, in the Fourth Circuit the largest share of the variation is attributable to differences in the substantial assistance rates.

So, what should we make of the data? It does not support the fear that the sky would fall after *Gall* and *Kimbrough*. On the other hand, it reveals troubling differences among circuits and even more from district to district, and also makes it plain the differences are caused as much (or more) by government sponsored departures than by downward departures and variances opposed by the government.

CHAPTER 19

FORFEITURE

Page 902. Add to "The history of federal forfeiture law"

From FY 2005 to FY 2006, total assets of the DOJ Assets Forfeiture Fund increased by almost 50%, to $2.05 billion. This jump is partly attributable to a major fraud case occurring near the end of FY 2006 that netted the Fund $337.5 million, though forfeiture revenue has been on the rise for several years. The Fund will return the money forfeited in the fraud case to victims. The Treasury Forfeiture Fund changed its net position from $236.8 million in FY 2006 to $361.4 million in FY 2007. This fund focuses on "high-impact cases," in keeping with the goal of federal forfeiture law to remove the economic incentives of crime. One such case was that of Michael Pescatore, who turned to a life of crime, despite being the first in his family to earn a college degree. Pescatore pled guilty to extortion charges connected to operating the largest criminal chop-shop enterprise on the East Coast, and was sentenced to 11 years in jail and ordered to forfeit over $12 million. The Treasury Forfeiture Fund sold his 14,000 square foot Long Island mansion for $8.3 million at auction, which it applied to his forfeiture debt. According to the Fund, "high-impact" cases provided over 84% of its forfeited cash proceeds in FY 2007, up from 72.90% in FY 2006.

In FY 2006, the Assets Forfeiture Fund shared a grand total of $297 billion with state and local law enforcement agencies. The Treasury Forfeiture Fund distributed almost $33 million to state and local law enforcement bureaus in FY 2007. Local law enforcement agencies have increasingly come to rely on forfeiture revenues (from both federal and state forfeitures) to enhance their budgets. In theory, sharing federal forfeiture funds provides agencies with the tools they need to fight crime and relieves pressure on state and local budgets. Left unchecked, however, there are also powerful financial incentives that may lead to the development of undesirable results and practices, see text at 902-903. Congress took aim at this problem when it passed the Civil Asset Forfeiture Reform Act of 2000, P.L. 106-185, making numerous changes in the procedures for civil–but not criminal–forfeiture to provide greater protection to property owners. For example, the Act increased the government's burden of proof in contested forfeiture proceedings to a preponderance of the evidence (rather than probable cause), and it required a "substantial connection" between the offense and the property to be forfeited. However, recent exposés indicate that some practices have developed that may be considered corrupt.

In 2008, National Public Radio aired a four-part series on seized drug assets, giving numerous examples of how the lure of revenues from asset forfeiture shaped (or deformed) enforcement policies. Here are a few examples:

- Texas law enforcement seized over $125 million in assets in 2007. (Note that the state of Texas received the most assets from the Treasury Forfeiture Fund in 2007, followed by New York and Florida.) Texas agents know that every year billions of dollars in drug money travel towards Mexico in the southbound lanes of their highways, and they tend to focus efforts there, rather than the northbound lanes carrying drugs into the U.S. Are you surprised that there is more of an effort to stop the money flowing south than the drugs flowing north? Is that a problem?

- In Robeson County, North Carolina, a long investigation called Operation Tarnished Badge has resulted in guilty pleas from every deputy in the Drug Enforcement Division of the Robeson County Sheriff's Office, and over 20 officers in total. According to media reports, two deputies seized millions of dollars in drug money and kept some for themselves, stashing stolen proceeds in a hydraulicly powered hiding place beneath stairs in an officer's home. They were also hired to train other police in the art of highway forfeiture – and in one South Carolina county, they allegedly operated on commission, keeping ten percent of the funds seized during training.

- Even when law enforcement agencies never reach this level of corruption, drug seizures sometimes result in odd budget decisions, such as Camden County's decision to purchase a $90,000 Dodge Viper for its DARE program using seized funds.

On the other hand, there can be significant law enforcement benefits from forfeiture, and there are even arguments in favor of the Texas decision to focus on drug money rather than drugs. Drug organizations are for-profit enterprises and, logically, disrupting their cash flow reduces the economic attraction of drug dealing. Moreover, shifting enforcement emphasis to the economics of the drug trade may reduce incarceration rates, which currently reflect significant racial disparities. Indeed seizing the proceeds of drug sales may result in more proportional punishment, because it hits more culpable drug kingpins harder than couriers or small time dealers.

Still, situations like those described in the NPR series raise concerns that forfeiture is breeding a law enforcement culture that depends on a robust drug market for its survival. Is there a way to regulate the use of forfeited funds to preserve some incentives but cabin them sufficiently to avoid corruption and prevent forfeiture from driving the law enforcement agenda? Perhaps Congress should consider the approach taken by some states, which divert forfeited funds away from the individual agency that made the case to a state-wide law enforcement fund or to a more general fund benefitting other government programs, such as education.

Forfeiture issues also came into the spotlight briefly in the fallout from Enron's collapse. Former Enron CEO Kenneth Lay was convicted of conspiracy, fraud, and making false statements, but his conviction was abated when he died while the case was being appealed. The abatement, which effectively erased his conviction, had a major impact on the ability of both the government and Lay's victims to reach his assets. Civil forfeiture is available, but it does not reach substitute assets. Victims may seek to collect in personal civil litigation, but they are not able to rely upon Lay's "abated" criminal conviction to establish liability. Accordingly, to date Lay's family has been able to retain much of his wealth. A legislative effort to overturn the judicially created abatement doctrine as applied to criminal forfeiture was unsuccessful, as were efforts to authorize the pretrial restraint of assets for purposes of restitution.

Page 930. Add to Note 4.

In the shadow cast by *Bajakajian,* text at 917, Congress made findings intended to support forfeiture of the full amount smuggled in violation of the new bulk cash smuggling criminal statute, 31 U.S.C. § 5332. Congress expressly stated that its purpose in enacting the bulk cash smuggling statute was not only to criminalize the act of bulk cash smuggling itself but also "to authorize forfeiture of any cash or instruments of the smuggling offense . . . and to emphasize the seriousness of the act . . . ." USA PATRIOT Act, Pub.L. No. 107-56, § 371(b), 115 Stat. at 337. Congress also drew attention to two other factors in support of its forfeiture remedy. First, the act of bulk cash smuggling is often a warning sign of drug trafficking and terrorism. Second, because those who attempt to smuggle bulk cash are typically easily replaceable low-level employees of larger criminal organizations, "only the confiscation of the smuggled cash can effectively break the cycle of criminal activity of which the laundering of the bulk cash is a critical part." *Id.* at § 371(a)(5), 115 Stat. at 337.

The first appellate court to rule on an excessive fines challenge under the bulk smuggling act concluded that these findings were sufficient to distinguish *Bajakajian* and sustain forfeiture of the full amount smuggled. In *United States v. Jose*, 499 F.3d 105, 110-11 (1st Cir. 2007), the court noted that the Congressional findings demonstrate the legislature's view of the gravity of the offense for purposes of the constitutional proportionality analysis. The court also noted that under the bulk smuggling statute the cash constitutes the corpus delicti of the crime, which establishes a form of inherent proportionality. In contrast, *Bajakajian* emphasized that the defendant in that case had not been smuggling, and that it was perfectly legal for him to transport the money in question. This supported the Court's conclusion that there was no relationship between the reporting violation and the amount of money the defendant was transporting.

Page 937. Add to Note 3.

Questions continue to arise regarding defense efforts to challenge the government's ability to freeze assets before trial. The courts have distinguished between two different procedural points before trial. The lower courts have generally held that an adversarial hearing is not required *prior to the restraint* of assets alleged to be forfeitable. The law is only slightly more favorable to defendants after such assets have been restrained. The majority rule is that a *pre-trial hearing regarding restrained assets* is required only where the defendant makes a prima facie showing that there is no probable cause for the forfeiture and his Sixth Amendment right to counsel is implicated. However, the recent case of *United States v. E-Gold, Ltd.*, 521 F.3d 411 (D.C. Cir. 2008), seems to depart from the general trend by requiring no special showing by the defense, at least in a limited class of cases. The government obtained a seizure warrant depriving E-Gold, Ltd. of $1.4 million in assets alleged to be involved in an unlicensed money transmitting business, and as a result E-Gold, Ltd. was unable to retain counsel. Balancing the competing interests, the court recognized that the government had a strong interest in avoiding the disclosures that would inevitably occur at such a hearing and that its interest in grand jury secrecy was a weighty one. Nevertheless, it held that "the constitutional right to due process of law entitles defendants to an opportunity to be heard at least where access to the assets is necessary for an effective exercise of the Sixth Amendment right to counsel." The court found it unnecessary to reach the question whether there would have been a pure due process right to such a hearing if the right to counsel had not also been at issue.

Page 941. Insert at the end of section 2.

What if a person who has been injured by the defendant wants to bring a private lawsuit seeking a civil recovery that would conflict with the government's efforts to forfeit the same property? May such a victim challenge the government's pretrial restraint of forfeitable assets? This situation arose in the case of *United States v. Holy Land Foundation for Relief and Development*, 493 F.3d 469 (5th Cir. 2007) (en banc). The restrained property belonged to a foundation alleged to have raised funds in the United States for a Palestinian terrorist organization. The restraining order was challenged by the administrator of the estates of individuals killed during a terrorist attack in Israel. The administrator obtained a default judgment against the terrorist organization in the United States and levied writs of execution on the foundation's bank accounts in order to satisfy the judgment, only to find these efforts frustrated by the government restraining order.

In criminal cases, Rule 32.2 provides that the court issues a forfeiture order that is final as to the defendant at the time of sentencing, and then considers the claims of any third parties in an ancillary proceeding. In the *Holy Land* case, the Fifth Circuit held that these post-trial ancillary proceedings are the exclusive remedy for the typical third-party claimant, who has no standing to contest a criminal forfeiture before trial. The court noted, however, that terrorist victims may stand on a different footing under the Terrorism Risk Insurance Act of 2002 (TRIA), Pub.L. No. 107-297, 116 Stat. 2322, 2337. TRIA provides:

[n]otwithstanding any other provision of law . . . in every case in which a person has obtained a judgment against a terrorist party on a claim based upon an act of terrorism . . . the blocked assets of that terrorist party (including the blocked assets of any agency or instrumentality of that terrorist party) shall be subject to execution or attachment in aid of execution in order to satisfy such judgment to the extent of any compensatory damages for which such terrorist party has been adjudged liable. TRIA § 201(a).

The terror victims argued that this section of TRIA works as "legal kryptonite" allowing them to reach the assets "blocked" by the restraining order. The Government contended that TRIA has no application to the criminal forfeiture scheme, which does not "block" restrained assets but merely says how and when they will be disbursed. The *Holy Land* court declined to reach the merits of the TRIA issue, because it had not been raised in the district court.

If the issue had been properly presented, how should the court have ruled? Think again about the *Lavin* case, in the main text at 941. Section 853(c) provides property that is subject to the statute "shall be ordered forfeited to the United States" unless the third party claimant establishes "that he is a bona fide purchaser for value of such property." Although Lavin had obtained a default judgment against the defendant for fraud, his claim against the forfeited assets was rejected; he was not a BFP, because he did not acquire his rights through purchase or sale. The same analysis may apply to the judgments obtained by the estates of the terrorist victims. If so, the estates can appear at the ancillary hearing after the trial, but they will be denied relief. Thus the criminal forfeiture scheme as a whole may eventually deny–or in some senses "block"–their recovery. (Note that federal law also provides for some "restitution" to crime victims, but it is doubtful that the estates would be able to qualify as victims of the offense for which the *Holy Land* is being prosecuted. The use of forfeited assets to benefit victims is also discussed in the note that follows.)

It might be some time before the families of these victims, who were killed in a 1996 drive-by shooting in Israel, have a final resolution. The government's first case against the Holy Land Foundation ended in a mistrial in 2007, but the government has decided to go through a retrial, which is scheduled to begin on August 18, 2008.

Page 916. Add note 9.

Under some circumstances, 21 U.S.C. § 853(p), text page 908, authorizes the forfeiture of property that does not itself have any connection to criminal activity. If the "proceeds" of a crime, or the property that "facilitates" the crime are not available (because, for example, they cannot be located with due diligence or have been placed beyond the jurisdiction of the court), § 853(p) allows the government to forfeit "substitute property."

In addition, although the statute does not expressly mention this alternative, many courts have entered money judgments as orders of forfeiture. As a conceptual matter, these orders are something of a puzzle, since they depart so radically from the idea that a specific res is being removed from the defendant because of its connection to a crime. Indeed, forfeiture money judgments lack even the nexus that connects "substitute property" to some specific forfeitable asset. Why does the government seek such orders, and how does such a "forfeiture" differ from a criminal fine? Forfeiture money judgments are not subject to the maximum statutory fines applicable to each offense. They allow the government to avoid the tracing issues that plague many forfeiture cases. Forfeiture money judgments are usually jointly and severally imposed on all the defendants in a conspiracy, and in many cases this can work to the government's advantage. Another benefit is that forfeiture money judgments are not limited by the amount of money in the defendant's possession–or any conceivable ability to pay the judgment.

Despite the lack of a clear conceptual (or statutory) basis for money judgment forfeitures, the courts of appeals have generally upheld orders of forfeiture entered as money judgments. *See United States v. Misla-Aldarondo*, 478 F.3d 52, 73-74 (1st Cir. 2007) (holding that it suffices that the amount of the money judgment is traceable to the underlying crime). What do you think of this development? If the main purpose of forfeiture is to remove the economic power of criminals or to strip them of assets gained or used illegally, why should the government be able to forfeit something that the criminal does not have? Note that proponents of forfeiture characterize it as the most effective means of preventing dissipation of property for the benefit of crime victims. Through a process called "restoration," such assets, after conviction and forfeiture, are often simply turned over to the courts to disburse to victims pro rata in satisfaction of restitution orders.

Page 943. Insert at the end of section a.

The USA PATRIOT Act also added 18 U.S.C. 981(k), which provides that a person who deposits illicit funds into an interbank account is considered the owner of the deposited funds. This provision was added to prevent foreign banks from raising the innocent owner defense, see text pages 941-43. A bank can defeat the government's claim to the funds, however, if it has "discharged all or part of its obligation to the prior owner of the funds," 18 U.S.C. § 981(k)(4)(B)(ii)(II). A court interpreted this provision for the first time in *United States v. Union Bank for Savings & Investment (Jordan)*, 487 F.3d 8 (1st Cir. 2007). The court gave the provision a pro-government interpretation, rejecting a variety of arguments by the bank concerning the term "obligation." It also held that the bank could not challenge the forfeiture under the Excessive Fines Clause, because the forfeiture was not intended to punish the bank.

251